CREATIVE MARGINALITY

CREATIVE MARGINALITY

Innovation at the Intersections of Social Sciences

**MATTEI DOGAN
AND ROBERT PAHRE**

Routledge
Taylor & Francis Group
LONDON AND NEW YORK

First published 1990 by Westview Press

Published 2019 by Routledge
52 Vanderbilt Avenue, New York, NY 10017
2 Park Square, Milton Park, Abingdon, Oxon OX14 4RN

Routledge is an imprint of the Taylor & Francis Group, an informa business

Copyright © 1990 by Taylor & Francis

All rights reserved. No part of this book may be reprinted or reproduced or utilised in any form or by any electronic, mechanical, or other means, now known or hereafter invented, including photocopying and recording, or in any information storage or retrieval system, without permission in writing from the publishers.

Notice:
Product or corporate names may be trademarks or registered trademarks, and are used only for identification and explanation without intent to infringe.

Library of Congress Cataloging-in-Publication Data
Dogan, Mattei.
    Creative marginality : innovation at the intersections of social sciences / Mattei Dogan and Robert Pahre.
        p. cm.
    Includes bibliographical references.
        1. Interdisciplinary research. 2. Social sciences—Research.
I. Pahre, Robert. II. Title.
H62.D613 1990
300.72—dc20   89-48096
                                                                                    CIP

ISBN 13: 978-0-367-01466-7 (hbk)
ISBN 13: 978-0-367-16453-9 (pbk)

CONTENTS

Preface ix

Introduction 1

PART ONE
SCIENTIFIC INNOVATION AND OBSOLESCENCE

Introduction 7

1 Defining Innovation in the Social Sciences 9

2 Patrimonies: Incremental Advance and the Distorting Effects of the "Star System" 19

3 The Paradox of Density 29

4 Does Citation Measure Innovation? 37

5 Cemeteries for Books 45

PART TWO
FROM SPECIALIZATION AND FRAGMENTATION TO HYBRIDIZATION

Introduction 51

6 Specialization in the Social Sciences 53

7 Hybridization: The Recombination of Fragments of the Social Sciences 63

8 Fragmentation by Geographical Area Versus Analytical Fragmentation 77

vi CONTENTS

PART THREE
THE CRUMBLING WALLS
OF THE FORMAL DISCIPLINES

Introduction 83

9 The Fate of the Formal Disciplines:
From Coherence to Dispersion 85

10 Why Interdisciplinarity Is a False Notion 115

PART FOUR
THE INTERPENETRATION OF DISCIPLINES:
THE PROCESSES OF HYBRIDIZATION

Introduction 121

11 The Diffusion of Concepts Across Disciplines 123

12 Borrowing Methods 131

13 The Impact of Technology 141

14 The Cross-disciplinary Repercussions of Findings 143

15 The Influence of Theories 147

16 Perspectives, Paradigms, and Praxis 153

17 Hybridization of Academic Journals 161

18 The Balance of Trade Between Disciplines 165

PART FIVE
GALLERY OF HYBRIDS: CREATIVE MARGINALS

Introduction 169

19 Three Ideal Types of Social Scientists 171

20 Intellectual Migration Across Disciplines 175

PART SIX
CROSSROADS: FOUR ILLUSTRATIONS

Introduction 185

21 Historical Sociology and Sociological History 187

22 Junctions Between the Social Sciences
and Life Sciences 203

CONTENTS vii

23 International Political Economy:
A Fusion of Several Subfields 217

24 The Hesitant Exchange Between Economics
and Psychology 225

Final Remarks: The New Kaleidoscope
of Social Sciences 229

Bibliography 237
Author Index 249
Subject Index 258

PREFACE

We are often asked how we came to write such a book, so unrelated to the more traditional academic fare that usually engages us. We are a political sociologist and a political economist. The first was trained in philosophy and history and is now a sociologist who has worked mostly in political science, while the second has training in political science and economics but has also published research in linguistics. Many of our colleagues are similarly hyphenated political scientists. Originally we intended to explore the ways in which political science is interwoven with the other social sciences. However, we quickly discovered that the various subfields in contact with political science are themselves in contact with different subfields in disciplines further abroad. These subfields, too, each had their own contacts in turn. The topic refused to be limited, and it carried us along with it.

The phenomenon soon appeared to be general throughout the social sciences. Discussing the idea among colleagues in other disciplines not only confirmed our suspicion but seemed to strike a responsive chord among many of them. Their responses encouraged us to continue our examination of all the social sciences, resulting in the present manuscript.

We have made an effort to bring together evidence for our thesis gathered from dozens of scholars in nine disciplines in reviews of their own fields of knowledge: political science, sociology, economics, history, anthropology, philosophy, geography, psychology, and linguistics. Covering nine disciplines is impossible single-handedly; among those whom we call as witnesses—and often cite directly—are many of the most eminent social scientists in the world. Having such allies on the research fronts scattered throughout the social sciences strengthens our confidence in our thesis.

We should confess one sin. We know that our examples are biased in favor of political science, sociology, economics, and history. Psychology, especially, receives less attention than it warrants. Despite this bias, we believe the breadth of examples is large enough so that we may state that the process is general to all social sciences.

No one can possibly master the social sciences today. We were fortunate to have the advice and comments of many other social scientists along the way, who as a group cover sizable expanses of the terrain. None have seen the entire manuscript in its final form, and it is obviously true that none of them are to be held responsible for our errors. We are, however, most grateful for the suggestions of the following: Nermin Abadan-Unat, Jeffrey Alexander, Geoffrey Bergen, Alfred Diamant, Ann Hinckley, Jack Hirshleifer, Scott James, Arend Lijphart, Jacques Maquet, Jennifer Pahre, Rhys Payne, Fred Riggs, Guenther Roth, Thomas Schwartz, Richard Sisson, Richard Sklar, Leo Snowiss, Sharon Snowiss, Ralph Turner, Michael Wallerstein, Eugen Weber, Jerzy Wiatr, David Wilkinson, and Ciro Zoppo.

Mattei Dogan
Robert Pahre

INTRODUCTION

As the title of the book suggests, the main idea we develop is that innovation in the social sciences occurs more often and with more important results at the intersection of disciplines. This is both cause and effect of a continual fragmentation of the social sciences into narrow specialties and the recombination of these specialties across disciplinary lines into what we term "hybrid" fields.

By "intersection" we mean an area where two specialized subfields of different formal disciplines overlap. This is not a book on "interdisciplinary" research—we reject the very notion; instead of broad catch-all "interdisciplinary" research, we find it is more realistic to combine two narrow specialties. The core of the book analyzes the two halves of this process: first, that scientific specialization brings about the fragmentation of disciplines into narrow subfields; and second, that as specialization reaches its natural limits, innovative scholars will seek to recombine these fragments into hybrid fields. We will show that by moving from the center to the periphery of a discipline, crossing its borders and penetrating the field of another, a scholar has a better chance to innovate. In fact, one can survey most of the important new work in a given field simply by walking along its boundaries.

We begin our discussion by insisting that scientific progress is incremental, arguing against a view of science that highlights the roles played by a few "stars." We address citation-counting, a practice often used to measure innovation, and we question the validity of such counts. Innovation, though a mass phenomenon, occurs at different rates in different fields; paradoxically, progress is slower in those areas with large numbers of scholars. Once masses of scholars enter a field, the major innovations have already been made. This is the "paradox of density."

Next, we discuss the twin processes of scientific specialization and the fragmentation of disciplines into subfields and sub-subfields. Although specialization is important, what interests us more is the recombination of these fragments into hybrid fields, a hybridization that consequently rests on specialization. We illustrate this process with reference to various areas of research throughout the social sciences. Our references are not meant to be detailed analyses of the subject, but brief illustrations of our thesis.

In Part Three we review the nine social sciences from this common perspective. We show how each discipline has become fragmented and how scholars in some of these fragmented areas have built bridges to segments of other disciplines. Again, the intent is to illustrate the thesis, not to provide a detailed analysis of the research front in each discipline. This overview of the "fate of formal disciplines" demonstrates, in general, that an "interdisciplinary" synthesis of two disciplines is a misguided objective.

The process of hybridization is also analyzed through the ways by which scholars in various disciplines exchange the tools of their trades. We discuss the diffusion of concepts, the borrowing of methods, the impact of new technology, the influence of theories, the hybridization of academic journals, and the productive results of conflicts between paradigms. Scholars are aware of this borrowing and lending process, but it is rarely analyzed. We conclude Part Four with an overview of the "balance of trade" among the formal disciplines.

In Part Five we present three basic types of innovative scholars and argue that it is increasingly common for them to cross the borders of formal disciplines. These types reflect in part the histories of their disciplines, from pioneers to builders to hybrids. In our section on "intellectual migration" we briefly discuss the intellectual histories of dozens of scholars and analyze what features some of these scholars have in common.

In the last part of the book we closely examine four hybrid fields: historical sociologies, international political economy, psychology and economics, and biology and the social sciences. The fields were chosen for their variety.

Interestingly, most research in the sociology of science deals with very different issues and usually involves only the natural sciences. Both of these characteristics are found in Robert Merton's classic work, *The Sociology of Science* (1973), which examines the social and cultural contexts of science, raises moral and ethical questions about science, and studies scientific norms and reward systems, organization, recruitment, and other topics. The issues that Merton presents are all important, but our particular interests are quite different—even though

INTRODUCTION 3

they may be classified as part of the same broad field, the sociology of science.

There are many things this book is not. Although we would classify it as falling into the sociology of science, it does not treat most of the issues that are current in that subfield. For example, we do not explore why different groups of scholars hold particular views of social reality. We do not ask whether there are universally valid norms of science or whether the standards of Western science are the products of a certain kind of social structure and history. We do not discuss whether or not value-free social science is possible or desirable, nor do we ask whether social scientists actually pursue either value-free or value-laden social science. We also do not examine the activities of social scientists in policymaking or in other practical fields, although that, too, falls under the auspices of the sociology of science (see, for instance, Crawford and Biderman, eds. 1969). We explore neither the psychological and cognitive basis for epistemology in the sciences nor what Jean Piaget has labelled "genetic epistemology." It is fascinating to us, however, that current research in the philosophy and sociology of science finds it necessary to draw from genetics, psychology, and neurology, among other fields (see, for instance, Wilcox and Katz 1984).

We also do not discuss the philosophy of social science or the scientific validity of social science theory, except to observe that most social scientists recognize the existence of advances in the social sciences. We do not address how scientific communities construct knowledge in an epistemological sense or *how* such communities manage to come to at least temporary agreement on the scientific validity of certain theories, concepts, or data—we only observe that they *do*. Nor do we discuss any number of related issues in the "constructivist" school of the sociology of science, as in the works of Karin Knorr-Cetina, Bruno Latour, Michael Lynch, or Steve Woolgar. Many of these works have entailed ethnographies of natural scientists, typically in laboratory settings, which we have also intentionally avoided. These all raise interesting questions, but they are not central to our chosen topic.

More generally, we fall neither into the traditional sociology of science, "the elucidation of the set of normative and other institutional arrangements that enable science . . . to exist and function efficiently" nor into the sociology of scientific knowledge, which analyzes "what comes to count as scientific knowledge and how it comes so to count," as H. Collins defined these branches of the field in a recent review (Collins 1983: 266–267). The first tends naturally to focus on how scientists and their institutions interrelate with society as a whole—a focus that pulls scholars in this field away from science *per se* and toward the social foundations of science. The second rapidly becomes philosophical: These scholars either assume the existence of objective truth and ask how scientists manage to find it, or they assume that truth is relative and ask how scientists make their own statements accepted as facts. We seek to avoid such questions, not because they are unimportant but because they are not essential for the topic we have chosen to investigate.

In a sense, then, the book is intentionally quite limited, albeit limited by its generality and its brevity: We present an overview of the processes of fragmentation and recombination of fields in the social sciences, elaborate on the reasons behind these phenomena, and illustrate these processes at work.

We have been surprised to find little written on our topic, notwithstanding the many who have written on these related issues. Although there is much speculation about what is erroneously labelled "interdisciplinarity," there are almost no analyses of the process. Some have discussed it with relation to a particular subfield or even to an entire discipline. A few have even suspected the process to be general. The closest predecessors are a number of scholars at the University of Chicago (White, ed. 1956; Campbell 1969) and seven prescient pages in David Easton's *The Political System.* (1953: 100–106) Other authors have addressed individual disciplines, such as anthropology (Firth, ed. 1967; Mead 1961; Plakans 1986), economics (Hirshleifer 1985; Hogarth and Reder 1986), political science (Lipset, ed. 1969), and especially the relations between history and sociology. (Besnard 1986; Braudel 1962; Burke 1980; Cahnman and Boskoff, eds. 1964; Knapp 1984; Lipset and Hofstadter, eds. 1968; Thrupp 1957; Tilly 1981)

The process can be found throughout the social sciences. For an overview of all nine disciplines, a good place to begin is the monumental three-volume *Main Trends in the Social Sciences* (1970, 1978), prepared and published under UNESCO auspices. The contributors to that book review innovation in each social science, but there is no integrating framework, and only a few contributors address the hybridization of fragments of their disciplines.

From the standpoint of innovation, *Advances in the Social Sciences* (1986), edited by Deutsch, Markovits, and Platt, is quite useful. However, the intellectual connection between their book and ours is very weak. For example, they focus only on the 100 or so most important innovations, while we consider innovation a mass phenomenon; in fact, we denounce the "star system" implicit in their analysis. They also give very little attention to processes we address, such as scientific obsolescence or the diminishing returns to research in crowded fields. Our main theme, the recombination of fragments of sciences, receives discussion in only one paragraph in their book.

INTRODUCTION

Perhaps one reason why the recombination phenomenon has not been more studied is that it is of recent vintage. In face, we have seen more break-ups and recombinations throughout all the sciences during the past three decades than occurred in the previous millennium. Because the process in the social sciences is only a product of the past few decades, and because it has rapidly accelerated throughout this brief period, it is poorly understood. It is essential that today's social scientists obtain a thorough understanding of the specialization-fragmentation-hybridization process as opposed to the traditional concept of "interdisciplinary research."

There is no consensus as to what should be included in the social sciences. The core consists of sociology, anthropology, and political science. Most scholars would include economics, social psychology, and history. Psychology, geography, demography, archaeology, and linguistics are partially natural sciences, but an inclusive definition would encompass them as well: Although experimental psychology, social psychology, or linguistics may use methods familiar to the natural sciences, they are obviously sciences of man. Some subfields of philosophy, education, and urban studies should also be considered part of the social sciences. The difficulty in classification comes from the fact that each discipline is fragmented; the fragments, too, are fragmented. These subfields often refuse to be classified. For instance, although many would classify the history of art as belonging to the humanities, sociological approaches to the topic are widely used.

The problem is confounded still further when one takes an international perspective; definitions vary by country. Demography is a discipline in many European countries but a subfield of sociology in the United States; archaeology is often a separate discipline in Europe but a subfield of anthropology in the United States. In some countries, archaeology is closely tied to art (as in the collection of Vienna's *Kunsthistorisches Museum*), and in others it is a part of "prehistory" and therefore is embraced by history and the humanities. Faced with all these difficulties, we prefer a nondogmatic and inclusive approach to the question of definition.

PART ONE

SCIENTIFIC INNOVATION AND OBSOLESCENCE

Innovation is at the core of this book because we maintain that it is more likely to appear where at least two specialized subfields overlap. Innovation, however, is not easy to define. "Creativity," a term related to "innovation," is a very elusive concept notwithstanding a large body of psychological research on the topic. Some scholars have defined creativity as the novel combination of two or more ideas, without having explained precisely how this is done by creative persons. Such an interpretation is surely suggestive for our purposes, although to take this definition as an equivalent of innovation would make our thesis almost tautological.

We define innovation as the addition of something new, whether large or small, to the scientific project. It must be examined in its scientific context. Innovation is not merely unequally distributed among scientists, it is unequally distributed among scientific subfields. It is also unequally distributed within the same field over time. Innovation has a history in each field, and the accumulation of innovations produces a "patrimony" of knowledge.

Subfields have both cores and margins, and innovation is different in each. In a core, innovations are often smaller in scope, hemmed in by a crowd of other researchers sharing similar assumptions and blinders. In contrast, areas which are at the margins of two subfields show the greatest potential for innovation. Not only are the margins less densely populated, providing more room to grow, but successful combinations of material from two subfields typically allows greater scope for creativity. In fact, the greatest accumulation of incremental advances takes place at the intersections of fields.

This should not imply that combining two specialties will make the scholar a giant. A scholar need not be a star to be an innovative hybrid, and innovation is a mass phenomenon.

1
DEFINING INNOVATION
IN THE SOCIAL SCIENCES

Every self-respecting scholar wants to innovate. Some have grandiose ambitions; others would be satisfied adding a few bricks to the construction of the scientific edifice. How have earlier innovators arrived at their discoveries? Is it solely a matter of individual genius, or are there strategies which help a scientist make the most of whatever talent he or she has?

To answer this question we must first attempt to identify the innovators. In the United States, there are nearly 150,000 college-level teachers in the social sciences as a whole, on the order of 10,000 to 50,000 in each discipline. (see Clark 1987: 12, 55) There are another 30,000 or more in Japan, about 20,000 in West Germany and an equivalent number in Great Britain. Depending on the discipline and the country, there may be several thousand more Ph.D.'s, employed by government agencies, private research centers, and other institutions, who are active in research. Not all of these researchers publish, and not all published articles are useful for others. For instance, out of all the people who received Ph.D.'s in sociology in the United States in the 1930s and 1950s, more than half published at least one article or book; only a third of the total, or about two-thirds of the published authors, garnered one or more citations. (Chubin 1973: 188) How many of these latter could be considered innovators? It would be impossible to provide a consensual definition.

It is difficult to define innovation, in part because science can advance by small increments, at a snail's pace. Imagine, as one example among hundreds, a linguist studying the languages of inland New Guinea—unmapped territory, to say nothing of unstudied. Whatever this scholar learns is new, and may or may not be important for colleagues. Yet one cannot deny this work its novelty, and science advances. Some of these studies will produce discoveries of wider theoretical value—but it is difficult, if not impossible, to know beforehand which will prove to be most important. Many languages distinguish nouns on the basis of animacy, for instance, but a proper understanding of the role of this distinction in langugage awaited the analysis of the elaborate hierarchies of animacy in several Australian languages. The first intrepid grammarians of these languages could not have known this in advance. Ethnographers are another example; each culture studied adds to our knowledge, but only a few such works will achieve the wide importance of Bronislaw Malinowski, A. R. Radcliffe-Brown, or Margaret Mead. The differences are in large part attributable to the scholar's talent, of course, but there is also an element of chance which makes some cultures more interesting than others. Certainly anthropology would be different if the Trobriand Islanders studied by Malinowski lacked the trading institution of the *kula,* for instance.

We obviously cannot dismiss scholars who carry on such research as mere data collectors even if their own work is not of the same degree of importance as Malinowski's. After all, Copernicus' discoveries were only possible because of data collected by Georg Peuerbach and Johannes Müller. The next major discovery, Kepler's laws, would not have been possible without the vast improvement in planetary tables by Tycho Brahe. In the social sciences, Joseph Greenberg's study of language universals could not have been made without hundreds of grammars written by field linguists. Historically minded theorists in all social sciences are dependent on monographs written by historians who have sifted through a mass of primary sources. In any case, it is not always easy to predict ahead of time which data will be more interesting than the others.

Obviously good data collection is not pursued in a vacuum. The geographer Paul Vidal de la Blache stated the issue for geography succinctly in the preface to his *Atlas* (1894): "considered in isolation, the features that go to make up the physiognomy of the countryside are significant as facts; only when they are related to the chain of events of which they are a part do they become significant as scientific ideas." In political science, there are many articles every year which present the results of recent elections and discuss their meaning in depth. While valuable as data collection, such articles are much more useful if they use this new data to confirm or disconfirm existing theories. Then, such work is not only novel data collection but an innovative contribution to science. Both data and interpretation are obviously important, and data collection unrelated to interpretation and theory is usually trivial. Most data collectors are aware of the

DEFINING INNOVATION

danger and do interpret or theorize about their data; certainly the more innovative ones do.

Besides the fusion of novel data collection and innovative theories, innovation is also characterized by the fact that large bodies of work spring up around important hypotheses, even within narrow subject areas. We may take as an example two related hypotheses concerning the party systems of Scandinavia—the Rokkan hypothesis, which explains the origins and persistence of the basic five-party systems of Denmark, Finland, Iceland, Norway, and Sweden, and the Bull-Galenson hypothesis, which predicts the degree of radicalization in the social democratic parties of the region. Virtually every work on the politics of these countries makes reference to one or both of these hypotheses, refining their applicability to various subnational regions, to changing cleavages and to the appearance of new political issues, and testing their applicability in light of new knowledge. None have refuted the hypotheses outright, but they have as a group much improved them. It is through this kind of work that science progresses, and we must grant every refinement a degree of innovation. Nonetheless, the most important contributors were obviously Stein Rokkan, Edvard Bull, and Walter Galenson, without whom the further developments would not really have been possible.

These new theoretical and conceptual formulations are mirrored by others who have made methodological improvements in a given theory. Take a researcher who refines the innovative work of twenty years ago, using more sophisticated methods. There have been about a dozen who have improved the data and methodology of Seymour Martin Lipset's classic "Some Social Requisites of Democracy," confirming Lipset's thesis in a more persuasive fashion. This, too, contributes to science.

Other important works are revivals and refinements of forgotten research, rather than innovations in the sense of novelty. Alexander George's article on the "operational code" very explicitly attempts to revive the work of Nathan Leites. His clarifications and summary are important and useful, and probably more widely read than the original. Can we deny it the label "innovative"? Being able to resuscitate scholarship of the past in such a way that it is relevant to present debates is no mean feat.

All these refinements are at the core of what Thomas Kuhn (1962) calls "normal science." They take most things as given, and endeavor to improve on the remainder. We must remember, as Derek de Solla Price points out, that "Mountain peaks are not typical. You cannot judge all scientists by the standards of Newton and Einstein. You cannot judge the technological impact of science by the case of transistors." (de Solla Price 1975: 130) While less spectacular than revo-

12   PART ONE

lutionary science, gradual improvements are the main engine of the scientific project. No discussion of innovation can avoid them, even if "normal science" is not the only form of science.

It is tempting, but impossible, to determine a single scale of "innovativeness." There are many varied kinds of innovation, and their relative importance is impossible to judge. Is importance to be defined in terms of a profound essay almost incomprehensible to most other scholars, or should importance be seen in terms of the number of citations? The three volumes of the *World Handbook of Political and Social Indicators*, edited by Bruce Russett *et al.*, Charles Taylor, Michael Hudson, and David Jodice, were among the most cited books in political science in their day. Yet this is a different kind of innovation than the work which others have built using these data, just as Brahe's planetary tables were a different kind of innovation than Kepler's laws. Because they are so different, it is difficult to rank them on a single scale of "innovation."

Length is certainly not a measure of innovation. It does not indicate profundity, in contrast to what some scholars seem to believe. Three seminal essays by Frederick Jackson Turner, "The Significance of History" (1891), "Problems in American History" (1892), and "The Significance of the Frontier in American History" (1893), are only sixteen, twelve, and twenty-five pages long, respectively. On the other hand, the great historian Leopold von Ranke wrote fifty-four volumes, including a twelve-volume history of Prussia. Both were great historians, and it would be futile to rank one's life work against the other's, but Turner is far more innovative on a per page basis. His succinctness also helps make him widely read even today. The virtue of succinctness can be seen in its clearest form when a single article, in all its brevity, proves to be seminal. Paul Samuelson's original theory of public goods is only three pages long, but served as the basis for the study of an important topic in both economics and political science. W. S. Robinson's article, "Ecological Correlation and the Behavior of Individuals" (1950), is only six pages long but succeeded in driving scholars out of ecological analysis and into survey research in sociology, urban studies, geography, political science, and demography. Mark Jefferson's "The Law of the Primate City" (1939) in the *Geographical Review* is only seven pages long; he uses statistical methods to propose a theory at the interstices of geography and demography. There are also books in which only a single chapter is innovative. For instance, a single chapter in Daniel Lerner's *Passing of Traditional Societies* established for the first time a meaningful relationship between the processes of urbanization, literacy, mass media, and political participation. To do so, he used statistical techniques and material from several specialties. This chapter

DEFINING INNOVATION

is widely cited, usually by authors who do not cite the remainder of the book. The reader could easily think of other examples of innovative but brief works.

The most important aspect of innovation is that modern innovators do not span whole disciplines or even major parts of them, but at most only a few subfields each. As the examples of succinctness show, the catch-all interdisciplinary approach is by no means necessary, and is in fact undesirable. Specialization is essential. If we were to compile a list of the innovators in ten or so subjects or subfields, even related ones, we would find that the overlap of names is relatively limited. Take, for instance, the related literatures on neocorporatism and consociational democracy. Among the most prominent contributors to the study of neocorporatism we would include such scholars as Philippe Schmitter, Suzanne Berger, Gerhard Lehmbruch, and many Scandinavian scholars; for consociational democracies, Arend Lijphart, David Apter, Val Lorwin, Jürg Steiner, Gerhard Lehmbruch, Kenneth McRae, G. Bingham Powell, and many others. While the topics are related, the overlap of names is small.

Because of such specialization, it is easy to overlook innovations in subfields other than our own, out of detachment from the problems others are trying to solve. To avoid oversights, we should define innovation in terms of importance for those in the relevant fields. Only a specialist in a given subfield can define what is innovative in that area; this is, after all, the principle of peer review. We are not competent to decide this question for most specialties, and rely on the evaluations of others of what is important. In cases of ambiguity as to whether a given method, concept, or work is innovative, it is better to err on the side of inclusiveness. This is not to say that we should include everything which could possibly be considered innovative, but if we are in doubt about the innovativeness of a work, we are willing to suspend judgment. With thousands of publishing scholars in each discipline, we will leave definitive evaluation to each author's peers.

It is clear that innovation is a mass phenomenon, as can be seen by browsing through books and journals. The index of the *Handbook of Sociology* (Smelser, ed. 1988) lists approximately 3,000 names, and it is doubtful that each and every innovator in sociology made the list. The *American Political Science Review* has reviewed about 100 books in each issue over the last ten years, or 400 per year; the rate was about 200 per year in the 1960s. That is 8,000 in a quarter century, and it does not include all the books published in the discipline. Even if only one out of four was innovative, a conservative estimate, that nevertheless leaves us with 2,000 innovative books. The number of innovative journal articles must be enormous.

Of course, some attribute the explosion of publications not to innovation, but to the imperatives of "publish or perish." Certainly scholars are driven to publish. They are not, however, driven to cite the uninteresting work of others. We may use citations, in some respects, as an indication of innovation (see Chapter 4). The size of the *Social Sciences Citation Index* clearly shows the massive extent of citation, suggesting that there is indeed a lot of citation-worthy work being done throughout the social sciences. Naturally the extent of the innovation varies widely: the modal number of citations per article per year is one, while the mean is over four, reflecting relatively few articles each with very many citations. If no one in the specialty cites a given article in the ten years following its publication, we may safely conclude that it was not innovative (if we allow for a few exceptions). And the rest? We are inclined to be generous. Some, with a few citations, are minor innovations; others are earth-shattering; hundreds and hundreds fall somewhere in between. This is true in all of the formal disciplines.

What, then, is a minimal innovation? We may give several examples. Someone who works to improve a correlation coefficient from someone else's work does advance science, but in a minor way; the same is true of many works which explain residuals. Unimaginative experiments in psychology are also new, and may be useful for others, but are minor innovations. In economic theory, scholars often improve the mathematical proofs of other scholars by correcting errors or by making the proof shorter or more elegant; these, too, are innovations, but of a decidedly minor kind. At the other end of the spectrum we find Darwin.

It is impossible to determine accurately the distribution of works along any imaginary continuum of innovation, although estimates are possible. Some have suggested a rough "law" of scholarly productivity which suggests both that innovation is a mass phenomenon and that it is very unevenly distributed among scientists. According to the "Lotka-Price law of productivity," the number of scientists producing n papers is k/n^2, where k is a constant. In relative terms, this implies that for every one hundred scholars producing one article apiece, twenty-five other scholars will produce two each, eleven will produce three, eight will produce four, and four scholars will each produce five articles. As a result, approximately ten percent of all scientists produce about half of all scientific papers. Even so, the mass of scholars who publish only rarely do, as a group, produce a signficant volume of research. Citations seem to follow a similar pattern: in a study of the articles which three leading sociological journals published in 1960, twelve percent of the sample received fifty-five percent of the citations; about two-thirds of the papers were cited at least once, excluding self-citations (Oromaner 1977: 127). This is approximately what the Lotka-Price law

DEFINING INNOVATION

would predict. As another example, by our estimate only three or four percent of the 10,000 citations in the *Handbook of Sociology* (Smelser, ed. 1988) belong to the five "stars," Karl Marx, Max Weber, Emile Durkheim, Talcott Parsons, and Robert Merton; the other 97 percent are spread among 3,000 people. Again, this is roughly in accordance with Lotka-Price. Of course, we should not read too much precision into this "law," and we must remember that it says nothing of "innovativeness," an unquantifiable concept. Even so, as a rough rule of thumb which has empirical support in both publication and citation data, it is a reasonable working hypothesis on the distribution of innovation among scientists.

Some have explored the innovations at the highest levels of the continuum. Karl Deutsch, John Platt, and Dieter Senghaas (in Deutsch, Markovits, Platt, ed. 1986) have compiled an important list of twentieth-century innovations in the social sciences using much more exclusive criteria than we, defining an innovation as an "advance which makes a substantial contribution." The Deutsch-Platt-Senghaas list does identify some of the most important innovations in the social sciences, but few scholars can hope that their work will be of this magnitude. Furthermore, in some ways their list is rather curious, for they have a substantial bias in the direction of general *approaches* ("elite studies") as opposed to specific *findings* ("iron law of oligarchy"), and they do not in fact identify individual works at all. This means that a lot of innovative work, especially findings in specialized subfields which are not necessarily of relevance for the social sciences as a whole, are excluded. Their list also ignores cumulative advances, such as those by researchers filling in the substantive gaps between subfields by using already-discovered innovations. Furthermore, many important findings are inexplicably left out; Alex Inkeles (1986) has suggested a large number of innovations in sociology which are strangely absent, and the same could be done for each formal discipline. Another peculiarity of their list is the inclusion of "innovations" which are actually a matter of praxis: the Fabian Society's strategy of gradual social transformation, Lenin's revolutionary strategy, Mao's revolutionary strategy, the Soviet one-party state, and Gandhi's strategy of non-violence were all political innovations, but not scientific ones. Neither can these cases really be classified as innovations in public policy because their driving force was not applied social science—Lenin, for instance, was implicitly forced to deny much of Marx's theory of history.

Despite these problems, we can still learn from this inventory, and use it as a suggestive list of the most important innovations in order to understand what characterizes them. Deutsch, Platt, and Senghaas do explore some of the conditions for major innovations in the social sciences, such as the type of position held by the major innovators and their countries of origin. They discuss "interdisciplinarity" in one short paragraph, without giving any further attention to the process, but this brief mention suffices to confirm that "interdisciplinarity" has been an important source of innovation. Since 1930, over two-thirds of the innovations in the social sciences on their list were "interdisciplinary" by their criteria. This is an increase over the previous period, and substantiates our argument that the phenomenon is on the rise at least in the broadest terms.

The picture is most vivid in political science. Every innovation on their list in political science was "interdisciplinary" (even the innovations in praxis). It is apparently impossible to produce an innovation at the pinnacle of political science without surveying the disciplinary frontier. This reflects, in part, the fact that about half of the innovations in all the social sciences have applications in political science; the same is true elsewhere, and almost all of these innovations have applications in fields outside the discipline of discovery. Quite a few scholarly reputations have been made by successfully importing such innovations from their original discipline. Some of these importations are major innovations in their own right for the importing field.

Major innovations come from specialized fields in many disciplines and from their recombinations. Some are methodological, and come from mathematics or statistics, including quantification of social variables, econometrics, correlation, sampling, survey research, and computer simulation. In these cases, scientific innovation was the distillation of a body of mathematical or statistical theory and research into a form which could be applied to the human sciences. Early innovators in these areas came from all formal disciplines, and advances in one often spread quickly to the others.

Other innovations in the Deutsch-Platt-Senghaas inventory could be classified as theoretical. Functionalism comes from anthropology, where it is at least a methodological strategy, a useful checklist for field researchers, a reminder that many forms of social behavior have functional equivalents across societies. Others have suggested theories of functionalism, arguing that all societies must perform certain functions or perish. Structuralism comes ultimately from linguistics, usually borrowed by way of anthropology. Structural-functionalism, drawing from both, is today not only widely used in anthropology, where it was first developed, but in sociology and political science as well.

Some of the innovations on the list are best classified as concepts, although these concepts are clearly associated with certain groups of theories. Economic development, elite studies, social welfare functions, socialization, and social systems are all examples of this kind of innovation. "Economic development" is a concept grouping together a large number of economic phenomena, and the very act of categorization suggests interrelationships. Many other disciplines have borrowed the term as applied to economics and built new terms by analogy, such as political development; again, the term suggests certain interrelationships but does not require them. "Socialization" comes originally out of the concerns of psychologists and anthropologists but has found many applications in both sociology and political science. Again, many different theories of socialization are possible. The same could be said of elite studies, from sociology; social welfare functions, from economics; and social systems, based on an analogy to biological systems.

We see then that a majority of the most important innovations in the social sciences are cross-disciplinary. The exclusive definition of innovation used by Deutsch-Platt-Senghaas selects a manageable number of cases, and allows conclusions about the proportion of such innovations which are or are not located at the interstices of disciplines. This enables us to refine our thesis. There are many different levels of innovation, from the explanation of statistical residuals to the synthesis of huge bodies of knowledge. The farther up the ladder of innovation a work is, the more likely it is to be accomplished at the margins of a given discipline, at its intersection with another.

2

PATRIMONIES: INCREMENTAL ADVANCE AND THE DISTORTING EFFECTS OF THE "STAR SYSTEM"

Because innovations can be both large and small, science is often the adding of successive layers of sediment; even if an occasional volcano deposits a large volume, it does not obliterate the underlying geology. These sediments form a "patrimony," the product of past scientific labor which forms the basis for all research. In the natural sciences, even those sciences which have undergone radical shifts necessarily build on the research undertaken before them. Even revolutions were incremental:

> Major upheavals in the fundamental concepts of science occur by degrees. The work of a single individual may play a preeminent role in such a conceptual revolution, but if it does, it achieves preeminence either because, like (Copernicus') the *De Revolutionibus,* it initiates revolution by a small innovation which presents science with new problems, or because, like Newton's *Principia,* it terminates revolution by integrating concepts derived from many sources. The extent of the innovation that any individual can produce is necessarily limited, for each individual must employ in his research the tools that he acquires from a traditional education, and he cannot in his own lifetime replace them all. (Kuhn 1957: 183)

As the example of Newton suggests, major innovations rely on their patrimony. Major advances often come through a combination of parts of two disciplines, a process which needs to be more fully analyzed by historians of the natural sciences. For instance, biogeology draws from the accumulation of research in paleobiology, biochemistry, genetics,

20 PART ONE

geochemistry, sedimentology, and atmospheric and aquatic chemistry in order to understand the interaction of biospheric, atmospheric, hydrospheric, and lithospheric evolution in the earliest phases of the Earth's history. It would not be possible without the patrimonies of these earlier fields, and "Like plate tectonics also, the new biogeological paradigm has long antecedents in the work of a perceptive minority of forerunners." (Cloud 1983: 15) The accumulation of "normal science" is invaluable for "revolutionary" science.

Most technological innovations are also incremental; they streamline the production process, make the device more efficient, more user-friendly, or they save on maintenance costs. These innovations are by their very nature cumulative, and they rely on a vast body of previous work whether or not the innovators realize this. In the study of the history of technology, some have tried to untangle the sources of technological innovation but have found—not surprisingly—that "any innovation is built upon a great web of earlier developments in technology and science stretching back, certainly, to the Renaissance and even earlier." (von Hippel 1988: 132)

It is interesting that in technical innovation, major advances often draw from two or more patrimonies. Here, too, innovations are more likely to be the result of multiple perspectives. Gilfillan describes the process in shipping technology as follows:

In no case do we find a good invention for the merchant marine being made by a sheer landlubber, nor by a sailor, and scarcely by a ship's officer. To reform the ship basicly [sic] it has always been necessary to depend on some outsider, who yet had sealegs on him, knew his footing on water, while his head could see into other spheres of life—Mathematics, Physics, shore Engineering, Aviation. . . . (Gilfillan 1935/1967: 89)

As in the natural sciences and in technological advance, innovation in the social sciences is usually the result of a process, not a sudden breakthrough, and is the accumulation of work within a subfield. The process is more incremental than most would admit. Compare, for instance, any modern historian's extensive use of the work of other scholars with the rudimentary references made by ancient historians such as Thucydides, Herodotus, Ssu-ma Ch'ien (Sima Qian), the venerable Bede, or Ari the Learned. Yet they too had at least some patrimony at their disposal: Bede, writing in the eighth century, used the works of about one hundred authors, excluding the Bible and other primary sources. The patrimony in the field of English history goes back at least to then.

PATRIMONIES

Certain authors still question the existence of such patrimonies in the social sciences; Stanislaw Andreski (1972), for instance, goes so far as to compare the social sciences with "sorcery." Let us pose two thought experiments for the doubters. Imagine taking a classic in some subfield, such as Moisei Ostrogorski's *Political Parties* (1902), disguising it, and presenting it to a colleague as a recent dissertation. Would it be acceptable as a dissertation today? Or would its ideas, methods, and findings all look outdated, and in ignorance of a large body of research which has improved, refined, superceded, or replaced these ideas? We suspect that the dissertation review committee would have serious questions about the abilities of our fictitious candidate. Take as another example Max Weber's seminal chapter on "Domination and Legitimacy" in *Economy and Society*—a chapter which would be unacceptable for publication as an article in a major journal today. The ideas have been so well integrated into sociology that its poor organization, outdated vocabulary, and other stylistic flaws would preclude publication. (In fairness, these flaws can be attributed to the fact it was published posthumously.)

We trust that some doubters will concede the point. Each formal discipline has a patrimony, the capital accumulation of many scholars' labor. It is common property; although every concept has its creators and developers, they need not be cited every time the term is used. If we use the word "consciousness" or "capital," there is no reason to give their heritage. The same is true of methodologies. If we use two-by-two tables to generate typologies, we do not need to cite Paul Lazarsfeld; we can use game theory without citing the Marquis de Condorcet or John von Neumann and Oskar Morgenstern; we can be psychotherapists without citing Sigmund Freud. A study of historical geography suggests that methodological innovations are absorbed rapidly indeed into the patrimony, being either rejected or quickly absorbed into nonmethodological writings through which the methods are passed on. (Baker 1973: 349) Even the identity of the innovator often disappears into anonymity—how many modern demographers can name the first scholar who used statistical correlations? How many economists know who first constructed mathematical models of the economy? Manifestos and proposed research agendas suffer similar fates, as has Karl Deutsch's seminal article, "Toward an Inventory of Basic Trends and Patterns in Comparative International Politics." (1960) As a supplemental criterion, then, we may say that innovation is not just novelty, as in the world of fashion, but is a contribution to the patrimony.

Having such a patrimony to draw from means that each scholar can start his or her research at a much higher level than did their predecessors. A modern graduate student of astronomy is more knowledgeable than Copernicus or Newton; his equivalent in comparative politics knows more than Montesquieu or John Stuart Mill, and the Ph.D. candidate in geography, anthropology, or sociology is more knowledgeable than her most illustrious academic ancestors. The reason why students can be more knowledgeable—without, of course, necessarily having the reasoning capacities of these forebears—is simple: they have access to the discipline's patrimony. Knowledge has certainly advanced if we may say of a new work, as did Edward Misselden of Thomas Mun's *Discourse of Trade* (1623), "Wee felt it before in sense; but now wee know it by science." Understanding some phenomena in a scientific sense is a precondition for further advance.

The giants, too, rely on the patrimony, perhaps more than the graduate students: Karl Marx refers to Adam Smith on 296 of the 1721 pages of his *Theory of Surplus Value,* meaning that on more than one page out of every six he draws from the work of this single individual. Besides Smith, Ricardo, and other major figures, Marx also made many, often polemical, references to the less well-known scholars of his day. These, too, contributed to his thought and show that giants may stand on the shoulders of midgets. Many leading scholars of the past leave footprints which are most visible today as a result of their role as foils for the giants, from Marx's "Theses on Feuerbach" to Jean-Baptiste Say's "La Theorie de M. Ferrier."

Innovation does not arise in a vacuum, but develops out of the patrimony in conjunction with the scientist's own insight into that patrimony: "It is perhaps the most precious art of the scientist to develop almost a sixth sense, based on deep knowledge of his whole field, that can tell him which researches are likely to be promising and which not." (de Solla Price 1975: 142) Patrimonies provide an anchor, a point of reference. All scholars will know the classics of their patrimony, and these exemplars are the standard against which innovation is measured. All sociologists, for instance, are familiar with a few dozen important works, and all know that "good sociology" will in some way relate to the concerns of these classics or their more recent counterparts. Even so, the direction of research is always changing. Most sociologists, including the very best, will not have read Marx, Weber, Durkheim, or Parsons at all since the early years of their graduate training.

Because such classics exist, it may be possible to identify a central territory of a discipline. Sociology, in all its myriad forms, is concerned with how people form and break group bonds, how people make collective decisions, how differences in power or status affect these decisions, how people are socialized into groups, and how groups of people are found in relations of conflict and consensus. Social-cultural anthropology, too, has a vague core built on field observation of "cultures" and their meaning for members of a given society. Furthermore, anthropology is more acceptant of heterogeneity studied for its own sake—like linguistics but unlike economics. To see the importance of this "core" principle, imagine four articles, on Inuit (Eskimo) ritual, Inuit semantics, Inuit economics, and Inuit political leadership: the first two would not raise eyebrows among disciplinary colleagues, while the latter two would condemn the author as irrelevant and eccentric.

So disciplinary norms and standards exist, and we can even distinguish them if we are willing to allow the same principle to be found in more than one discipline. Notwithstanding such cores—or "paradigms"—disciplines are not unified, and in practice research is only weakly connected to the core. This is because the "cores" are definitions of subject and standards of research, free of specific content such as theories or findings. Once this content is introduced, researchers are propelled outwards—they do not lose contact with their origins, of course, but the connection is increasingly tenuous. Most work at the research frontier has little occasion to cite the classics except in a perfunctory way.

Because such classics exist, there is a tendency among scholars to over-emphasize the contributions of a few outstanding scholars and to forget the more modest contributions they built upon. Time necessarily contributes to this process, as the minor innovations are absorbed into the patrimony and remain largely as influences upon subsequent classics. These classics remain the major point of access to the patrimony, just as Michelangelo and other artistic giants remain the primary access to Renaissance art. Yet the Renaissance encompassed hundreds of talented artists, as a visit to Italian museums would show. For every Mozart, too, there were dozens of now-obscure composers, such as Antonio Salieri. The same is true in the social sciences, as is evident in the process of obsolescence. In a study of 145 sociological articles, the most heavily cited articles maintain a high rate of use for at least a decade while the infrequently cited articles receive most of their citations soon after publication. (Oromaner 1977: 130) Since they are cited to begin with, they presumably have something to add to knowledge, but their findings are apparently rapidly digested.

Only rarely is a major contribution later attributed to many scholars, although this is now true of the development of the theory of plate tectonics in geology. Yet the unsung researchers and their smaller advances nonetheless play a part, and focusing only on the contributions of the "stars" is unfair for the hundreds of scholars thus overlooked. In the natural sciences, Nobel laureates "repeatedly observe that eminent scientists get disproportionately great credit for their contributions to sciences while relatively unknown scientists tend to get disproportionately little credit for comparable contributions." (Merton 1973: 443) Even the princes of the scientific community criticize the exaggerations of the "star system."

Besides the question of justice, the star system may actually harm the cause of science. Robert Merton has argued that when transformed into an "idol of authority, it violates the norm of universalism embodied in the institution of science and curbs the advancement of knowledge." (Merton 1973: 457) The star system may also breed intolerance and tyrany. One extreme case is famous, the stagnation of Soviet linguistics and Soviet biology after Stalin's interventions on behalf of his favorite stars. Yet much less extreme cases occur constantly. Every scholar has heard horror stories about the tyrany of a certain journal's editor or of a certain faction's leader in a university department. Such behavior is often possible only because the star system makes the scholars in question seem more valuable than they really are.

The prevalence of simultaneous innovation shows very clearly the extent to which stressing a few stars is misleading. As Harriet Zuckerman notes, "The history of science is crowded with episodes of much the same discoveries being made independently and often at the same time by two or more scientists." (Zuckerman 1988: 542) For instance, Isaac Newton and Gottfried Leibnitz developed calculus at the same time, 1665–1666. Paul Broca is known for his demonstration that injuries to certain areas of the brain could impair speech, but his idea came from Ernest Aubertin, who had the misfortune not to find an appropriate clinical case of the phenomenon until after Broca. The naturalist Alfred Russel Wallace developed the theory of evolution in Indonesia at the same time Charles Darwin was developing the theory in London with Galapagos data; when Wallace began corresponding with Darwin, Darwin felt compelled to publish not only his theory but letters and notes showing that the theory predated his contact with Wallace. More recently, the AIDS virus was discovered at about the same moment by Montagnier in France and by Gallo in the United States. There are many such cases. Among the 264 Nobel laureates whom Zuckerman studied, seventy "were found to have been involved in multiple discoveries with other Nobelists, besides those with whom they shared prizes. . . ." (Zuckerman 1988: 545) This also happens in the social sciences. Gustave Le Bon and Gabriel Tarde both wrote on crowd behavior in the late 1800s and both offered mental contagion and the role of leaders as explanations why rational men can behave cruelly and irrationally in crowds. The law of diminishing returns was developed independently by three political economists in January 1815, Edward West, David Ricardo, and Thomas Malthus. Bertil Ohlin, Erik

PATRIMONIES 25

Lindahl, Gunnar Myrdal, and Michael Kalecki may all have anticipated parts of Keynes' *General Theory* by several years.

Simultaneous invention would not occur unless the innovation was "in the air." This phrase is too vague, of course. What really occurs is that two creative scholars, both familiar with the same patrimony, logically follow their predecessors in the same direction. Simultaneity would not occur without this logic behind it—it could not happen without a substantial patrimony on which both innovators build. Policy debates are often the catalyst for several scholars to move in the same direction. West, Ricardo, and Malthus all responded to the uses of contemporary economic reasoning in the debate over the Corn Bill of 1815, although Ricardo used the law of diminishing returns to attack the Bill, and Malthus to defend it.

The process of simultaneous innovation is ubiquitous, and not just at the high end of the scale. It is important to remember that "multiple discoveries are not confined to great discoveries, nor to any particular science, nor to any particular period." (Zuckerman 1988: 542) Many scholars have had the experience of discovering another working on the same topic in a similar way, making a simultaneous discovery whether great or small. Keeping such discoveries in mind helps us remember the exaggerations of the "star system" in science.

The star system greatly understates the role of thousands of scholars. A few examples from the social sciences will suffice to illustrate the problem. Any understanding of the effect of electoral mechanisms on party systems builds on the work of many scholars, to say nothing of parliamentary debates about proportional representation. One can make out some summits such as Maurice Duverger, Ferdinand A. Hermens, Douglas W. Rae, Anthony Downs, David Butler, Giovanni Sartori, and many others from Thomas Hare in 1859 and John Stuart Mill in 1862 to George van den Bergh (1956) and Enid Lakeman and James Lambert (1955), but they are part of a mountain range. To miss the range is to exaggerate the height of the peaks. Some of the most insightful were the politicians themselves: there is no democracy which has not had hundreds of contributors to the debate, from Madison's discussions in the *Federalist* papers to the participants in the political debate over proportional representation in France in 1986. The issues have been most recently explored by a large group of scholars in contributions to *Choosing an Electoral System,* edited by Arend Lijphart and Bernard Grofman.

Mass innovation, large patrimonies, and incremental advance are obvious in virtually every part of the social sciences. Take, for instance, the literature on the impact of technology on society and on technostructures. Again, one can make out some faces among the crowd:

Friedrich Engels, Thorstein Veblen, Joseph Schumpeter, Lewis Mumford, John Kenneth Galbraith, Jacques Ellul, Jean Fourastié, and Meadows *et al.* from the Club of Rome. Yet hundreds have added to the edifice, and it would be impossible to disentangle them all.

The economic theory of uncertainty and risk is no different. Certainly it includes work by Johann Bernoulli, Thomas Bayes, Kenneth Arrow, John Pratt, Oskar Morgenstern and John von Neumann, Frank Knight, Howard Raiffa, Michael Rothschild, Joseph Stiglitz, Jack Hirshleifer, Jacques Dreze, G. Debreu, and George Akerlof. Yet even this long list is dissatisfying. Many others, especially in subfields of capital markets, investment, stock markets, and insurance, should be added; a satisfactory bibliography of the topic would include dozens of articles, with almost as many authors represented. Furthermore, those articles rest on a much larger body of work which specialists in the various subfields would have to master. A still larger body of work lies behind all these articles and books, superceded by them in a cumulative fashion, but nonetheless contributions in their day. Various parts of the literature are relevant to almost any use of formal models in the social sciences, and in their non-formal aspects have implications for cognitive psychology, organizational behavior, and other specialties.

Elite studies are also the product of many scholars, with contributions both great and small. Setting aside pre-1900 figures, any review of the topic would include Moisei Ostrogorski, Vilfredo Pareto, Gaetano Mosca, Robert Michels, and Max Weber, among others, from before World War I. The inter-war period would add contributions by Moller von der Brück, Harold Lasswell, Joseph Schumpeter, and others. In the 1950s and 1960s understanding of the topic grew still further, with notable contributions by José Ortega y Gasset, Walter Dean Burnham, Raymond Aron, Floyd Hunter, Milovan Djilas, C. Wright Mills, Ralf Dahrendorf, Heinz Eulau, Susanne Keller, James Meisel, Donald Matthews, Dwaine Marvick, and many others. In the 1970s and 1980s over one hundred other scholars have built on a most impressive patrimony indeed, along a wide spectrum from Robert Putnam to G. William Domhoff.

Some have tried to quantify the extent of the patrimony in a given subfield. Looking back over the years 1930–1955 in the study of public opinion, Bernard Berelson writes, "The first edition of the Smith-Lasswell-Casey bibliography contained 4,500 items from the beginning to 1934; the second edition contained 3,000 items for the nine years from 1934–1943. The compilers of 1943 starred 150 'outstanding titles'; 60 percent of them had appeared since mid-1934." (Berelson 1956: 302) This means that in 1943, two percent of all titles ever published were still judged "outstanding." Even this low percentage implies a large

PATRIMONIES

absolute number, and many more titles would have to be considered valuable even if less than outstanding. We must also keep in mind that this large body of work already existed in 1955—the study of public opinion has since exploded!

In another large subfield, developmental psychology, about 2,000 articles, monographs, reviews, books, and book chapters were published each year in the early 1980s. (Cairns and Valsiner 1984) Extrapolating from such examples, we must conclude that the current patrimony of each of the social sciences is composed of several thousand books and tens of thousands of articles, most of them published in the last twenty years. Such an estimate can be broadly confirmed. The Library of Congress has approximately 200,000 books in geography, 30,000 in anthropology, 50,000 in psychology, 700,000 in economics, 200,000 in sociology and 200,000 in political science, 300,000 in American history, and 600,000 in the history of other countries. (American Library Association 1986) Many are quite old, of course, and not all of these books were innovative when published, but many made some contribution to the patrimony when they originally appeared. Detailed study of all these patrimonies is impossible, but the figures give a good picture of the relative size of the various patrimonies. History, not surprisingly, has the largest number of titles, and in the Library of Congress, American history alone has more titles than almost any other discipline. Psychology's total is surprisingly small, although analysis of the journals would probably find that it has an extraordinarily large amount of research reported in that format instead of in books. Most hybrid fields, because of their recent origins, do not appear at this level of generality in the cataloging system, so the available data do not permit detailed analysis for the vast majority of hybrids. The few which do have call letters all their own, such as human ecology and anthropogeography (2,000 titles), folklore studies (12,000), or social history (26,000), are dwarfed by the masses of volumes in the often descriptive "economic conditions" or area studies in political science and geography. This testifies to the hybrids' recent origins.

We can also try to estimate the size of the patrimony in the journals. Suppose that a sociological journal publishes five articles per issue, twenty per year, or 500 articles in a quarter century. There are, perhaps, 100 journals around the world which are relevant for sociology and which are at least twenty-five years old; these therefore include a total on the order of magnitude of 50,000 articles. Not all are innovative, of course; but if we use the Lotka-Price law as our rule of thumb we could hazard a guess that approximately half of the total innovativeness among those articles is to be found in the best 5,000—still an important number!

28 PART ONE

Berelson's discussion of the state of public opinion research also illustrates the extent of cumulative work. In a review of an illustrative list of the ten "most important" books as of 1930 and the ten most important books as of 1955, Berelson notes several trends. The titles prominent in 1930 were written over the course of a century; those on the 1955 list were all written between 1939 and 1953. Thus, the new appears to supercede the old. The more recent titles also exhibit what we call fragmentation, with the earlier titles mostly broad, theoretical, or speculative work, while the later titles are more narrow "field studies of particular and limited topics or a compilation of findings from such studies." (Berelson 1956: 304) These more particularized studies were really possible only because of the broad theoretical and methodological clarifications that preceeded them.

Throughout every specialty in every discipline we find such a patrimony. They vary in size and in age as well as in importance. While difficult to quantify satisfactorily, they are evidently vast. Nonetheless it would be a serious error to conclude, as did some short-sighted scholars at the turn of the century, that everything which could be invented had been and that the U.S. Patent Office should therefore close up shop. The social sciences have much more work to do.

3

THE PARADOX OF DENSITY

Innovation is a mass phenomenon. Masses of scholars have contributed to rapidly growing patrimonies throughout the social sciences. Can we then conclude that the quantity of innovation is related to the number of scholars working on the same topic? Ideally, of course, increasing the amount of effort applied to any given subfield would also increase the amount of innovative research in that subfield. Administrators, research institutes, and suppliers of grants often act as if this is in fact the case when they allocate their resources.

However, there are good reasons for taking a less sanguine view. Research in a given area is, like most things, ultimately subject to the law of diminishing marginal returns. As a result, "a major proportion of what participants see as innovative work is completed before the field has begun to acquire a signficant proportion of its eventual membership." (Lemaine *et al.* 1976: 5) While the field continues to accumulate knowledge, and the addition of more scholars to a subfield may increase the amount of innovative research done, it does so at a decreasing rate. The topic slowly becomes exhausted.

More ominously, adding additional scholars may not only produce proportionally less innovative research, but may even succeed in obfuscating past innovations. More commonly, advance is simply made more difficult and is less easily communicated out of the subfield to related areas. Theoretical hair-splitting, the use of opaque jargon, and over-quantification are common ways in which too many cooks spoil the broth.

For theoretical hair-splitting, consider an example from international trade theory. There exists a significant literature exploring the conditions under which different forms of "protection" such as tariffs, import quotas, and voluntary export restraints do or do not have equivalent effects. The question requires complicated mathematical analysis but is obviously of importance both for policymakers who must select from among these instruments and for explanations of interest group behavior on trade issues. Some leading scholars have debated under what conditions the social costs of lobbying for tariff reductions are different than the social costs of lobbying for less stringent import quotas; the models on both sides include important assumptions which do not have empirical referents. This is hair-splitting. At the very least, someone approaching the topic may legitimately question whether the mathematical sophistication necessary to answer this question has produced findings worthy of the skills of the researchers, some of whom have produced truly valuable research on related topics of international trade theory.

A concern for esoterica is often the product of having too many scholars concentrated in a given area. The same questions not only tend to be asked in the same way (which may or may not be a good thing), but are also answered in the same way (which is definitely not a good thing). Debates rage over minor points. Historical schools are a common example of this phenomenon, once their founders have asked, and begun to answer, the school's most interesting questions.

Theoretical hair-splitting is only possible in a dense field; in an underpopulated area, such arguments would be ignored. In a dense field, on the other hand, hair-splitting usually arouses the ego defenses of those whose hairs are being split. They respond in kind, and they too find an audience. This kind of scholarly energy could find more productive channels.

For opaque jargon, we need look no further than a well-known sociologist, Talcott Parsons. His theoretical work was frequently verbose, and his often unnecessary invention of terms has had an unfortunate effect on many of his followers in sociology, political science, and anthropology. The jargon may have the effect of obscuring innovative findings. To take another well-known example, the work of Claude Lévi-Strauss is not easy to summarize because of "the abundance of words and their vibrant ambiguity, and in part from the obfuscation in the critical literature that has grown up. . . ." (Freedman 1978: 81) In the case of jargon, the disciples often surpass their master, for this enables work which is less than innovative to cloak its weaknesses. Professional insecurities among the sociological community may also nourish the "professional deformation" of bad writing in sociology, argues Richard Hofstadter:

> As a lately arrived discipline, which has a strong drive toward generalization, sociology felt obliged to justify itself by taking on an air of profundity, and its practitioners fell into the trap of imagining that an

THE PARADOX OF DENSITY

idea gains in force and dignity the more abstractly it is expressed. (Hofstadter 1968: 12)

Living in a dense field lets them get away with it. Jargons, like natural languages, require some minimal speech community if they are not to disappear into the obscurity of extinct languages such as Manx or Cornish. Overcrowding can provide such a community, sometimes with deleterious effects on the advance of science. The jargon persists because the subfields in which it is used are sufficiently well-populated to give it an audience which can understand it. If the field were not so dense, no one would bother to read the work and its authors would learn through negative reinforcement how to write more clearly.

Jargon also cuts a scholarly community off from other subfields. Despite their relevance to one another, complains one anthropologist, "the languages of the physical anthropologist, the linguist, the archaeologist and the specialist in culture are almost completely turned in on themselves." (Matos Mar 1988: 205) Obviously, this makes communication across boundaries more difficult. Even if the jargon does not harm communication within a scholarly community it may have detrimental effects outside. Such is true of the language of mathematics, increasingly used in the social sciences. As one advocate admits,

> although mathematics serves as an integrating language for some, it serves as a barrier to entry for others. Some scholars, then, turn entirely to other endeavors; some make reference to the theorems and results that form the central part of the theory without fully comprehending their power or limitations; and still others, unable to understand why so many fail to appreciate the value of their research, return to the shelter of mathematical notation. (Ordeshook 1986: x)

Mathematical language and the jargon built around it, like other scholarly languages, hinders communication within formal disciplines and makes cross-disciplinary influence more difficult.

Overquantification is at least as prevalent as the vice of jargon. Because there are many statistically sophisticated social scientists in all formal disciplines, the statistically signficant but analytically insignificant has soil in which to grow. Because of this, small facts may attract fairly large audiences.

The "number crunchers" thrive by communicating with one another, revelling in their mathematical virtuosity. On the sidelines, the rest of the discipline may remain skeptical. After all, "precision" in the social sciences is often unnecessary. "Statements of greater or lesser value may be sufficient; rank ordering and ordinal scales may do; and statistical correlations, however explicit and controlled, are in themselves useless without the existence of an explanatory and empirically verified model which is consistent with them." (Belshaw 1988: 197) There are many social scientists who persist in ignoring such advice because they have colleagues who will read their work regardless; some varieties of econometrics are a notable example.

These scholars forget that some important phenomena cannot possibly be quantified; the non-statistical scholar may take solace in the knowledge that "it is impossible to know how many murders are committed which pass completely unnoticed." (Andreski 1972: 124) Nonetheless, many social scientists continue to produce superfluous quantification because there are other scholars who will consume it. Overcrowding helps make this possible. Scholars often cease to ask to what extent public opinion data, for instance, is useful or meaningful, and instead analyze them for their own sake.

The emphasis placed on quantification by many sociologists may lead to perverse results which violate common sense. Notwithstanding repeated warnings, the problem persists. Ralph Turner cites with approval the views of Carl Taylor in 1946: "I have for a long time worried about the fact that it takes young sociologists from five to ten years to recover from what happens to them in their graduate training. . . . if sociology is to develop into a useful discipline it must combine the type of knowledge and understanding which is derived by use of the most rigid technique of science and the type of knowledge that is known among practical men as common sense." (cited in Turner 1988: 28) As Turner notes, Taylor was in a decided minority of the time. This demonstrates once again that none of these vices can exist without a community of sinners. It is probably true that they are most easily practiced in a crowd, and may even be exalted there. In short, this is the "paradox of density," the tendency of densely populated subfields to produce less innovation notwithstanding the greater effort applied.

Density in the core opens up room for innovation at the margins of the field, on the frontiers. Ralph Turner describes the case in sociology as follows, based on his experience as editor of the *Annual Review of Sociology:*

> For several years it was my practice to write to authors of earlier review articles after five years, asking whether the field had now advanced enough to justify a new review of the same topic. Most of the responses were negative, but included suggestions of closely related newer topics in which substantial development had occurred. In many areas sociology has progressed principally by concentrated attention to a particular topic or paradigm until its novelty has been exhausted and its limitations well

THE PARADOX OF DENSITY

known. Attention then shifts to an alternative topic or paradigm that opens up new possibilities and seems more adequate than the old one. (Turner 1988: 23)

Research on the periphery anticipates this process, and is likely to be more important than that produced by the densely packed scholars in the center.

If innovation is more likely at the margin of a field, why does high density occur? In some fields, density is the result of having an unusually large patrimony. The field of "classics" is intrinsically interesting to many, and the large patrimony provides more than ample room for thought and discussion. On the other hand, even if you are brilliant, it is a challenge to say something new about Aristotle, Plato, or Cicero, although if successful the topic would obviously be of great significance. Similarly, there are mountains of books on Moses, Jesus, or Mohammed—but has the definitive book been written? Even the discovery of new manuscripts, such as the Dead Sea Scrolls, is not enough to stimulate such innovation. The problem is intellectual, and depends on the kind of question you ask and which perspective you take.

Patterns of graduate training also produce overcrowded fields. Like ships, a Ph.D. takes several years to produce, and the demand may be different at the end of the process than it was at the beginning. Graduates are trained in current fads, but find themselves part of a glut a few years later. Many believe that there are too many generative grammarians today because of training patterns in the 1960s and 1970s. As with the other vices of overcrowding, their existence makes scientific progress somewhat more difficult, for they nourish that which is no longer valid. One critic, tired by their "exclusive views" and "impatient discussions," complains that their "Theories of the psychological reality of generative description and its genetic determination so far remain without valid support and do not become more persuasive by continuous repetition. . . ." (Katicic 1988: 236) Yet the generative grammarians remain strong throughout the discipline of linguistics.

Such groups are often successful in reproducing themselves, in part because their students are the teachers of tomorrow. In the humanities, almost all who earn the Ph.D. go into college teaching; in the natural sciences only about twenty percent do. (de Solla Price 1975) We do not have figures for the social sciences, but clearly many economics Ph.D.'s go on to work for government and business. A much smaller but still significant percentage of political scientists work for government, while most anthropologists probably teach. Whatever the figures, this means that density is much more driven by teaching needs in the social sciences than in the natural sciences.

As a result, both the supply of and the demand for teachers generate some overcrowding. In the United States, for instance, there is a great demand for teachers of American politics. Yet teaching is a different function than research; for research purposes some topics in American politics resemble an overcrowded city. There is not only competition for new topics among scholars, but the stability of the American political system means that new phenomena cannot be generated in the real world fast enough to meet the needs of scholars. Work reaches a kind of plateau, with only occasional increases in elevation. Innovative books on the American presidency, for instance, rarely appear, and most scholars in the field never have the opportunity to produce one.

It is easy to dismiss Americans as ethnocentrists, but they are not the only ones. The universities of every country have a need to teach their own history; history is therefore often an overgrown field. Particularly glorious periods in each country's history seem the most overcrowded of all. Naturally the Greeks of today are enamored of ancient Athens; the Italians are most attracted to ancient Rome and medieval Venice; British historians relish the Empire. An extreme case is Iceland, where a sizeable plurality of all academics in the entire country study the Saga period, whether the researcher is a historian, literary scholar, linguist, or jurist. Overcrowding also results when new nations create subfields to justify their national identity. The East European countries are a well-known example; the same thing takes place in Africa, the Middle East, and Southeast Asia today.

Ethnocentric history is only one example of a high density of scholars. Each nation seems to produce a national specialty with a crowded roster of scholars. Scandinavian sociologists over-study social stratification; British sociologists over-study the ruling class; Latin American economists over-study dependency; and Yugoslavs of all formal disciplines over-study self-management. Paul Lazarsfeld provides a few more examples, noting that Finnish sociologists, thanks to their close contact with the State Liquor Monopoly, often study alcoholism, while Indians are most concerned with studies of castes and villages. (Lazarsfeld 1970: 121–127) Naturally there is some logic to all these choices, but it does make innovation more difficult in these areas.

Density may also be nourished by the fact that some questions will have ever-changing answers, thereby attracting researchers. One may ask what the time is almost continually, without getting the same answer twice in a day. Similarly, much survey research on attitudes obtains always novel data, although this research does not often change the manner in which scholars understand the problems at issue. Those who study recent elections, too, perform the labor of Sisyphus, for no sooner

THE PARADOX OF DENSITY 35

is one election analyzed than another one is held which will require their attention.

All these dense areas are the mainstream. These topics are extensively researched and then exhausted. Political culture, after the publication of Gabriel Almond and Sidney Verba's *The Civic Culture,* recruited adepts in many countries, inspiring a series of survey research. By the end of the 1970s, however, enthusiasm waned, and even the concept is little used today except in textbooks. Earlier, studies in Europe of "national character" had experienced the same rise and fall.

It is clear that it is more difficult to innovate in these overcrowded subfields, although not impossible; nonetheless, the potential is greater outside them. Clearly, "The creative mind will typically be attracted by problems which are overlooked, or not recognized as anomalies by his colleagues." (Shapiro 1968: 60) Even so, the potential for innovation varies substantially from one field to the next. For cultural anthropology in the 1930s and 1940s, the absence of data, concepts, and theories meant that any step forward was likely to be significant. The void in the study of clientelism, similarly, made it possible for scholars in several dozen countries to innovate in this subfield simultaneously.

There are many ways out of the problems associated with greater density. One is fragmentation, jettisoning surplus scholars to related topics where density is not a problem. Often events will create new topics, and scholars will move into the vacuum, recognizing that older problems have been largely exhausted. The study of totalitarianism attracted many innovators in the 1940s, such as Hannah Arendt and Carl Friedrich. Similarly, the perceived crisis of the welfare state in the 1970s and 1980s was a topic of great potential because the phenomenon was widely, but erroneously, believed to be new.

When faced with a new phenomenon or when a scholar becomes interested in a relatively unstudied question, the first task is choosing an adequate conceptual framework. When David Apter (trained in anthropology, political science, and sociology) asked in *Ghana in Transition* whether Ghana would become democratic, a modified application of Parsonian theory from sociology proved itself useful. Analogies may also suggest avenues of borrowing from other specialties. In international relations, for instance, an analogy with economic markets (firms/ states, profit-seeking/power-seeking, equilibrium/balance of power) has suggested an application of economic reasoning to other topics. Similarly, Claude Lévi-Strauss's structural anthropology was inspired at least in part by an analogy to structural linguistics.

These examples bring us to the most common road out of high density: interaction with the outside. Economics tells us that adding a scarce factor to a production process built on an abundant factor generally makes both more productive. The same is true in research, and adding elements from the outside to an overcrowded field can make a big difference. Those fields with reduced potential for innovation can probably benefit the most from cross-fertilization. Marginality is the opposite of density, and a good route out of its problems.

While we hesitate to formulate it in terms of a sociological rule, it nonetheless seems that the higher the density of scholars in a given field, the less likely innovation is per capita. Foundations who award research grants therefore face a difficult task when deluged by applications from scholars in an overcrowded field. The paradox of density suggests they look for those applications showing the greatest potential for interaction with other fields.

4
DOES CITATION MEASURE INNOVATION?

Mass innovation and the paradox of density interact to make the analysis of scientific advance more difficult. Citation analysis might help clarify the problem. Winding through the process of innovation past and present one confronts the question of citation time and time again. In fact, citation studies are an important part of the sociology of science.

Some suggest that the number of citations a scholar receives, as listed in a publication such as the *Social Sciences Citation Index* (*SSCI*), is a good proxy for measuring the degree of importance of their innovation. Indeed, the number of citations correlates fairly well with other indices of quality such as professional reputation and, where applicable, Nobel prize winners.

Nonetheless, there are many reasons to be skeptical. Obviously citation is not innovation. Citation indexes do not indicate whether the cited work is referred to twenty times in a given article or only once— yet the difference, as all scholars know, is vast. A large number of citations are merely perfunctory, nods in the direction of scholars working on similar topics, an indication that the author is familiar with the relevant literature, or an attempt to establish a kind of intellectual heritage or legitimacy; an example we shall leave anonymous is, "From Aristotle through Locke, Rousseau and Tocqueville up to the multitude of contemporary studies, this analysis has been attempted again and again." In other cases, the heritage is not cited at all, again skewing the tally; according to two specialists in citation study, this "occurs most frequently when a scientist's work has had such a deep impact on the field that the ideas have become part of the accepted

38   PART ONE

paradigm and explicit citation is not considered necessary." (Cole and Cole 1972: 370) Such works have joined the anonymity of the patrimony.

The question deserves more study, but some findings indicate that the number of perfunctory citations is quite large. In a study of citations in theoretical high energy physics, for instance, Moravcsik and Murugesan found that

> A large fraction (two-fifths) of the references are perfunctory. This raises serious doubts about the use of citations as a quality measure, since it is then quite possible for somebody or some group to chalk up high citation counts by simply writing barely publishable papers on fashionable subjects which will then be cited as perfunctory, "also ran" references. (Moravcsik and Murugesan 1975: 91)

Furthermore, perfunctory citation may be self-reinforcing. Any scholar who is frequently perfunctorily cited gains status which makes his future work more visible regardless of its worth, a kind of "halo effect." Cole and Cole note that "Scientists gain visibility originally by publishing significant research. After such visibility is gained, they enjoy a halo effect as their research gains additional attention because of their visibility." (Cole and Cole 1972: 370) This inflates the number of citations for future work by that scholar whether innovative or not. Again, this calls into question the use of citation counts to measure innovation.

More ominously, the number of citations a work receives cannot be viewed without reference to the paradox of density. If major innovations are indeed less likely in subfields which are densely populated by scholars, minor innovators in such fields may nonetheless garner large numbers of citations simply by virtue of being surrounded by many others. A major innovator at the interstices of fields, on the other hand, may have difficulty finding a large audience, although we could expect that those who do cite him would do so in a more than perfunctory manner.

From the standpoint of the social sciences as a whole, citations are also problematic because the size of disciplines varies enormously: psychology is easily the largest, while anthropology, for instance, is relatively small. This means that innovations in psychology receive many times more citations than innovations in anthropology. It is certainly not self-evident that the psychological innovation is therefore more important than the anthropological one.

Another problem for cross-discipline comparability is the fact that each discipline has its own norms of publication and citation. In some natural sciences, it is not uncommon to publish a score or more articles

DOES CITATION MEASURE INNOVATION? 39

each year. In a sense, the standard for publication may be a single "finding," with its relevance and implications suitably explained. In many social sciences, on the other hand, an article built around a single regression analysis would be unacceptable.

It should also be noted that the *SSCI* measures only citations in articles, not books. Disciplines vary significantly in their ratio of books to articles. Psychology is largely dominated by journal articles, while historians must produce books whether or not they also write articles. Many disciplines are in transition: economists publish fewer and fewer books today, although they are not infrequently expected to collect their papers together in book form in order to receive major promotions; political scientists seem to be following their example in mathematically oriented subfields. In a transitional or divided discipline such as political science, using the *SSCI* will overstate the degree of innnovation in public choice and understate advances in political theory.

Individual authors also vary in citation habits. Broadus notes that "Two writers may use the same number of books, pamphlets and periodical articles, yet one may make footnote references to twenty and the other to thirty items." (Broadus 1971: 236) If a frequent publisher and generous citer likes your work, you will receive far more citations than if this visible scholar were less productive, but this would not change the value of the work. Of course, variations due to this cause will even out for a large sample of scholars, but it will skew the tally for any individual, most of whom do not receive many citations each year.

The result is that citations seem a curious measure of anything, and we cannot use them as a measure of innovation. Of course, we would like to be able to correlate "innovation" and "hybridization," but this is not feasible, and even if successful, it would be misleading. However, it does remind us that although hybrids are more likely to be innovative, it is by no means true that monodisciplinary scholars are necessarily less productive. Some such figures have been very important for their own discipline but relatively unimportant for the others. Noam Chomsky and Milton Friedman were each cited over 3,500 times between 1981 and 1985 according to the *SSCI*, a very high figure. Both are monodisciplinary scholars, and are cited primarily by colleagues in their own discipline. Other great scholars are hybrid, many of whom have found a large audience in various fields. Max Weber, also with about 3,500 citations in this period, is a famous example; Talcott Parsons, with a similar number of citations, has an audience in sociology, political science, and anthropology. Karl Marx was cited 1,500 times between 1981 and 1985, as was Seymour Martin Lipset; both are hybrids with wide audiences in many fields (interestingly, the balance between them was slightly different in 1966–1970, with 1,800 for Lipset and 1,100 for Marx). There are also some scholars cited almost entirely outside their own discipline, such as the economist Mancur Olson, with about 1,000 citations mostly by political scientists.

Among the most cited social scientists in the early 1980s are such men as B. F. Skinner (3,000), cited by philosophy, sociology, anthropology, psychology, and others; Paul Samuelson (3,000), more monodisciplinary than Skinner but nonetheless cited by both economists and political scientists; Robert Merton and Emile Durkheim (2,500 each) both have wide audiences outside sociology. Durkheim is a good example of longevity, in contrast to his contemporary, the geographer Paul Vidal de la Blache, who is cited only a few dozen times. This difference is understandable, since Durkheim was more theoretical and Vidal de la Blache more descriptive.

There are many surprises in the *Social Sciences Citation Index:* Thomas Kuhn (2,700) is cited as often as Aristotle (1,500) and Plato (1,100) together. John Maynard Keynes has only 2,000 citations in the same period, more than Schumpeter (1,600) but less than that of Milton Friedman (4,000). Other noted economists are far behind, such as Wassily Leontief (800) and Gordon Tullock (800).

The three core figures of anthropology, Malinowski, Radcliffe-Brown and Evans-Pritchard, have between them only as many citations as the psychologist O. F. Kernberg. Clearly the reason is that there are many more psychologists than anthropologists. This also explains why Freud is cited 13,600 times, to our knowledge more often than any other scholar in the social sciences. The major figures in political science, Gabriel Almond, Robert Dahl, Karl Deutsch, David Easton, V. O. Key, Sidney Verba, and Kenneth Waltz, like their colleagues in anthropology, have a relatively limited audience: Each is cited fewer than 500 times over these five years, and even together these seven scholars have fewer citations than Chomsky. This also reflects the diversity of political science and the relative cohesiveness of linguistics.

In short, it is far from clear what the number of citations really indicates. It may simply be popularity, as in the case of Lenin's almost 6,000 citations versus Darwin's 1,700 and Pareto's 500. This is not the rank order of innovation.

For this reason, quantifying innovation is difficult for us. We can give many examples, present illustrations, analyze the overall process, and discuss its importance for scientific advance. We cannot, however, quantify it. We cannot count the number of innovations and of innovators. Our reader will have to think of his or her own specialty to evaluate the extent of the phenomenon we discuss. Instead, we must go at the task indirectly, selectively, and subjectively, while trying to

DOES CITATION MEASURE INNOVATION? 41

keep the sample as reasonable as possible. The result is admittedly inadequate, but we hope suggestive.

A few other uses of citation data are worth exploring if we keep in mind their serious deficiencies. Some data strongly suggest that the extent of cross-fertilization in the social sciences is remarkable. The only studies we are aware of which begin to address the problem are a series of articles by Jean Laponce (1980, 1983), discussed in Chapter 18, and the sources cited in an article by Broadus. (1971) These data can easily be criticized, but they are the only available. These surveys attempted to determine how many citations made by scholars in a given discipline are citations to others in the same discipline, and how many are citations to outsiders. Economics makes less use of other disciplines than its sister fields: 35 percent of the citations from books were to sources outside the discipline (1949) while only 28 percent of the citations from articles were to the outside (1945–1950). If we assume that, in general, books are more difficult to get published than are articles, and that they are therefore more innovative on average, then these crude data suggest that works of greater innovation are more influenced by other disciplines than the less innovative. The same is true of sociology. In books on sociology, a remarkable 85 percent of the citations are to the outside (1948–1949), while only 61 percent of the citations from articles are (1947–1948). The only time series data we have suggests that leading sociological journals are becoming *less* cross-fertilized, however; 67 percent of the citations in 1950 against 57 percent in 1965. If our hypothesis is correct, this would suggest that the average article in sociology in the mid 1960s was less innovative that the average article in the early 1950s—a not untenable conclusion. Political science is less cross-fertilized than sociology, but more than economics; in books, 69 percent of the citations are to outside the discipline (1948–1949). To review all these data—the best available— is to see both how many scholars cross the borders of their "native" discipline, and how little students of citation analysis have been able to ascertain about the subject.

Having admitted the problems, we might also examine a list of the most widely cited authors in a formal discipline. We have such information for political science. (in Finifter, ed. 1983) Among recently deceased scholars: V. O. Key, in his exemplary work on American politics, applied two sociological methods to mass political behavior— ecological analysis and survey research; Harold Lasswell, a professor of law who made his largest contributions in psychology, is of great importance for political science; Raymond Aron was a philosopher, a sociologist, an economist, and a historian, drawing on each field; Stein Rokkan was a political comparativist combining data from history and

42   PART ONE

sociology, and concepts from sociology, geography, and history, in his genealogical tree of political parties in Western Europe.

The list of the most cited living scholars, again limiting ourselves to those whose major work is in political science, also includes men who have crossed the borders of their discipline: Gabriel Almond, who borrowed anthropological concepts to build several important theories; Karl Deutsch, who is very knowledgeable in a number of subfields of philosophy, history, economics, cybernetics, and history of science, with his most important contributions in political science coming from his juxtaposition of these subfields; Seymour Martin Lipset's works are as relevant for sociology as for political science, and no one has integrated these two fields more than he into the hybrid of political sociology; Mancur Olson, Jr., used the theory of collective goods, taken from public finance, to explore topics in interest group behavior, which has enormous relevance for many political scientists; and Jürgen Habermas, who has a great capacity for synthesis of a variety of subfields of sociology, philosophy, political science, and developmental psychology.

Another related way to approach the problem is to take a list of important books in a single discipline from some survey. The editors of *PS* (Spring, 1983) asked a number of political scientists to list what they thought were the three to five most significant books for their work. Clearly such lists are unsatisfactory in many ways, but we may nonetheless take the responses as a selection of some significant books in political science. We will exclude the classics such as Hobbes, Marx, and Weber, and in the interest of brevity we will list only those which appear on at least two lists: V. O. Key, Jr., *Southern Politics*; John Rawls, *A Theory of Justice*; Gunnar Myrdal, *An American Dilemma*; E. E. Schattschneider, *The Semi-Sovereign People*; Robert K. Merton, *Social Theory and Social Structure*; Anthony Downs, *An Economic Theory of Democracy*; and Angus Campbell et al., *The American Voter*. All are hybrids, cross-fertilized by sociology (Key, Merton, Myrdal), philosophy (Rawls), economics (Downs), or social psychology (Campbell *et al.*). In fact, not all of these authors are political scientists, but brought the tools of their discipline to the study of political problems.

We also have subjective information for one field, a large one. Ronald Inglehart (1983) lists three "landmark" volumes of the behavioral revolution published in the early 1960s: Seymour Martin Lipset's *Political Man* (1960), Campbell *et al.*, *The American Voter* (1960), and Gabriel Almond and Sidney Verba's *The Civic Culture* (1963). All are hybrid. *The Civic Culture* "applied concepts drawn from sociology, social psychology and psychological anthropology . . ." (Inglehart 1983: 433); the authors of *The American Voter* included a social psychologist as well as political scientists. To take another subjective list, Alfred G.

DOES CITATION MEASURE INNOVATION?

Meyer (1975: 115) selected as the six best works in Soviet and East European studies from 1950 to 1975 books by Jerry F. Hough, Joseph S. Berliner, Robert V. Daniels, M. Lewin, David Joravsky, and Kenneth Jewitt: an economist and "two or three" historians. All these examples are in political science, but the phenomenon is not limited to that discipline. Other examples will be found throughout this book.

Such lists are necessarily subjective, and perhaps in ten years a more objective list could be compiled. To do so will require that citation data be used with greater sophistication than is implied by the simple citation count. After all, through citation "Scientific papers are assembled by a process rather like knitting or the way in which pieces of a jigsaw puzzle are held together by interlocking with their neighbors." (de Solla Price 1975: 125) While qualitative studies have been done for the natural sciences, the social sciences have received far less attention. Cross-citation data may help delineate the boundaries of subfields as well as showing areas of high cross-fertilization. Other data would show whether a given scholar is widely cited only within her subfield or by other specialties as well. Qualitative studies of citations would show which citations are perfunctory, which truly build on the previous work, and which overturn the cited piece. Such studies would also make it possible to list individual works which are "major" or "minor classics" in the subfield, as well as to identify those scholars whose bodies of work are deemed most important. This kind of research has been done for individual subfields, such as public choice (Downing and Stafford 1981), but dozens of such studies are required. To do the same for the social sciences as a whole is well beyond the capabilities of any one project until many more of these specialties have been mapped.

5
CEMETERIES FOR BOOKS

Almost all research results are less frequently cited with time. Cumulative innovation, the growth of patrimonies, and the paradox of density combine to bury older scientific innovations. Obviously some hang on much longer than others, but all eventually succumb and become of only historical value.

Social scientists are not immortal. Innovative research merges into the patrimony as it dies, while a lot of the work in overcrowded fields is stillborn. It would be unfair to ask how many books and articles are still alive today. What matters is that most of them were innovative when they appeared: the editors and referees of the journals judged the articles worthy of publication, and judged many of the books worth reviewing in their journals.

We may take as an example political science. There are about 300 journals published each year which are of relevance for this discipline. One might generously admit that most of the articles in these journals bring something new to their subjects—otherwise, the editorial board would not have selected them from among many others for publication. Yet if someone were to go to the library and browse through a journal of thirty years ago, he would find that 80 to 90 percent of all articles have lost any significance. Of course, if this browser were to look only at those articles selected for the top dozen journals in a discipline, they would appear to have aged more gracefully. Even so, what was innovative in political science thirty years ago is, with some exceptions, dead or dying today. The mortality of articles is much lower for history and geography than for sociology or economics. The very maximum life expectancy can be found among articles in the most prestigious journals, such as the *American Journal of Sociology*. Of the 43 articles published in volume 56 of this journal (1950–1951), 20 were not cited at all in 1981–1985 and had apparently died. Most of the rest were on their last legs: 14 were cited only once in that five-year period. Only five of the 43 articles approached or exceeded the level of one citation per year: two were cited four times each, one five, one seven, and one eight times. The most vibrant two are Melville Dalton's "Informal Factors in Career Advancement" and Edwin H. Sutherland's "The Diffusion of Sexual Psychopath Laws." We have no explanation for their longevity. Since science is a cumulative enterprise, the deaths are perfectly understandable; the journals are layers of sediments of knowledge before becoming cemeteries.

So, too, with books. One reader of an earlier draft of this essay expressed skepticism about our discussion below of Quincy Wright's *A Study of War* because "it isn't cited any more." We may take this comment as an inadvertent criterion for deciding when something has been fully incorporated into the patrimony, with "any more" the key phrase. Wright's book was seminal for a generation, and widely cited; having been fully incorporated into that generation's work, it is now a largely uncited part of the patrimony. It, like so many other works, has passed the torch of learning to the next generation. We are reminded of Marc Bloch's comment on a different subject, "If it seems sterile now, that is only the price that all intellectual movements must pay, sooner or later, for their moment of fertility." (Bloch 1954: 15)

Innovative older work gradually fades away. In fact, obsolescence is an important aspect of the growth of any patrimony. One can determine the extent of advance in a given field in part by the rate of obsolescence. Certainly it varies across formal disciplines: a natural science grows "from a very thin skin of its research front, whereas philosophy and history grow from knowledge that may be quite old. . . ." (de Solla Price 1975: 126) Aristotle's philosophy is timeless, his natural science hopelessly outdated, and his social science somewhere in between.

Many books die, and are interred in stack annexes; others remain alive. It is difficult to ascertain what determines their life expectancy. Mortality can occur for technological reasons. This is obviously true in physics, astronomy, or chemistry; Lavoisier's scales look quaint today. Methodological improvements can have the same effect. In the social sciences, most quantitative works based on aggregate data published before 1950 are outdated today, because W. S. Robinson's article, "Ecological Correlation and the Behavior of Individuals" (1950), succeeded in driving scholars out of ecological analysis and into survey research, itself made possible by technical advances. Only after the computer revolution, twenty years later, did it again become possible to do methodologically sophisticated analyses of aggregate data—as argued in *Quantitative Ecological Analysis in the Social Sciences,* edited by Mattei Dogan and Stein Rokkan (1969). The revival of ecological studies also

CEMETERIES FOR BOOKS

takes strength from the methodological work of Erwin Scheuch on the "individualistic fallacy," which has had an important impact on survey research by sociologists, political scientists, and social anthropologists. Nonetheless, a few important works survived the twin attack of technology and the ecological fallacy; the logic of Durkheim's research on suicide remains important, even though the calculations were all performed manually.

Such longevity is not easy to explain. Murray S. Davis (1986) argues that a certain rhetorical program was essential in order for Marx, Durkheim, Weber, Simmel, and Freud to become classics. This rhetorical pattern made these authors' arguments seductive to their audiences.

The range of a theory may also explain longevity. Robert Merton made a powerful case for theories of the "middle range" in the social sciences, as those theories are best able to combine meaningful theory and empirical evidence. It seems that such theories are also more long-lived; grand theories quickly succumb to the attacks of the specialists and die a premature death, while narrower projects are rapidly absorbed by those in the middle range.

Other cases of longevity show simply that some questions remain important, and the broad approach of early scholars may still provide important points of reference. Andre Siegfried's *Crise britannique au XXe siecle,* written in the early years of this century, will be of relevance as long as Britain's economy continues to decline. Werner Sombart's question, why there is no socialism in the United States, continues to intrigue many scholars. The questions asked by Alexis de Tocqueville and Lord Bryce about American democracy have also remained relevant.

On the other hand, some innovations are forgotten and not appreciated for many years. John Mitchell was the first to discuss the type of stars now known as "black holes," in 1783; the Marquis de Laplace made similar suggestions independently a few years later. Both were forgotten, and Laplace even left the idea out of subsequent editions of his *The System of the World.* The idea did not reappear until 1928 when Subrahmanyan Chandrasekhar worked out the requisite mathematics with the aid of quantum mechanics; the Russian Lev Davidovich Landau made a similar discovery at about the same time. Both Chandrasekhar's teacher, the eminent astronomer Sir Arthur Eddington, and Albert Einstein attacked the idea, and it was forgotten again. Only resurrected around 1970 and not widely accepted for some years after that, this early work was ultimately one of the reasons why Chandrasekhar was awarded the Nobel prize in 1983. Robert Merton gives additional examples:

The history of science abounds in instances of basic papers having been written by comparatively unknown scientists, only to be neglected for years. Consider the case of Waterston, whose classic paper on molecular velocity was rejected by the Royal Society as "nothing but nonsense"; or of Mendel, who, deeply disappointed by the lack of response to his historic papers on heredity, refused to publish the results of his further research; or of Fourier, whose classic paper on the propagation of heat had to wait thirteen years before being finally published by the French Academy. (Merton 1973: 456–457)

Many examples of revivals could be given in the social sciences. Arthur Bentley's theory of interest groups was stillborn in 1908 but revived in the 1950s by David Truman. In economics, Slutsky's equation (1915) was rediscovered by J. R. Hicks and R.G.D. Allen in 1934 and by Henry Schultz in 1935; Ramsey's solution (1928) was rediscovered after World War II largely by Paul Samuelson. Charles Horton Cooley's *Theory of Transportation* (1894), was exhumed a century later for the study of "Giant Cities as Maritime Gateways." (Dogan, 1988) Kaname Akamatsu's "flying geese" model of industrial development in follower countries predated Western analysis of the advantages of backwardness such as Alexander Gerschenkron or Raymond Vernon by several decades, but was not discovered by Western scholars until fairly recently. Cournot's mathematical treatment of economic theory was not appreciated for at least a half century. The work of the Russian economist Kondratieff on fifty-year economic cycles was revived when the next depression came due.

Some resurrections are the result of a prophecy confirmed. Phillips Cutright's article, "National Political Development: Measurement and Analysis" (1963), predicted which countries would soon become democratic and which existing democracies would collapse. Reading the article today, we are forced to admire his perspicacity. We may also note that this article, of great importance for comparative politics, was published in a sociological journal, the *American Sociological Review.*

Some dead or dying books stimulated scientific progress in the course of their assassination. One important example is Henri Pirenne's thesis, best stated in *Mohammed and Charlemagne,* which is no longer accepted but which generated a huge literature attacking and modifying it. Max Weber's *Protestant Ethic and the Spirit of Capitalism,* too, is not generally accepted today but stimulated much research on the origins of capitalism. The Fischer school on the origins of World War I is another case of such "creative destruction," and many other examples could be given. Progress means that the new replaces the old. No matter how wise a scientist is, he and his work are condemned to

CEMETERIES FOR BOOKS

senescence or obsolesence. Only Shakespeare and Homer are immortal—yet the first is probably the pseudonym of the seventeenth Earl of Oxford and the second may never have existed as a single individual at all.

In a forest, dead or decaying trees are usually fertile soil for saplings. Such nurse logs contribute to the process of growth and renewal in nature. So, too, the patrimony serves as fertilizer for the field as it grows graduate students into professors. Important research from yesterday's frontier becomes distilled into new textbooks. In many fields of the natural sciences, graduate students read introductory textbooks which cover increasingly narrow topics; the findings presented are sufficiently well accepted to be formalized in such teaching materials. Many subfields in the social sciences have such graduate-level textbooks. Yet, although the existence of advanced textbooks is a sign of advance, the relative scarcity of graduate textbooks may be taken as an indication of how much more work there is to be done in the social sciences.

PART TWO

FROM SPECIALIZATION AND FRAGMENTATION TO HYBRIDIZATION

Patrimonies are always changing. They grow, of course; yet they also fragment, and scholars in these fragments interact with one another. The subfields, too, divide as they grow, like amoebas. Specialization within each fragment leads to further advance; neither specialization nor fragmentation is to be deplored. At the same time, there are limits to this growth within the framework of a single discipline or subdiscipline. Overcoming these limits requires that something be brought in from outside. As each fragment interacts with others outside its discipline, many pairs recombine and form new subfields, which develop patrimonies of their own.

There are two stages of the process. At first a topic is studied in two different disciplines. As progress is made, the two communicate. Often a new hybrid field is institutionalized, and recognized as separate from its two parents.

While it may sound ironic, scholars innovate first by excluding successively more variables and then subsequent scholars innovate by bringing successively more variables back in. In early phases of research, including all relevant factors leads to a superficial treatment of each, and in-depth study of the more important is essential. This ultimately proves too one-sided, however, and what was once excluded must be judiciously reintroduced. This is hybridization, a process by which specialized knowledge from different subfields is combined. A hybrid field results from the overlapping of two or more fringes from different disciplines. As a result of this process, the social sciences no longer resemble the image most people have of them.

6
SPECIALIZATION IN THE SOCIAL SCIENCES

As patrimonies grow, they become unknowable by a single person. Ralph Turner gives an apt description of this process in sociology:

> In the 1930s and 1940s the aspiration to be a general sociologist was still realistic. There was a sufficiently common body of core concepts and a small enough body of accumulated research in most fields of sociology that a scholar might make significant contributions to several, and speak authoritatively about the field in general. It is difficult to imagine the genius necessary for such accomplishments today. (Turner 1988: 34)

Turner rightly stresses the importance of the patrimony's expansion for subsequent fragmentation. As such disciplines grow, they fragment; most parts become the patrimonies of individual subfields. A rare few, the classics, are passed down in the hagiography of formal disciplines.

Specialization is also necessary as a discipline progresses from broad speculative approaches to more empirical studies and hypothesis testing. No scholar can master all empirical reality, and moving from the level of the abstract to the concrete naturally forces one to narrow down, to specialize.

Disciplines and subfields also fragment along epistemological, methodological, theoretical, and ideological lines. To those in the field, the theoretical and ideological divisions are likely to seem more important than the others. Divisions of ideology and epistemology may well be irresolvable, in fact; divisions along theoretical lines or between alternative "paradigms" can be overcome; divisions of subject matter and conceptual inventories are still more easily combined.

Many of these differences, and often the most significant, come from the fact that two scholars studying the same topic may have very different neighbors and contacts. They may borrow from completely different intellectual sources, and use methods which do not complement each other. Imagine three scholars working on French politics, one using game theory, one using sophisticated statistical methods, and a third presenting empirical analysis expressed in the vernacular. They simply do not speak the same language, and are usually interested in different topics. They will not communicate. Instead, the first may talk to other game theorists in economics or to applied game theorists in international relations, the second is likely to communicate with statisticians and social psychologists, while the third is more likely to communicate with historians and sociologists. People also specialize in this manner, and disciplines fragment along these lines.

Specialization is a recent phenomenon, as can be seen by browsing through old course catalogues. Before World War II, the course catalogue even at mighty Harvard is pathetic by modern standards. In 1902–1903, the social sciences were, with the exception of economics and history, barely represented at all. The courses offered in history were incredibly parochial, all dealing with either European or American history. "Government" was a recognized subfield within history, and the courses offered in this subfield were also parochial—various topics of American government, English government, canon law, Roman law, and international law. Psychology received similar treatment as a subfield of philosophy, and courses were offered in experimental psychology and comparative psychology. What we know as anthropology was represented by the department of "American Archaeology and Ethnology"—like history and government, very ethnocentric. Linguistics did not have a department of its own, but philology was a well-developed subfield within the departments of German, French, Latin, Greek, and Semitic languages. At the turn of the century, economics was the most developed social science. Although it had not broken into formal subfields, it had a relatively large faculty and many course listings. There were several courses in each of the subfields of economic history, industrial and labor organization, money and banking, economic crises, international trade, finance, accounting, and economic theory. It even included sociology, which did not exist as a department or subfield, and which could have been found only in a single introductory course taught in the economics department, "principles of sociology."

By the 1924–1925 academic year, the social sciences had expanded and some had even begun to fragment. Nonetheless, Harvard's course offerings still make it look like a community college of today. (So, incidentally, does its tuition of only $300 per year.) History had discovered the Far East, the Spanish Empire, and several countries of Latin America. "Social and intellectual history," an analytical fragment,

SPECIALIZATION IN THE SOCIAL SCIENCES

appeared. Economics now had recognized subfields, in economic theory and method, economic history, applied economics, and statistics. These two most developed social sciences had also spawned the first hybrid— a series of courses in the subfield of economic history, cross-listed in both departments.

Government had split off from history and was now a department of its own. It even had subfields: modern government (that is, the governments of the United States and Great Britain), law and political theory, and international law and diplomacy. Like any good community college today, it also had several courses in state and municipal government. Anthropology had also made its appearance as a department, encompassing the subjects earlier found in American Archaeology and Ethnology. It offerred topics in anthropological methods, primitive societies, physical anthropology, criminal anthropology, ethnology, and a series of courses in the "races and cultures" of Europe, North America, South America, Oceania, Asia, and Africa. Education, too, had emerged as a department by 1924–1925, although only three courses were offered. On the linguistics front, philology was beginning to emerge from the language departments, and two courses were taught in a new subfield of "comparative philology," one in historical linguistics and one on the phonology of several European languages. Psychology was not yet a department but was organized as a formal subfield of philosophy. The field had grown, and it encompassed experimental, comparative, and abnormal psychology, as well as a number of courses in psychological processes and physiology. Sociology was still not to be found at all.

Out West the situation is similarly bleak at this time. Berkeley's anthropology department had only two people in 1927; sociology did not exist; there were no graduate courses in psychology; political science did not teach any foreign topics at all, but referred interested students to the history department. In the best tradition of American universities, the institution lays its stress on more practical topics such as agriculture.

Thanks to documents such as these course catalogues, it is possible to pinpoint the final stages of the fragmentation of the social sciences from one another and the early stages of their internal divisions. Of course, in the natural sciences and in philosophy taken in the broadest sense, the fragmentation is far older. The history of science is a history of the multiplication and diversification of disciplines, as a brief review makes clear. Richard Merritt reminds us that when Moses came down from Mt. Sinai, "he brought not only the ten commandments but also a secret protocol in his pocket which divided knowledge into divinely-inspired academic disciplines." (World Congress of Political Science,

Rio de Janeiro, 1982) This protocol cannot be found in the Vatican archives, but we know that it outlined seven disciplines: logic, mathematics, geometry, grammar, rhetoric, music and astrology. These borders between disciplines remained sacred until the seventeenth century, when a few heretics challenged them.

Over the course of the following century, heretics were able to add a few new disciplines such as optics or chemistry. It is difficult to pinpoint the moment when the proliferation of scientific disciplines increased rapidly, and we may leave this point to the historians of science. Let it suffice to agree with Harriet Zuckerman that "the boundaries of the sciences have changed greatly since 1901. Scientific specialities now exist that were not dreamt of in Nobel's time." (Zuckerman 1977: 51) While Nobel might have guessed that the contours of the sciences would change, he evidently did not anticipate the speed of the transformation and proliferation. What is more, he could not have expected new branches of science such as molecular biology or plate tectonics.

A similar process occurred in the social sciences. The origins of these disciplines are to be found in philosophy, of course. Philosophy eventually divided into two branches, natural philosophy and moral philosophy, which were later to become the natural and social sciences. Each branch continued to grow, with predictable consequences: "under the impact of the rapid expansion of knowledge, this evolution ultimately led each of the social disciplines to branch off from the parent stem." (Easton 1953: 100) Classical political economy was among the first to break away under the leadership of Adam Smith, Thomas Malthus, and David Ricardo. In the course of the 19th century, Auguste Comte and others constructed sociology as a distinct discipline, followed by similar trends at the end of the century in anthropology, psychology, and political science. Political economy then became economics as we know it today; before and after World War II social psychology began to form as a separate discipline at many universities.

Each of the disciplines began with a strong nucleus before dividing and growing. The distance from the center to the border varies from one discipline to the next, in part because of their different subjects and their different ages. Some have even begun to implode, to contract; demography is the clearest example. More typically, disciplines go through cycles of expansion and contraction as younger hybrids grow and then leave the nest.

The growth of patrimonies is accompanied not only by the fragmentation of former disciplines but by increasing specialization of scholars. Just as the development of distinct disciplines depended on a growing patrimony, so too did increasing specialization; indeed, David Easton

SPECIALIZATION IN THE SOCIAL SCIENCES

argues that "without the progressive accretion to the fund of social data in each generation, there would be no need or purpose behind specialization." (Easton 1953: 100) This specialization, by permitting the in-depth study of a given topic, makes possible a more complete understanding of the phenomenon under investigation.

Before approaching a big topic, it is necessary to break it into its component parts. Obviously, monocausality does not exist, but it may be useful at some stages in research to assume that it does. While everything is related to everything else, some things are more related than others, and cohere into specialties. Price, supply, and demand are a good example, and gravitate naturally towards the field we know as economics. Identifying and grouping such phenomena is a necessary first step towards their study. Separation and classification are essential elements of conceptualization, and the circumscription of a subfield makes it easier to formulate problems.

Specialization has many advantages. Besides providing refined techniques, methods, and questions, specialization can provide context. How many laymen, given a translation of the Dead Sea Scrolls, could ascertain their significance? Or, more tellingly, how many laymen could sort the important texts from the routine, the surprises from the expected? This is the problem faced in archival research: anyone could read their country's diplomatic archives, but how many can make sense of them?

By exposing the weaknesses of existing theories, narrow specialization may force scientists in innovative directions. Such was true of Nicholas Copernicus: "The blinders that restricted Copernicus' gaze to the heavens may have been functional. They made him so perturbed by discrepancies of a few degrees in astronomical prediction that in an attempt to resolve them he could embrace a cosmological heresy, the earth's motion." (Kuhn 1957:184) Specialization has other advantages. It provides researchers with valuable methods and tools so that each scholar need not develop them anew. Refinements in methods may also be more easily transmitted among specialists. To see the importance of these tools, imagine a field linguist trying to write a grammar without concepts such as noun, verb, phoneme, morpheme, and declension. Many native speakers are not consciously aware of grammatical inflection, so the contributions of those ancient Sanskrit, Greek, and Roman grammarians who developed these concepts have provided important tools for all subsequent linguists. Other techniques, such as the comparison of minimal pairs, are somewhat more recent but no less essential.

Specialization has its weaknesses, of course, but need not be deplored in its entirety. Thomas Kuhn argues that "Although it has become customary, and is surely proper, to deplore the widening gulf that separates the professional scientist from his colleagues in other fields, too little attention is paid to the essential relationship between that gulf and the mechanisms intrinsic to scientific advance." (Kuhn 1962: 21) Scientists need no longer justify first principles, but may take them for granted and strive to explore their more subtle or esoteric ramifications.

Narrowness also makes for simplification which, if acknowledged to be limited, can help sort out the complexity of the real world. As Marc Bloch argues, with "*homo religiosus, homo oeconomicus, homo politicus,* and all that rigamarole of Latinized men, the list of which we could string out indefinitely, there is grave danger of mistaking them for something else than they really are: phantoms which are convenient providing they do not become nuisances." (Bloch 1954: 151) While specialization is essential, we must be aware of its limitations.

Specialization is a process. As a field grows, its practitioners generally become increasingly specialized and must inevitably neglect other areas of the disicipline. It is for this reason that scissiparity, the amoeba-like division of a discipline into two, is a common process of fragmentation. The division of physics into physics and astronomy, and the division of chemistry into organic chemistry and physical chemistry, are two important examples in the natural sciences. In the social sciences, what was originally the study of law divided into law and political science; anthropology split into physical anthropology and cultural anthropology; psychology broke up into psychology, social psychology, and psychotherapy and psychiatry.

The fragmentation of each discipline can also be observed at national and international meetings. Everyone who has participated at a gathering of several thousand people such as the International Sociological Association or International Political Science Association has noticed the absence of coherence: twenty or thirty panels run simultaneously, most of them mobilizing only a handful of people. The plenary sessions attract only a small minority, with most participants uninterested in issues encompassing the entire discipline.

The result of such divisions is that each formal discipline gradually becomes unknown and unknowable, or at least unmanageable. No theory or conceptual framework can continue to encompass the entire field. In sociology, Talcott Parsons was the last to attempt such a unification, but he was not successful and no modern sociologist could be. Parsons

> exaggerated the internal unity of the discipline; such descriptions, if applied today, would appear almost ludicrous. Rather, the themes have

SPECIALIZATION IN THE SOCIAL SCIENCES

been and are increased specialization of inquiry, diversification of both perspectives and subject matter studied, and considerable fragmentation and conflict. There appears to be no present evidence of an overarching effort at theoretical synthesis of the sort that Parsons sought to effect, and little reason to believe that such an effort is on the horizon. (Smelser 1988: 12)

As Smelser notes, it is not just subject matter but also perspectives and ideology which divide a discipline. Scholars often try to minimize these differences, in the hopes that both sides can learn from one another despite the distance between them. Occasionally the gulf is frankly recognized; when discussing the causes of the Great Depression, a leading non-monetarist could say of a leading monetarist that "Schwartz and I do not seem to have any common ground on which to discuss our historical stories. How can we talk about the historical facts when we perceive them so differently?" (Temin 1981: 122) Even within a relatively narrow area of economic history, the divisions appear insurmountable.

As this example suggests, the advance of knowledge is not the only force driving fragmentation. For one thing, it is partially dependent on broader social forces: one reason for this fragmentation was the tenfold expansion of faculties and student bodies in the last two generations in almost all Western democracies, and with no small thanks due to veterans' scholarships under the G.I. Bill in the United States.

Institutional forces can have a similarly important effect. Donald T. Campbell (1969) has presented a picture of overlapping specialties, clustered into isolated and artificial "disciplines." Training, collective resource allocation, and institutional forces help hold these disciplines together for reasons which have nothing to do with encouraging innovative research. These clusters tend to be drawn in upon themselves, leaving gaps in knowledge between disciplines. To fill these gaps, he suggests training scholars to specialize in these gaps. Scholars should not attempt to become generalists with a broad familiarity with two or more disciplines, for this will leave them with only a superficial familiarity with the specialized knowledge necessary for innovation. If institutional forms could be found to encourage specialization in the gaps between disciplines, he argues, the sciences could approach a "fishscale model of omniscience," in which all subjects are covered by a series of overlapping specialties, without leaving gaps between them. Campbell believes that once the "fish scales" cover all the territory available, science can progress without leaving gaps in knowledge. While suggestive, he neglects the dynamics of the process. No static world of "omniscience" could ever last, in part because of the reasons Campbell gives and in part because of the processes of innovation, the building of patrimonies, fragmentation, and the problems of density. The major innovators in his fish scale world would still be found at the places where scales overlap, and not in the centers of each one. The social sciences are always dynamic.

Nonetheless, Campbell's institutional focus does help explain why the patterns vary so widely from one country to another. Much of what is political science in the United States would be categorized as sociology or law in Europe. Historical linguistics has a stronger base among the philologists of language departments in Europe than it does in the United States, where it is more closely tied to linguistics. What is in Germany *"Anthropologie"* is "physical anthropology" in the United States, while the American "social-cultural anthropology" is often recognized as "ethnology" outside the U.S. Germany has departments of *Staatswissenschaften,* which have no parallels elsewhere, combining aspects of what others would recognize as public finance, economics, administrative science, history, statistics, and sociology. Such examples illustrate the substantial arbitrariness in the assignment of border areas to one formal discipline or the other.

The issue is a comparatively recent one. One indication of the modern rate of specialization is the number of new disciplinary associations founded in a given period, which shows a rapidly increasing rate of specialization in the United States from 1880 to the present. Only 3 disciplinary associations date to before 1840, 5 to 1840–1859, and 4 to 1860–1879. The period from 1880 to 1899 saw a marked increase, to 27 such associations, followed by 43 in 1900–1919, 58 in 1920–1939, and 77 in 1940–1959. The rate in the next twenty years was almost double that of the previous twenty, with 150 new disciplinary associations formed, over forty percent of the total of 367. (Clark 1987: 37) Besides the sheer numbers, the nature of these disciplinary associations has also changed greatly. The first three associations, the American Philosophical Society (1743), the American Academy of Arts and Sciences (1780), and the American Statistical Association (1839) cover much more ground than recent additions such as the Tissue Culture Association or the Society for the Anthropology of Visual Communication. It is difficult to tell precisely when the phenomenon hit the social sciences, because the available data are not broken down into academic divisions. However, the decades after 1880, in which the rate of growth increased so rapidly for all disciplines, also saw the first social science associations. We may date the origins of the process to then, with the rate of specialization increasing ever since.

Because the social sciences have only recently become sufficiently well-developed to fragment, the question of appropriate boundaries is

SPECIALIZATION IN THE SOCIAL SCIENCES

similarly young. It was only in the 1920s that the social sciences were institutionalized as such, in the form of the Social Sciences Research Council and the Division of the Social Sciences at the University of Chicago. At that time, fragmentation was still rudimentary, primarily at the level of whole disciplines. Since then the degree of fragmentation has been impressive in each of the formal disciplines in the social sciences.

Before 1930, sociology consisted, with notable exceptions, of only a few core fields, among them family, social stratification, and urbanism. Part of "sociology of family" is today related to demographics and the rest has remained a living field only in textbooks; most scholars have moved out towards new hybrids such as social history or women's studies. Social stratification and class are basic concepts throughout the social sciences, especially in sociology, political science, anthropology, and economics. Urbanism, for its part, is now an enormous independent field of its own, expanding into other formal disciplines, and often institutionalized today as "Urban Studies," having left the nest of sociology.

Specialization in political science began in the period when it fragmented from other disciplines such as history or sociology. Political science as an academic discipline began by explaining politics in its own terms, leading to some innovative work such as the research of Woodrow Wilson. However, by the time Wilson had left the discipline for politics, the legal-institutional approach he and others had developed was already past its prime. Charles Beard, for instance, had already shown the need to expand into other subfields for explanations of political behavior; the economist Arthur Bentley had done the same, although his work was not appreciated for decades. This set the precedent, and today a political scientist stubborn enough to try to explain politics solely in terms of politics is unlikely to get very far. As a result, John Gunnell's comments on the development of political theory could just as easily be applied to the other subfields of political science: "Dispersion is less a symptom than the very condition of the field. The condition grew out of the events of the 1960s, became clearly manifest in the 1970s and defined the state of the field by the beginning of the 1980s." (Gunnell 1983: 4) In political theory, this "dispersion" sent scholars off into several other disciplines, including philosophy and economics.

Fragmentation has been continuous and rapid. The subfield of political theory, for instance, was officially divided into three subsections by the APSA Biographical Dictionary: historical, normative, and empirical. The 1973 Directory separated out methodology, with divisions into epistemology and the philosophy of science, as a separate subfield, and subdivided political theory into systems of ideas in history, ideology systems, political philosophy, and methodological and analytical systems. The 1982 Directory began to stem the tide, dividing political theory only into political theory and philosophy, formal or positive theory, and methodology, "but these categories are not particularly descriptive of the field or the ten percent of the members of the APSA who designate themselves as primarily political theorists." (Gunnell 1983: 32)

The same trend is visible in all subfields of political science. International relations, for instance, has changed greatly in the last twenty years. While the core of the field was originally diplomatic history—the explanation of diplomacy in terms of diplomacy—this has shrivelled up and died as the field has moved into security studies, foreign policy and public opinion, crisis management and decisionmaking, international political economy, and mathematical models.

The fragmentation makes many uncomfortable. The Guideline Paper of the 1988 International Political Science Association Congress on the theme "Toward a Global Political Science," lamented that "there is a clear danger of Political Science becoming not one but a multiplicity of disciplines divided by geographic area and functional specialty." The concern strikes us as quaint, if endearing.

7

HYBRIDIZATION: THE RECOMBINATION OF FRAGMENTS OF THE SOCIAL SCIENCES

The specialization of the sciences is the first stage of the process of innovation. The continuous reintegration of specialties across disciplines into hybrids is the next. As in botany, a hybrid is a combination of two different branches of knowledge in a manner that improves the species. Unlike some biological hybrids such as mules, scientific hybrids are not sterile; Jean Piaget suggests that a better biological analogy may be the "genetic recombinations" of molecular biology, "which prove more balanced and better adapted than pure genotypes." (Piaget 1970b: 524) Hybrids are of two basic types. The first becomes institutionalized, either as a subfield of one formal discipline or another, or as a permanent cross-disciplinary committee or program with regularized exchanges among scholars from different disciplines. Others remain informal. These informal hybrids are often hybridized topics, rather than subfields *per se*. An economist interested in questions of development, for instance, is likely to have many contacts with similarly inclined economists, political scientists, historians, sociologists, and perhaps anthropologists. Yet it is hard to imagine this topic ever becoming an institutionalized hybrid field.

The reasons for hybridization are straightforward: in brief, specialization leaves gaps between subfields as they divide. One good example is developmental psychology: "From its rather feeble origins, at the turn of the century, as a vague and ill-defined attempt to bridge the gap between psychological (or behavioral) and biological development, developmental psychology has grown to its present status as a separate and major research field encompassing, in principle, virtually all developmental research in psychology and neurobiology." (Hall and Oppenheim 1987: 92) This is by no means an unusual case. Such new fields, filling the gaps between two existing fields and drawing from both, are ubiquitous.

Some may confound recombination and synthesis. The difference is most clear in history. In our terms, an innovative recombination is a blending of scientific fragments, whereas a synthesis brings a humanistic unity, a new interpretation, a personal or stylistic achievement. Arnold J. Toynbee's theory of history is a synthesis of the best kind; Fernand Braudel's *The Mediterranean World* is a recombination of segments of social sciences, largely history and geography. Perry Anderson's *Lineages of the Absolutist State* is largely synthesis, while Karl Wittfogel's *Oriental Despotism* is largely recombination. Recombination requires scientific advance in the fields from which it draws, while synthesis can occur without such advance.

Because it requires scientific advance, hybridization is a fairly recent phenomenon. It is insufficiently noticed even in the natural sciences, although it occurred first there: The physics community emerged in the mid-nineteenth century, "formed by the merger of parts of two previously separate communities, mathematics and natural philosophy (*physique experimentale*)." (Kuhn 1969: 179) The fruition of this hybrid had been a long time in coming; Sir Isaac Newton had written his *Mathematical Principles of Natural Philosophy* over a century earlier. Many other examples could be given, from biochemistry to astrophysics.

The same process is visible in the social sciences. In the early stages of its development, a new discipline is often an aggregation of specialties from a variety of other fields. John G. Gunnell (1983) writes that "to some extent, political science at the time of the creation of the APSA (American Political Science Association, founded in 1903) was less a distinct discipline than a holding company for a variety of endeavors that were in various ways related, but no longer easily resided in other disciplines." Other disciplines, such as economics, sociology, anthropology, and linguistics, exhibit a similar pattern in their founding years because, as Cyril Belshaw notes, "every discipline had an interdisciplinary beginning, since there was by definition no tradition of professional limitations at the time of emergence." (Belshaw 1989: 2) In many cases, it is accidental whether the discipline's name betrays its hybrid origins: social psychology makes clear its ancestry, while anthropology does not; economics—formerly known as "political economy"—has chosen to turn its back on its former breadth.

Today, the more important process is not the creation of new disciplines, but the formation of new, hybrid subfields. Because it is a feature only of recent decades, hybridization is frequently overlooked; it receives very little attention in the monumental UNESCO collection

HYBRIDIZATION: THE RECOMBINATION OF FRAGMENTS

on *Main Trends in the Social Sciences,* for instance, which organized most of its material as if it fell neatly into disciplines. Just as some seem to believe that the social sciences can be neatly categorized, many others persist in pursuing the holy grail of "interdisciplinarity"—a word which should be banished from the language as virtually devoid of real meaning today. The fragmentation of each discipline makes this impossible, for it leaves gaps between the specialties in addition to those left by the division of the social sciences into formal disciplines. Hybridization sometimes bridges these gaps, and sometimes fills them completely. However, no single project can tackle more than one or two such gaps.

Another reason why hybridization is not well understood is that much of the exchange between formal disciplines takes place in the so-called "invisible college." The first such college was an informal grouping of amateur scientists in the 1600s which later became the Royal Society. European scientists and philsophers formed many more such communities in the 18th century, as Voltaire's extensive correspondence demonstrates. At that time, the invisible colleges were thoroughly international. The number of such colleges has since grown exponentially, through journals, associations, conferences, correspondence, telephones, computers, and facsimile machines. Invisible colleges may be monodisciplinary or hybrid, and this book includes many examples which suggest that the hybrid colleges are more likely to be innovative. Unfortunately, there are few sociological studies of the shapes invisible colleges take which might further support us in this hypothesis; Derek de Solla Price could still write in 1975 that the phenomenon of invisible colleges "might well be the subject of an interesting sociological study." (de Solla Price 1975: 168) Yet such colleges obviously are important, and are essential for the development of an intellectual community. In most university departments there are only one or two scholars representing each specialty, so they must communicate with their intellectual cousins in other departments, at other universities, or in other countries. Because such communication is usually very important for their research, clearly more study of these colleges is needed, especially for the social sciences.

Sciences advance by such interaction. The process is straightforward. As old fields advance, they accumulate such masses of material in their patrimony that they split up. Each fragment of the discipline then confronts the fragment of other fields across disciplinary boundaries, losing contact with its siblings in the old discipline. A sociologist specialized in urbanization has less in common with a sociologist studying social stratification than he does with a geographer doing research on the distribution of cities; the second sociologist has more in common with her colleague in economics analyzing income distribution than she does with the first sociologist. A political scientist researching political socialization reads more literature on the agents of socialization (family, church, school, street-corner society, cultural pluralism, etc.) than on the Supreme Court, legislative processes, party leadership or the recruitment of higher civil servants. Those working on the subfield of security studies have little recourse to the literature on political socialization or industrial relations, but rather "economics, psychology, military strategy, history, mathematics, and nuclear physics and engineering all must be tapped in their applications to politics to conduct security studies in the nuclear age." (Zoppo 1988: 1) Analogously, psychologists studying child development are much more likely to use developmental physiology or the linguistic literature on language acquisition than they are to study clinical psychology.

While in contact, related subfields from neighboring disciplines exchange concepts, theories, and personnel. Those subfields that interact over a period of time often form innovative hybrids, a process general throughout the natural and social sciences. Jean Piaget has pointed out, with reference to the social sciences that "one of the most striking features of the scientific movements of recent years is the increased number of new branches of knowledge born precisely from the union of neighboring fields of study, but in fact adopting new goals that impact upon the parent sciences and enrich them." (Piaget 1970a: 56) These are the hybrids.

There can be no hybridization without previous fragmentation, although not all fragments hybridize. Because of the size of the patrimonies today, specialization is essential. This enables the researcher to build on the work of her predecessors, for recombination is meaningless without the earlier advance in two separate fields. Marc Bloch correctly argues that "the work of reintegration can come only after analysis. Better still, it is only the continuation of analysis, and its ultimate justification." (Bloch 1954: 155) The resulting reintegrations benefit both from specialization and breadth.

There are many hybrid fields throughout the social sciences, and the combinations are many and varied. Child development includes developmental psychology, developmental physiology, language acquisition, and socialization. Indo-European studies encompasses historical linguistics, archaeology, prehistory, and botany. Scholars in the subfield of criminology come from law, sociology, social psychology, psychology, urban studies, economics, and political science. The study of artificial intelligence encompasses formal logic from philosophy, grammar and syntax from linguistics, and computer programming from computer

HYBRIDIZATION: THE RECOMBINATION OF FRAGMENTS   67

science. Folklore studies includes historical linguistics, cultural anthropology, social history, and comparative literature.

Those fields that do not interact outside the discipline generally stagnate, as we discussed under the paradox of density. Unidisciplinary research on a given issue is subject to diminishing returns, and at some point, additional factors must be brought to bear on the topic. As a result, "pathbreaking ideas within any specialty usually come from cross-referencing ideas from other specialties or disciplines, rather than from research that is narrowly focused within the specialty. Specialties that become isolated typically become moribund without the infusion of new ideas from outside." (Turner 1988: 25) Although surrounded by colleagues, a scholar can very easily become insulated in the center of a discipline. Moving to the periphery is essential.

Hybrid scholars are often interested in the interplay of variables, and this may lead them to study many different phenomena. Kurt Lewin, a leading psychologist before and during World War II, was interested in a wide range of psychological behavior, including cognitive process of learning and perception; motivation; interpersonal reward, punishment, conflict and influence; leadership, social climate, group standards, and values. "Although his interests changed and developed, he nevertheless carefully adhered to a central theoretical tenet: that to represent and interpret faithfully the complexity of concrete reality situations requires continual crossing of the traditional boundaries of the social sciences. . . ." (Lippett 1968: 266) Lewin is by no means an isolated example.

In other cases, the concern for the interplay of variables leads hybrids to the position of "hybrid critics" who use their understanding of several fields to highlight and criticize the lacunae of their formal discipline. T. E. Cliffe Leslie was a sociologist and economist whose early work centered on the land problem, especially in Ireland. He later turned to questions of economic methodology, "apparently as an outgrowth of a cross-fertilization between his studies of the land problem and the ideas of Sir Henry Maine" under whom he had earlier studied law. (Fetter 1968: 260) He was particularly critical of rigid deductive theories and abstractions in economics, stressing instead historical systems and acute observation of modern conditions.

In fact, one of the features of a hybrid is to be disturbed by the gaps which arise between fields. Besides gravitating toward these gaps in their own research, these scholars will often attempt to highlight the arbitrariness of boundaries or the irreality of gaps. As one example among many, Charles McIlwain "was profoundly disturbed by the divorce of political science and history." (Bachrach 1968: 511) He worked to bring them together under the auspices of political theory.

Similarly, Halford Mackinder argued that "one of the greatest of all gaps lies between the natural sciences and the study of humanity. It is the duty of the geographer to build one bridge" over this abyss. (cited in Gilbert 1968: 515) He developed one such bridge in his famous "heartland" theory, which examined the role of the geographical pivot area, central Asia, in world history.

By moving into such gaps, hybrids will often discover phenomena others had simply missed. Johann Jakob Bachofen was a jurist, anthropologist, and classicist, who drew not only from ethnography but also the Greek and Roman classics. While he wrote primarily on legal history and on symbolism, his book *Mutterrecht* (matriarchy) was seminal for modern social anthropology. John Ferguson McLennan is another example, a Scottish lawyer struck by the prevalence of "symbols" and "totems," contemporary survivals of earlier forms of legal and customary behavior. In order to account for these survivals, he developed a theory of cultural evolution from archaic polyandry, fraternal polyandry, and then monogamy and polygyny. While his theory is no longer accepted, in the course of this research he invented and developed two important concepts, exogamy and endogamy, which are of wide importance in anthropology today. Like Bachofen, his hybridization was essential for the discovery of important categories of social institutions.

As hybrid specialties form, they generally attract researchers from neighboring specialties, especially stagnant ones; Lemaine *et al.* note that "the scientists moving into a new field tend to come from . . . research areas which have experienced a pronounced decline in the significance of current results. . . ." (Lemaine *et al.* 1976: 5) The colleagues they leave behind find it more and more difficult to make progress, while the innovators press on regardless of the boundaries they face. As Piaget describes it, "the object of any innovatory trend is to push back the frontiers horizontally and to challenge them transversally. The true object of interdisciplinary research, therefore, is to reshape or reorganize the fields of knowledge by means of exchanges which are in fact constructive recombinations." (Piaget 1970b: 524) Such recombinations are essential to the scientific project.

This is very clear in the pattern of Nobel prize winners today. There are many combinations of subfields not officially represented within Nobel's framework. The most fertile of these hybrid subdisciplines include biophysics, biochemistry, mathematical physics, quantum biophysics, neurophysiology, neuro-chemical physiology, and so on. One of the most important of these, molecular biology, is a good example of the process we discuss, for it "had its origins in individual decisions of a small number of scientists . . . trained in diverse fields, among

HYBRIDIZATION: THE RECOMBINATION OF FRAGMENTS

them physics, medicine, microbiology and crystallography." (Baltimore 1978) While not recognized as belonging to hybrids, scientists working at such interstices are the usual prize winners in the now-ancient fields of "biology," "chemistry," or "medicine." In fact, the great changes that have occurred contribute to the growing conviction that the categorization of the Nobel prizes has become increasingly obsolete and that they no longer correspond to the contemporary contours of scientific fields. With the exception of economics, the social sciences are not eligible for Nobel prizes, even in "hard" subfields of psychology or linguistics. One would think that scholars such as Jean Piaget or Noam Chomsky are worthy of the honor, although it would be extremely difficult to give the award in the deeply divided disciplines of history, anthropology, sociology or political science.

Without giving awards, we can recognize those early scholars who worked to establish the independence of their field institutionally and intellectually. The psychologist Floyd H. Allport was a founder of social psychology as a scientific disicpline. Eugen Ehrlich, trained in law, was the founder of the sociology of law. William Cunningham was primarily responsible for the establishment in England of economic history as a degree-giving discipline distinct from both of its parents. Besides producing work of high quality in and of itself, he also succeeded in demonstrating the importance of economic history for both history and economics—a goal of any hybrid. The same can be said of Émile Levasseur, the father of modern economic history in France. He was most concerned with "incorporating the material, concepts, and methods of the social and economic sciences into the study of history. . . ." (Fohlen 1968: 261) Not satisfied solely with such imports, he then turned around and brought history back into economics. This served to bring French economics away from its earlier abstract and speculative tendencies towards history and statistical data.

Hybridization appears in all fields. Charles A. Ellwood spent his life trying to establish psychological sociology; he was influenced by W. I. Thomas and George H. Mead in social psychology, John Dewey in psychology and philosophy, Albion Small and Gustav Schmoller in economics and Friedrich Paulsen in philosophy. The ultimate result was his book, *Some Prolegomena to Social Psychology* (1898), "the first presentation of social psychology to be firmly based on the principles of academic psychology." (Barnes 1968: 31) His most well-known work, *Sociology in Its Psychological Aspects* (1912), took advantage of biologists, comparative psychologists, and hybrids such as Charles Darwin, Lloyd Morgan, E. L. Thorndike, Jacques Loeb, William James, and J. R. Angell.

Each subfield has such a figure. Ralph H. Brown was a pioneer in historical geography, by which he meant not the effect of geography upon history but the "geography of the past." George Sarton, although trained in mathematics and the natural sciences, soon became interested in the history and philosophy of science; he spent his life working to establish this topic as an independent discipline.

Not all hybrids become formally recognized as subfields, but remain instead bodies of research on a hybrid topic. The study of traditional empires, which also goes under the heading of "oriental despotism" or "the Asiatic mode of production," spans political science, sociology, economics, anthropology, history, and geography. Important books, such as Karl Wittfogel's *Oriental Despotism* or S. Eisenstadt's *Political Systems of Empires,* encompass two or more of these formal disciplines. Studies of peasant society are found scattered throughout anthropology, history, sociology, political science, and economics. They also include hybrids such as economic anthropology, as in Raymond Firth and B. S. Yamey, eds., *Capital, Saving and Credit in Peasant Societies* (1964). Research on another hybrid topic, the welfare state, can be found in political science, economics, sociology, and history.

In other cases, a potential hybrid may face a choice of becoming an institutionalized subfield or a looser and informal community of research; in a review of the nascent field of biopolitics, Thomas C. Wiegele decided against presenting it as a field and instead "as a potentially intimate part of every subfield in the discipline." (Wiegele 1979: 3) It is not yet clear in which direction the future of biopolitics, if any, lies. It may become a subfield of political psychology.

One of the most notorious new hybrid domains is women's studies. Its growth is spectacular. From its origins in the early 1960s as a social movement, it had become in less than fifteen years one of the most visible hybrid subjects, recruiting researchers from all social sciences. Yet it is usually not an institutionalized hybrid field, because the debate between those who advocated a formal program or department and those who preferred to change their original disciplines from within has been resolved against "segregation." Today, about 30,000 courses on women's studies are offerred each year in American universities, creating an enormous invisible hybrid college, having produced hundreds of books in recent years and communicating through hybrid journals. All social sciences have been affected by the concept of gender.

The study of major events, too, is usually uninstitutionalized even when hybrid. Among those who study the fall of the Weimar Republic there are historians, sociologists, psychologists, political scientists, economists, and literary critics. Successful work looks at parts of the picture, at the intersection of two or more subfields. *The Authoritarian Person-*

HYBRIDIZATION: THE RECOMBINATION OF FRAGMENTS

ality by Theodore Adorno *et al.*, draws from personality theory, socialization, and the study of political ideology. Peter Merkl's *The Making of a Storm Trooper* (1980) examines changing patterns of political socialization with cross-disciplinary views showing how a large cohort of young males born in 1902–1914 were hitting the job market at the height of the Great Depression. Of course, political variables such as the differences in voter mobilization and loyalty between the Communists, Socialists, Center, and the Nazis, on the one hand, and the various bourgeois and nationalist parties on the other, cannot be ignored when studying the "political" question of Weimar's fall, but neither can the other variables be left out. Economic factors, such as the material foundations of different positions on the tariff question in 1929–1933 play an important role in the coalitions of Weimar's final years, as argued in David Abraham's controversial book, *The Collapse of the Weimar Republic.* Are these scholars cutting Germany into slices, with each studying an isolated aspect? No—the historian becomes a sociologist, psychologist, and economist, the economist becomes a political scientist, and so on. If the work is good, the discipline of the author is immaterial.

Narrower topics are not immune to this crossing of borders. Someone researching the choice between revolutionary and reformist strategies in the German Social Democratic Party (under its various names) reads books from intellectual history, political theory, German politics, political parties, trade unions, and economic policy. When published, the finished research could be categorized as part of several of these subfields. As an example, the English translation of Miller and Potthoff's *History of German Social Democracy* (1983) is classified by the Library of Congress Cataloging-in-Publishing program under "History—Socialism—Germany," with the call number HX273.K5313, while the same book is classified by the British Library Cataloguing in Publication program under "Sozialdemokratische Partei Deutschlands," with a call number in political science, JN3946.583. Of course, both classifications are in some sense "correct."

There are many examples of this classification problem in many subfields. Innovative authors often approach a topic in such a way that the reader cannot tell what discipline the author belongs to. To take only one example among many, Alfred Diamant's *Austrian Catholics and the First Republic* (1960), written by a political scientist, could easily be mistaken as a book by a historian or a sociologist.

Librarians have trouble classifying such books, and no matter how much care they take in classification, they must in the end assign them a call number arbitrarily. While a book may be found in several places in the card catalogue (or computer), it can be on only one shelf at a

72 PART TWO

time. A given book, no matter how hybrid, will therefore find itself shelved among sociologists, anthropologists, or historians. Would the authors of these books be able to say where they would most like their books to find their home?

How many books in a given formal discipline, published in the last two decades or so, cross the borders of their discipline in some way? To answer this question accurately would require more expertise than anyone is capable of possessing. Suppose we take a sample of 1,000 books in sociology, for instance. We would have to know, for each book, how innovative it is, and the extent of its penetration into other disciplines. It would be possible to use a large research team for this task, but inter-coder reliability would likely be poor.

Systematic inventory of the major journals in many social sciences would show that a significant proportion of the authors of their articles are from other disciplines. We may give one example: of the 76 contributors to volume 82 of the *American Political Science Review* (1988), 55 were political scientists and 21 from outside. Of these 21, philosophy, applied mathematics, and economics are the most common disciplinary affiliation. Closer inspection would show that most of the 55 political scientists, although insiders from an organizational standpoint, make use of material from other formal disciplines.

It is clear, then, that hybridization is ubiquitous. Moreover, hybrids can beget further hybrids. This is especially true in the natural sciences, which have reached higher degrees of fragmentation and hybridization than have the social sciences. A fruitful alliance has recently developed within physiology between endocrinology and neurophysiology, neuroendocrinology. This is a second generation of hybridization. On another front, genetic biologists and biological anthropologists have recently used analysis of mitochondrial DNA (transmitted solely by females) to map out prehistoric migrations. Perhaps this will create a hybridized "genetic paleontology." Genetic epistemology, as another example, is a hybridization of genetic psychology and epistemology.

While there are fewer multi-generational hybrids in the social sciences, some have begun to form. Phonetics, which developed most rapidly as a scientific subfield in the form of the hybrid called physiological phonetics—as in the work of Jens Otto Jespersen, Jones, Palmer, Paul Éduouard Passy, and Henry Sweet—has now moved towards neurophysiological phonetics, a third generation hybrid. Political anthropology may see the same development as the inadequacies of the prevalent structuralist approach became more evident; Maurice Freedman (1978: 42) argues that the structuralists' focus on unconscious behavior has left a gap which may be filled by game theory, which analyzes the intentional behavior of individuals interacting with one

HYBRIDIZATION: THE RECOMBINATION OF FRAGMENTS

another. There are today many scholars moving into areas which we will only later be able to recognize as third, fourth, or fifth generation hybrids.

It is important to realize that, once created, hybrids are subject to the same inherent problems as their parents. After some time, hybrids can become sterile, and if they do not give birth to a second generation of hybrid subfields in time, their line will die out. Theology, for instance, was long a stagnant discipline until a variety of borrowed methods resuscitated it. Led by the Tübingen school and such theologians as Ferdinand Baur, Friedrich Schleiermacher, Barthold Georg Niebuhr, and Johann Josef Ignaz von Doellinger, by the second half of the nineteenth century, "Germany had already established itself as the world's centre for advanced study in theology, employing modern methods of biblical criticism, historical investigation, and evidence from geology, biology and other sources." (Kennedy 1980: 105) This historical-textual criticism has, for its part, since stagnated, but is now interacting with the subfields of historical anthropology and historical sociology in its attempt to understand, for instance, the social content of the message of the Hebrew prophets. This effort has proven to hold great meaning for other areas of theology, such as liberation theology. The pattern in theology has parallels elsewhere: a report of the American Association for the Advancement of the Humanities described political theory as a field that had "died and been reborn several times" (cited in Gunnell 1983: 34), and in each case its rebirth was midwifed by another discipline. As another example, throughout the social sciences, it seems that the once-productive marriage of many statistical subfields (regression, factorial analysis) and most subfields of sociology, political science, and other disciplines has brought forth quite a few scholars who have not yet produced viable progeny.

Marxist political economy is another example of how what was once an innovative synthesis can become sterile if it ceases to to interact at the borders of other disciplines. Innovative Marxists have been forced into subdisciplines Marx never dreamed of, and this has been the driving force behind advances in Marxism, which is for most purposes its own formal discipline. The Austro-Marxists fertilized Marxism with neo-Kantian philosophy, the work of Ernst Mach, and the Austrian marginalist school of economics. (see Bottomore and Goode, eds., 1978) However, they tended to stay too close to Marx, and were often too ideological; their activities as a political movement are another matter entirely. Even so, they were the first to use the more recent findings of other social sciences to rejuvenate the Marxist corpus, and out of this school came the first empirical, sociological, Marxist social science.

The Frankfurt School, centered at the Institute of Social Research as it migrated from Frankfurt to New York and back again, innovated by striking out in a different direction. Denying the possibility of a positivist Marxism, they sought to develop a "critical theory" of society. Almost all the major figures drew from parts of several formal disciplines: Max Horkheimer (philosophy, sociology, social psychology), Theodor Adorno (philosophy, sociology, psychology, cultural criticism, musicology), Erich Fromm (psychoanalysis, social psychology), Franz Neumann and Otto Kirchheimer (political science and law); the same is true of the second generation figures, such as Arkadij Gurland (economics, sociology), Jürgen Habermas (philosophy, sociology, linguistic philosophy and philosophy of science), and Claus Offe (political science, sociology). These scholars escaped the sterility of many other Marxists by striking out into other subdisciplines.

The most recent innovations in Marxist political economy are no different. G. A. Cohen's *Karl Marx's Theory of History: A Defence* (1978) drew from traditional English philosophy in writing what Jon Elster called a "revelation." "Overnight it changed the standards of rigor and clarity that were required to write on Marx and Marxism." (Elster 1985: xiv) Elster himself has helped raise those standards still further, especially in his *Making Sense of Marx* (1985), which borrows a number of concepts and methods from philosophy, economics, history, sociology and political science. John Roemer's *General Theory of Exploitation and Class* (1982) uses formal economic models and the philosopher John Rawls' notion of alternative property arrangements, in his attempt to to construct a new Marxist theory of exploitation. Adam Przeworski and Michael Wallerstein have, similarly, used formal economic models to address the questions of working-class consent and of the constraints on state redistributive policies in capitalist democracies. All of these scholars have, in different ways, used a wide range of fields in efforts to escape the sterility of Marxism.

In Marxism as in any field, the borders are in fact the frontiers. Border skirmishes in the sciences expand these frontiers, and also creates new borders, and new gaps between fields. At times, these gaps may coincide with old, long-stagnant, specialties. As the hybrids form second-generation hybrids, they often rediscover these former fields and expand on previous findings.

This process explains what seems to be fads. Joseph Ben-David has described one fad in sociology as follows: "In the forties and fifties mathematically trained sociologists pressed for the development of statistical methods especially designed for sociology, and considered econometrics irrelevant for sociologists. Today the trend is almost completely reversed." (Ben-David 1973: 41) Many, like Ben-David, lament such

HYBRIDIZATION: THE RECOMBINATION OF FRAGMENTS

fads, but they are only a problem if the results of the previous cycle are not rediscovered and must be developed anew.

What is important is the cyclical layering of sediments in different directions and at different levels, each adding to the work of the previous "fad." The subfield of phonetics, for instance, has produced a successful cycle of fads. While acoustical phonology is now out and physiological phonology is once again in, as it was before World War II, "this is not a circle but a spiral; the new trend is more than physiological; it is *neuro*physiological." (Kim 1978: 161) Even without a change in name, the gains of specialization can put a recurrent hybrid on a new level of understanding, as it has political economy: "today's political economists have not simply reproduced the studies of earlier (and perhaps neglected) generations of political economists. The professionalization of both Economics and Political Science led to major advances in both fields, and scholars now understand both economic and political phenomena far better than they did a generation ago." (Frieden and Lake 1987: 4) More accurately, the advances have been made in a number of distinct but related subfields, but the point is the same. Being aware of the history of the discipline can help scholars avoid duplication of effort, and scholars who can draw on older bodies of literature transform fads from wasteful repetition into one facet of the advance of patrimonies.

If such cycles are to be productive, they are also very dependent on specialization and narrow recombinations. While discussing the "reintegration" of "disciplines," David Easton reminds us that "there can be no doubt that to continue creative additions to social knowledge at the higher levels of inquiry, the distinctions among various areas of research will have to be maintained." (Easton 1953: 101) Where we differ from Easton is in our appraisal of the likely pattern of these distinctions. Specialization exists, but is not static: the pattern is one of constant flux as the cores of old subfields burn up, much like the cores of old stars, and as scholars at the margins create new centers of research which eventually grow dense in turn.

The process of fragmentation and hybridization may have another effect, causing entire fields to "migrate." Ethnomusicology has changed from being a field of anthropologists who know a little about music to musicologists who know a little about anthropology, as Freedman describes it: "as the musicians and musicologists have begun to espouse ethnomusicology, the anthropologists, in the narrow sense of that term, have appeared largely to disengage themselves from its study." (Freedman 1978: 59) Something of the same has happened to most fields of political science:

76 PART TWO

> early in this century judicial politics by its various names was somewhere near the center of the study of politics, because of the legalistic approach that pervaded so many fields. But gradually the rest of political science drifted away from a concern with law, thereby severing a link with the judicial politics field. With that link gone, for several decades there has been something of a gulf between judicial politics and other fields of political science. (Baum 1983: 196)

Actually, it is both the subfield of "public law" and political science as a whole which have migrated.

We must end this discussion with a word of caution. Biologists know that not all attempts at hybridization are successful. Some are simply not viable, while others are viable but sterile. The same is true of potential hybrids in the social sciences and it is often true that an actual attempt is required in order to determine whether or not the potential exists. Imaginative scientists will see more easily which attempts are likely to bear fruit. Theoretically, combining just the ten disciplines would produce about 100 hybrids, but in reality there is a recombination of the far more numerous subfields, so the actual number is far higher than that. Of these theoretical combinations, not all exist and not all can exist. Because they are constantly in motion, it would be impossible to enumerate them.

Such dynamics make the process of recombination difficult to capture. What was virgin territory quickly becomes overpopulated, like much of southern California. While difficult to observe as it occurs, the process does leave tracks, and has implications for the formal disciplines under whose ostensible auspices research takes place.

8
FRAGMENTATION BY GEOGRAPHICAL AREA VERSUS ANALYTICAL FRAGMENTATION

There is no great university anywhere in the world today which lacks a series of area research centers, each focusing on a given continent or world region. The idea is of course good—among a group of specialists from several disciplines who share a common fund of historical and cultural knowledge, scholars may find it easier to communicate across disciplinary boundaries. Ideally, this intellectual openness begins during graduate training and lasts throughout a scholar's career. As Lucian Pye notes, "The experience of gaining background knowledge from courses in other disciplines has possibly left those with a foreign area interest less intimidated by disciplinary boundaries and more willing to absorb the skills and knowledge of related disciplines. . . ." (Pye 1975: 9) For instance, the Africanist David Apter studied not only political science and sociology at Yale but also anthropology at Oxford. After graduate training, area studies centers and conventions are important sources of extra-disciplinary contacts, and may stimulate hybridization. These informal connections are the greatest promise of area studies.

Even so, the geographical approach may not be the best strategy for creative work. Useful communication is a chancy affair. One can combine knowledge of subject material from several subfields without necessarily creating a cross-disciplinary hybrid. Geographical area specialists generally know vast amounts of detail from the subject matters of several formal disciplines, and are well acquainted with a wide range of different theories which explain this data. On the other hand, within each area center one all too often finds a potpourri of scholars who have only a territory in common. Many area studies programs need further fragmentation in order to stimulate innovation.

Furthermore, researchers studying similar topics but with different area focuses may work in parallel, without their work being intertwined. Scholars studying the role of religion in South Asia, for instance, would unnecessarily limit themselves if they ignored the role of religion outside that area, since most of the religions of that diverse subcontinent are also found outside it.

Similarly, the differences in the language and history of Japan, Korea, and Taiwan have kept most scholars from analyzing these countries' economic development in tandem. Yet even a superficial glance at these countries' economic and political history since the 19th century shows an extensive division of labor, trade, and flows of capital and labor even before Japan's infamous "Greater East Asia Co-Prosperity Sphere" and far in advance of Korea's and Taiwan's current status as "newly industrialized countries." To the extent that area specialists focus on one country alone for reasons of language, they miss these interrelationships.

In part, the limitations of the area studies approach stem from the fact that most area centers were not created for analytical reasons. As W. J. M. Mackenzie reminds us, "These centres in most cases grew out of demand; a particular area became important to foreign policy and to public opinion. . . . It must be confessed that this way of proceeding does not commend itself strongly to social scientists. The objects of such institutions are generally political rather than scientific. In teaching they are apt to give students an acquaintance with many disciplines and mastery of none." (Mackenzie 1970: 191) This is superficial interdisciplinarity, not hybridization.

Of course, other area studies centers were created to correct an imbalance in resources allocated to study the various countries of the world. Certainly, many horror stories can be told about these imbalances of only a few decades ago, and area programs have performed a real service in rectifying the problem. However, the need for such corrections is, at least in principle, a temporary one.

Hybridization does not usually result from area studies *per se,* but from issue-centered research which concentrates in a given region. The study of development or modernization often took place in conjunction with area studies centers, in such a way that hybridization could occur. Scholars from different formal disciplines found in the theory of development a focus which enabled them to analyze the interrelationship of patterns of political, economic, or social change in a specific regional setting.

FRAGMENTATION

In other cases, area studies may highlight the weaknesses of existing theories, stimulating the formulation of new ones. For instance, the inappropriateness of Western approaches to democratic stability led Nobutaka Ike to develop a theory of stable patron-client democracy in *Japanese Politics* (1970); analogous vacuum-filling in East Asian studies can be found in Robert Lifton's *Thought Reform and the Psychology of Totalitarianism* (1961) and Chalmers Johnson's *Peasant Nationalism and Communist Power* (1962). All three of these books benefit not only from intimate knowledge of the area but also from debates outside it, and each can make contributions beyond East Asia.

It is obvious that theories can benefit greatly from area studies. Any theory developed in one social context may have failings when applied to another, suggesting new issues and often bringing a field into contact with other formal disciplines. For instance, Karl Marx and Max Weber each sought to apply their theories to India and China, and the effort led in Marx's case to the partial formulation of the "Asiatic mode of production." India has since proven to be an important test case for theories of development, in work by David McClelland, Karl Deutsch, Reinhard Bendix, and Barrington Moore, to name but a few.

In each of these cases, the contribution is less geographical than analytical. Nonetheless, some regions lend themselves more to analytical distinctions than others. Some fields, such as East Asian studies, are traditionally dominated by historians. To the extent that this remains true, nonhistorians may be able to make major contributions. The presence of a vibrant community of native scholars in a wide range of formal disciplines may also stimulate hybridization, both among themselves and with outsiders, as the study of Latin America shows. The importation of advanced methodology and theory may depend upon the difficulty of the language for Westerners to learn: where English, French, or Spanish are useful, as in Latin America, South Asia, West or South Africa, or the Philippines, area studies have been more open to external innovations. Soviet and East European studies, East Asia studies, and Near East studies have been much less open. (Pye 1975: 14)

As this suggests, specialization in an area may impose blinders of its own, mirroring the blinders of non-area specialists. The logic of area studies often brings scholars to over-emphasize the cultural and historical foundations of contemporary society, just as generalists underplay these variables. Furthermore, important questions are often not asked in area studies narrowly defined. It would be interesting to compare Argentina and Australia as recent lands of European settlement with very different political and economic outcomes. Similarly, there is not yet any systematic comparison of black Africa and Latin America despite the potential of such a topic in many subfields.

In the end, the usefulness of area studies probably depends on the analytical coherence of the individual countries found in the region. It might make sense to have a center for Middle Eastern Studies, since this delineates not just a geographical area from Morocco to Pakistan but a coherent religious area, to a large degree also a coherent cultural area, and to some extent a similar socioeconomic stage of development. Nevertheless, there are huge differences between these countries, in historical legacies, in political systems, in patterns of urbanization, in economic structure, in social stratification, and in openness to the West. Successful work must address conceptual issues, as did, for instance, Michael Hudson's study of legitimacy and cultural identity in the Arab world. Southeast Asian Studies has great difficulties in this regard, as it is not even geographically—much less culturally, economically, or politically—coherent. On the other hand, studies of comparative communism in Eastern Europe were originally able to benefit from both a geographical and conceptual delineation.

It is true that Latin American Studies has contributed notably not only to the knowledge of this continent but has also generated theories of more general applicability, such as dependency theory. African studies have had much less impact than Latin American studies, but there are scholars such as David Apter, James Coleman, Carl Rosberg, Richard Sklar, and Crowford Young, whose work is of relevance outside the geographical area.

There are remarkably few centers for West European Studies in the United States or for American studies in Europe. A geographical focus is not needed for these countries since their study is delineated by well-developed analytical distinctions. Perversely, as Harry Eckstein (1975) argues, Western Europe is the most cohesive "area" in most objective respects as well as the area most distinct from all others, but it is also the least likely to have institutionalized area programs esablished for its study. The "geographical" unity and distinctness are even more pronounced if one includes other "European" countries such as Canada, Australia, and New Zealand. While the U.S. is well studied because of the large number of American social scientists, "area studies" leads most scholars to neglect Canada—a significant country on the world stage whose total GNP is greater than Brazil's. Canada suffers in a kind of area studies limbo, neither "European" nor "American." Only a few countries have included it into the "area" framework, as in the British field of "Commonwealth Studies" or the Soviet Union's Institute for the Study of the United States and Canada.

FRAGMENTATION

Even if formally included in an "area," smaller countries are ignored whether or not they are theoretically interesting. American scholars of Western Europe, for instance, study mostly France, Britain, West Germany, and Italy, whether or not such studies are always appropriate. Few scholars interested in economic planning in a capitalist economy have compared the two best cases, postwar France and Norway—instead, many have studied planning in France and Great Britain. Until the 1970s, "The rich diversity of experiences in the smaller European democracies has been almost lost to comparative theory. . . ." (Lorwin 1968: 113) Some are still lost. There are many analogies between Finland and Germany in the period 1919–1933, from the roles played by the two wings of a divided labor movement down to the role of an aging war hero narrowly elected President during a period of increasing "fascist" agitation. Democracy survived in the one and not in the other—yet there is no comparative study of the two in any language other than Finnish, despite the obvious relevance of such a study to the important question of why the Weimar Republic collapsed.

To some extent, the existence of area studies as a subfield might stimulate innovation when hybridized. Lucian Pye (1975) argues that there emerged in the 1950s and 1960s a division between disciplines and area studies paralleling that between theory building and data collection. Clearly, interaction could benefit both. Robert E. Ward (1975), on the other hand, argues in the same volume that the distinction between behavioral (often theoretical) and area studies approaches is largely spurious; most area specialists are concerned with extra-regional issues, theories, and methods, in part because disciplinary connections remain essential for appointment and promotion in most cases. Nonetheless, there is often at least a perceived distinction between the theorists back home and the monograph writers in the field even though some are exporting locally grown theories back to the theorists, who can learn from them in turn. Studies of patron-client relations grew out of area studies, for instance, but remind us of phenomena found throughout the world.

Area studies labor under many handicaps in the pursuit of scholarly advance. The geographical divisions paradoxically cut across the analytical distinctions which are essential for fragmentation, specialization, and recombination. On the other hand, area specialists could conceive of their research as potential focal points for the interaction of several subfields. It is obvious that most disciplinary boundaries are the products of Western social science, and therefore also of the structure and problems of Western society. Economics, for instance, clearly owes its present form to the problems of a capitalist market economy. Where such an economy does not exist (or has not until recently existed), the "economic"—production and distribution under scarcity—is often regulated by "social" relationships, many of which are nonetheless susceptible to economic "rational choice" analysis. (see, for instance, Godelier 1974: 614–625) An area specialist can draw on her knowledge of such "noneconomic economics" to cross-fertilize several related subfields and to add important insight into the topic of non-capitalist economics. Non-Western studies, if conceived in terms of attacking and rearranging Western disciplinary boundaries, should be able to make significant contributions. Area studies is probably not the best strategy for either comparative analysis or cross-disciplinary approaches unless the research focuses on a specialized field.

PART THREE

THE CRUMBLING WALLS OF THE FORMAL DISCIPLINES

The twin processes of fragmentation and hybridization, discussed in the previous part, have greatly affected each of the social sciences. Fragmentation is fairly well appreciated in the academic community. University departments recognize fragmentation by dividing themselves into subfields. Textbook writers also recognize fragmentation; most write not an introduction to an entire discipline, but an introduction to a given subfield or sub-subfield: international economics, urbanism, physical anthropology, or social geography. Scholars are also aware of the increasing differences between them as each specializes into an increasingly narrow area.

As this happens, many try to rediscover the unity of what had been a unified discipline. This should not imply that there was once a golden age of unity in each social science, for this was never the case. Nonetheless, some do try to rediscover the legendary unity of their formal discipline. At some point in its development—usually in the folly of youth—each discipline attempts to exploit its potential for imperialism, imposing its perceived unity upon others and trying to place itself in the center of the social science solar system. However, fragmentation is already too great to sustain such unity. As the disciplines mature, they outgrow this phase, and their hegemonic views decay.

This failed imperialism does leave behind a generation of mulattoes, born of a union of the imperialists and the natives. They may create new nations themselves. Other hybrids result from a more conventional marriage of equal partners from different families. It is these latter generations which are of relevance today, not the founders of the ancestral line.

Notwithstanding the contemporary disunity of these disciplines, some intellectual boundaries can be drawn, although in any such exercise it is still hard to tell what keeps the disciplines apart. What determines boundaries is often less a question of subject matter than of method, theory, and conceptual framework. Social and cultural anthropology, for instance, can be set off from other social sciences largely on the basis of ethnographic methodology. Economics is distinguished by its core theories of microeconomic and macroeconomic behavior, while much sociology is characterized by a large toolbox of common concepts (role, status, structure, system, group, and so on).

Even so, the recognition of departments in universities has limited value for research. Jencks and Riesman rightfully point out that "A discipline is at bottom nothing more than an administrative category. The various subdisciplines within biology or history or psychology, for example, have only the most limited intellectual relationship to one another, and the same is true in every other field. They are grouped together mainly because the men working in them went through the same sort of graduate program and have some residual feeling of common identity." (Jencks and Riesman 1969: 523–524) Left without consistent boundaries, each discipline's walls are porous, as are their divisions into subfields. The real mapping of scientific knowledge today highlights the importance of subfields born by recombining segments of older disciplines. A brief review of the subfields in the social sciences shows the extent to which they are in fact more closely linked to subfields across departmental boundaries rather than within them; as Riesman has succinctly stated, "every field harbors within it greater differences than those which divide it, on the average, from neighboring fields." (Riesman 1956: 336)

The administrative division of schools of arts and sciences into divisions of physical sciences, social sciences, and humanities, is not immune to the process. This frustrates some administrators. Lawrence Kimpton, then Chancellor of the University of Chicago, complained that "it is alarming to note that history moves into the humanities, that economics becomes mathematics, that anthropology and psychology ally themselves with biology, and that geography is at home with the physical sciences." (Kimpton 1956: 349) This overlapping is inevitable; administrators cannot stop it. We make no recommendations about what administrators can do in response to this trend; a few others have made some speculative suggestions, such as Donald Campbell (1969), Pierre de Bie (1970), Asa Briggs and Guy Michaud (1972), and Joseph Ben-David (1973). It is, in any case, by no means clear that administrators need do anything at all.

9

THE FATE OF THE FORMAL DISCIPLINES: FROM COHERENCE TO DISPERSION

At almost all universities, hiring, promotion, peer review, teaching, and administration are organized along disciplinary lines, and each discipline jealously guards its sovereignty in these areas. On the research front, however, these disciplines increasingly see their sovereignty threatened by hybrid organizations and research communities which interpenetrate them. Like many nation-states today faced with a deluge of transnational organizations, corporations, and trade, these disciplines believe that they have greater autonomy than they actually do.

The processes of specialization and hybridization have wreaked havoc with the traditional organization of the social sciences. Each formal discipline becomes more and more diversified internally and at the same time more and more open for exchanges with other disciplines.

Just as most disciplines lack a strong core, there is no central discipline in the social sciences as a whole. Moreover, there is no hierarchy of social sciences, and the order of our presentation that follows implies no such hierarchy. Philosophy and history are simply the oldest and most fragmented disciplines, so we discuss them first. Economics and linguistics, while not the youngest, are the least fragmented, and we save them for last. The others are discussed in no particular order, although we grouped neighbors such as political science and sociology together and also put geography, psychology, and anthropology next to one another because they straddle the natural and social sciences.

PHILOSOPHY

Philosophy, the oldest discipline, has not only fragmented but has lost its fragments over time: from mathematics to theology, physics to psychology. The symbol of the original discipline remains only in the title "Doctor of Philosophy" (Ph.D.), now given to scholars from physics to literature. Each fragment split off as its patrimony became unmanageably large and as specialization within the fragment set in:

> sciences such as psychology, sociology and logic became detached from philosophy not because their problems were established once and for all as scientific and of no concern to philosophy . . . but simply because progress towards greater knowledge requires that problems should be identified and that those on which no agreement is possible at a given moment should be set aside and all attention focused on subjects in which joint investigation and verification are possible. (Piaget 1970a: 13)

By implication, philosophy reigns in the domain where investigation and verification are impossible. This is not an easy task.

In the early stages of this fragmentation, we see "giants" who are hybrids of philosophy and a new field. They take advantage of both the speculative and unverifiable from philosophy and the growing scientific nature of the new field. A good example is the hybridization of philosophy and economics. F. A. Hayek suggest that a list of England's "great economists, if we leave out only two major figures, might readily be taken for a list of great philosophers: Locke, Hume, Adam Smith, Bentham, James and John Stuart Mill, Samuel Bailey, W. S. Jevons, Henry Sedgwick, down to John Neville and John Maynard Keynes." (Hayek 1956: 472) It would be easy to multiply the examples for other disciplines and other countries: Montesquieu and Auguste Comte as both philosophers and sociologists, for instance.

As a result of this continual emancipation of its fragments, philosophy is only a residual category today, with subfields in logic, the history of philosophy, ethics and value theory, and metaphysics and epistemology. Yet how long can even these last? Logic is in contact with mathematics, computer science, and linguistics; the history of philosophy with intellectual history; ethics with political theory and welfare economics. Is there something common to these subfields which justifies retaining philosophy as a field where welfare economists, syntactic linguists, and intellectual historians can meet?

F. A. Hayek (1956: 472) has suggested one role for philosophy, at least where it is in contact with the social sciences, in the development of scientific ethics and epistemology. All social scientists address the

THE FATE OF THE FORMAL DISCIPLINES

problems of ethics, and questions of scientific method are typically more troublesome for social scientists than for natural scientists. If Hayek is correct, then all scholars should be given at least a modicum of training in the field.

Philosophy might also evolve to cover that which goes beyond the limits of knowledge. In many ways, philosophy is returning to interact with the natural sciences, increasingly neglecting the social sciences. The encounter between philosophy and some subfields of physics is fascinating. Quantum physics provides plenty of material for metaphysics to explore. Heisenberg's uncertainty principle tells us that there is a trade-off between what we can know about the location of a particle and what we can know about its motion. Pauli's exclusion principle keeps these unlocatable particles from colliding. Electrons move from one energy shell to another without entering the space in between. Matched particles of matter and antimatter may appear out of nowhere only to collide and disappear again. The limit of logical formalization, which can be found in a variety of forms from Gödel to Wittgenstein and others, is another good bone for philosophers to chew on. In all these areas, the philosophical problems are formidable.

HISTORY

Another ancient discipline, history, has had better success keeping its unruly offspring within the fold. Because of this it is perhaps the most fragmented discipline of all. A historian of medieval thought has little in common with a historian of 19th century politics; a historian of Chinese dynasties can find little common ground with a historian of Middle American empires. Even in one area in a given time period, history fragments into sub-subfields: one does not study "Medieval History," but medieval constitutional and legal history, medieval social and economic history, medieval ecclesiastical and religious history, or medieval intellectual and cultural history. Each of these becomes legitimate hunting grounds for the historically minded legal scholar, and for specialized sociologists, economists, and other social scientists. The extent of the specialization means that history is in fact one of the busiest areas of cross-disciplinary combinations, as political history's primacy has been challenged by a series of specialties: social history, cultural history, economic history, psychological history, intellectual history, and so on.

These changes are evident in the history and future of the famous French journal *Les Annales*. Beginning with borrowings from geography, sociology, and economics, "The *Annales* elabored not a definition but a *practice* of social history." (Revel 1986: 174) However, the use of these outside disciplines for the study of social history in the style of the *Annales* seems to have reached the limits of its innovative potential. The current leaders of the school recognize this, and are searching in other areas today. Having already found inspiration in geography, sociology, and anthropology, the editors of the *Annales* are now in search of new frontiers in a manifesto on the occasion of the journal's sixtieth anniversary: "At the margins of the discipline there exists provinces which history claims, curiously without having tried to secure the means of imposing its imperialism. . . ." (*Les Annales* 1988: 293) The journal has set its sights now on these areas.

As in the case of the *Annales*, it is possible to trace the geneologies of some of these hybrids. Some five or six hundred American sociologists now identify themselves as historical sociologists. How did this happen? As is the usual case, fragmentation left gaps. Some historians, abandoning the chronological approach and their discipline's bias in favor of narrative history, moved toward sociology and other social sciences. At the same time, many sociologists felt limited by studying only contemporary societies, or believed that to understand modern societies they had to study their predecessors. Eugen Weber would illustrate the historian turned sociologist, in his work on 19th century France, while Reinhard Bendix or Charles Tilly illustrate the sociologist turned historian. Today, sociology and history are both distinct and difficult to distinguish. Many have attempted to delimit their frontiers, but the problems this entails illuminate the extent of their interpenetration, as well as the tendency of both disciplines to evolve from imperialism to dispersion. We will discuss these issues further in Chapter 21.

Besides being a social science, history is also part of the humanities. This probably explains why history is unique among the social sciences in that it is also possible for novelists to make important contributions to the field. Among the classic novelists, the works of Balzac reflect historical research and present a sociological picture of French society in his time. Many other classics from all European countries could be mentioned. Two recent examples of historical fiction are Giuseppe di Lampedusa, who did extensive historical research for his *Gattopardo*, an important book for understanding the Sicilian aristocracy of the time of Italian unification; and Umberto Eco, who used monastery archives and an extensive reading of medieval theology for *The Name of the Rose*, providing an unmatched portrayal of medieval monastery life.

There is no intellectual core of the field in most departments of history today. History is but an aggregation of specialists; as one member of the discipline admitted, "what holds the lot together are

THE FATE OF THE FORMAL DISCIPLINES   89

simply a common concern for time as an essential component in the narrative of human affairs and a particular skill in the manipulation of the remnants (overwhelmingly documentary) of past times." (Rutman 1986: 121) Some do not even share the concern for time but prefer diachronic analysis. There are no common theories or common methods. Historians communicate very little among themselves, except within subfields. They are extroverted scholars, and borrow much from their neighbors. The pages of the journal *History and Theory* are one of the few means by which they may share findings by relating them to problems of causality, epistemology, theory of history, and so on. Given this picture, of what use for research is a department of history today?

Of course, fragmenting history into its component periods and nations, as is done formally among historians, understates the shared approaches of historical "schools," the extent of common beliefs about how history differs from other social sciences, and above all, neglects the widely accepted "historical method." On the other hand, it is easy to overstate the uniqueness of the historical approach, but certainly there are intellectual reasons why sociologists, political scientists, and economists present their theories in the first chapter of their books, while historians save theirs—if any—for the final chapter.

It is also true that the historical method is a moving target, thanks in large part to changes from the outside, from across disciplinary boundaries. Mabillon and the Bollandists borrowed new techniques of biblical criticism; Niebuhr and Ranke took advantage of the methods of classical philology. "In turning to the social sciences for new insights and new techniques, historians today are only continuing a practice which has been followed at every turning-point in the development and refinement of historical studies in the past." (Barraclough 1978: 273) Not only is the historical method not absolute, but even this common denominator of the discipline changes as a result of contact with the outside. As is true elsewhere, the process is nothing if not dynamic.

ANTHROPOLOGY

The field of anthropology is an excellent example of our thesis. Cyril Belshaw goes so far as to say of the field that "interdisciplinary connections are essential corpuscles in the lifeblood of anthropology, without which it would cease to be effective." (Belshaw 1989: 17) Its origins are to be found in a number of separate bodies of research, in ethnology, archaeology, egyptology, antiquarianism, sociology, and ancient history. Early anthropologists came from these fields and others, including biology, psychology, law, music, geology, medicine, philosophy, and geography. "The very richness and variety of its interests lead inevitably to fragmentation into a number of semiautonomous subdisciplines, practically all of which, moreover, must share their subject matter with some other well-established and independent field of study." (Greenberg 1968: 305) At a minimum, these include archaeology, with close ties to paleontology and other natural sciences; physical anthropology, linked to biology; and social-cultural anthropology, which reaches out towards the other social sciences.

Anthropologists are propelled outwards in two ways. First, observing that some feature is of great importance to a given society may lead anthropologists to study that feature more generally. This brings them in contact with other disciplines: analyzing symbolism may lead them to linguistics or psychology, analyzing art may take them to art history or sociology, and so on. The second major path outwards can be conceived as an accumulation of examples of the first, creating a new field which is a multicultural study of some phenomenon. Observing reciprocal gift-giving in a series of cultures led anthropologists to form the hybrid of economic anthropology, for instance, and similar histories of observations were responsible for the development of political anthropology, the anthropology of religion, the anthropology of development, and so on.

At its inception, anthropology was strongly influenced by Charles Darwin and other biologists. The search for the "origin of species" led naturally to the search for the "origins of culture." "Original culture," the early anthropologists assumed, would doubtless be found in some locale at least as remote as the Galapagos, such as Polynesia or New Guinea. Anthropology was born a comparativist discipline, and exalted cultural heterogeneity, looking mostly at non-literate non-Western societies. Paradoxically, the early Darwinian evolutionists argued that "primitives" had no history, justifying ahistorical ethnography; yet, despite its obvious shortcomings, the approach did make progress.

To overcome the limitations of ahistoricism, Bronislaw Malinowski, A. R. Radcliffe-Brown, and others developed structural-functionalism, which is perhaps anthropology's most well-known theory. Structural-functionalism drew initially from the work of Marx, Max Weber, and others. Its practitioners today may be open to cognitive anthropology, social psychology, political anthropology, and so on. At the same time, structural-functionalism proved so useful that it was borrowed in turn by both sociology and political science, and is central to Talcott Parsons and Gabriel Almond.

All of anthropology is remarkably interpenetrated by others. In the UNESCO review of the field, Maurice Freedman (1978) suggests that there are five main fields of research in anthropology: kinship, politics, law, economics, and religion. To list these topics is to see the potential

THE FATE OF THE FORMAL DISCIPLINES 91

for hybridization with sociology, political science, economics, and jurisprudence. The anthropological study of kinship, for instance, is now being drawn out into areas overlapped by other disciplines. In "primitive" societies, kinship relationships are often the dominant framework for much social behavior, economic, political legal, and religious. As anthropologists give greater attention to the role of kinship in modern societies, they inevitably tread into the sociological family, the economic household, and the processes of political socialization.

In other areas, it is fair to say that this potential has only been partially exploited, but the anthropologists are not to be blamed. The overwhelming majority of political scientists, for instance, know little political anthropology beyond structural-functionalism in the forms borrowed by Almond, Easton, and others. The asymmetry is perhaps starkest in economic anthropology, whose anthropological practitioners must know economics, whereas few economists are versed in anthropology—or know much about non-market societies more generally.

Even if the influence has not been mutual, economic methods have been useful for anthropology. Clifford Geertz has argued that the economic theory of information explains the pattern of "clientelism" in bazaars as well as the persistent pattern of intensive haggling (in lieu of the comparison shopping found in modern economies). Richard Posner suggests that this analysis has implications for other institutions in pre-literate society, and argues that this theory can help bring together anthropological observations on food sharing, polygamy, kinship groups, usury laws, patterns of "gift giving," legal processes, property rights, contract law, family law, tort law, and criminal law.

As this suggests, other anthropologists have reached out towards law and the study of dispute settlement mechanisms. African lawyers such as the Nigerian T. O. Elias have played an important role here by studying tribal law, often in cooperation with anthropologists. This intersection of anthropology and jurisprudence has grown large enough to be organized as the Scientific Commission on Folk Law and Legal Pluralism, under the auspices of the International Union of Anthropological and Ethnological Sciences but also recognized by the International Association of Legal Science.

Anthropology's interaction with other formal disciplines are quite diverse at the current research front. Over the last two decades, social-cultural anthropologists have developed interests in many new areas, including urban anthropology, peasant studies, migration, social and cultural ecology, personality and culture studies, and comparative primatology. This subfield thus has tentacles reaching out into parts of sociology, geography, psychology, and biology. Cultural anthropology and cultural geography may not have identical perspectives, but they share the same territory, particularly in specific geographical areas; the borders between anthropology and human ecology are largely arbitrary. For its part, "Political anthropology . . . fully recognizes history, even if originally it intended to devote itself to the study of societies-without-history. The anthropologist has become a historian." (Izard 1988) There is also a British tradition linking philosophy and anthropology, including some philosophers who are also field anthropologists such as Gellner and Jarvie.

Anthropology and psychology have interacted in several areas. Pioneers such as Seligman and Rivers used medical-psychological approaches in their fieldwork; among other topics, they sought to measure and interpret differences in sensory perception. Gregory Bateson and Clyde and Florence Kluckhohn, among others, used psychoanalysis in anthropology. Some psychiatrists have recently reversed the flow by applying anthropology to their research. Arthur Kleinman, for instance, uses anthropology to rethink the aetiology and definition of psychiatric illness.

Anthropology is more honest about its hybridization than most, as can be seen from the names the discipline gives its offspring. It covers the subfields of biological anthropology, cultural anthropology, linguistic anthropology, social anthropology, political anthropology, the anthropology of social action, archaelogy, regional cultures, and the theory and methods of anthropology. Is there anything that ties these subfields together while setting them apart from other fields? As we have argued, most of these subfields have closer ties to subfields in other disciplines—biology, sociology, linguistics, political science, and paleontology—than they do to their sibling subfields.

Extensive interaction with the outside is also found in archaeology, a subfield which often fits the rest of the discipline poorly at best, and which is a formal discipline of its own in many countries. Archaeology is a fusion of four main lines of research: classics, antiquarianism, geology, and anthropology. Sigfried de Laet argues that "multidisciplinary" approaches in archaeology "have come to be so vital that they are now an integral part of research practice" and that progress there "would no longer be conceivable without them." (de Laet 1978: 207) To take an obvious example, advances in the methods of dating has important applications in archaeology. More surprisingly, so does astronomy. Chou Hung-hsiang, a professor of Chinese at UCLA, and the astronomer Kevin D. Pang of NASA's Jet Propulsion Laboratory have teamed up to use ancient Chinese astronomical records to solve several dating problems of early Chinese history such as the founding of the Xia dynasty. They also demonstrated that these data are consistent

THE FATE OF THE FORMAL DISCIPLINES

with one another and with astronomical theory and can be taken as accurate by modern astronomers.

Other natural sciences also stimulate advance in archaeology. The study of the natural environment in which prehistoric man evolved naturally brings archaeologists to the work of geologists, paleontologists, paleographers, and others. At the same time, examining the introduction of agriculture and the domestication of animals brings in zoologists and palynologists. More recently, specialists in medicine have collaborated in the new hybrid of paleopathology. Paleontology, too, is in search of new research tools: the use of the electronic microscope in the analysis of tooth enamel has been helpful, and the chemical analysis of fossils has furnished information about the diet of the individuals examined. (Rukang 1988: 294) Each successive wave of external influence has contributed to the field.

It is difficult to determine whether anthropologists communicate more among themselves or with their neighbors. The distance covered by anthropology in one generation can be marked by two milestones. In 1948, Radcliffe-Brown saw in anthropology the "Science of Society," incorporating sociology, economics, psychology, political science, and others. Only twenty years later one could read instead that "a general anthropologist equally at home in all areas is now generally regarded as a mythical hero whose like is no longer among us." (Chang 1967: 227) Dependence on the outside is usually freely admitted; one eminent anthropologist testified that "Without the contributions of other classical disciplines such as philology, archaeology, epigraphy, and papyrology, nothing of what I have done in an anthropological perspective would have been possible." (Vernant 1985: 2) This is a classic statement of the hybrid scholar.

GEOGRAPHY

Geography is a "crossroads science, a science that resides at the confluence of the natural and human sciences, a synthesis of approaches originating elsewhere." (Claval 1988: 1) Shakespeare wrote that all the world's a stage. While the Bard was not referring to the world in a literal sense, it is nevertheless true that the earth is the stage on which human affairs unfold. Geography studies that stage; to the extent that the staging affects the play, it interacts with all of the social sciences. Because of this, at the turn of the century, some geographers in France and in Germany claimed for geography a central place, a dominant role at the crossroads of all social sciences.

Like all such disciplinary imperialisms, this proved to be untenable, and the discipline is very fragmented today. The discipline's heterogeneity is at least partly the result of the diversity of its origins. In the United States, geography developed out of geology, in Germany out of "earth science" (*Erdkunde*), in France out of history, and in Britain out of those interested in management of the Empire. (Mikesell 1969: 228) The result of these manifold origins is a discipline spanning both the natural and social sciences.

Systematic interaction with the social sciences dates to the first few decades of the century. Isaiah Bowman combined physical and human geography into a type of regional geography as well as writing an influential book on political geography. In his *Geography in Relation to the Social Sciences* (1934), he refused to define geography—in effect joining us in arguing that geography, like other social sciences, lacks a core—but did describe the role of the geographer as follows: "Besides being an explorer, a measurer, a describer, and an interpreter of the features of the earth, the geographer is a synthesizer of the data of his subject according to those realities of experience called *regions,* and this brings him to fraternize with the historian, the economist, and the sociologist." Since these words were published, geographers have continued to do precisely this.

The discipline's breadth can be seen in the multiplication of hybrid subfields. The discipline now encompasses the subfields of human geography, cultural geography, biogeography, geomorphology, climatology, medical geography, economic geography, political geography, urban geography, environmental science, regional geography, and cartography. Each subfield relates directly to specialties outside the discipline—to take only examples from sociology, these would include human ecology, environmental sociology, rural sociology, and urban studies. In short, "For any student of terrestrial space, the natural sciences, history, the social sciences and the humanities have always had something to say, but different interests have sometimes favoured closer contacts with one field, sometimes with another." (Claval 1988: 21)

These outside fields have made some of geography's most important advances. Although Polybius was well aware of the importance of geography for history, current advance at the intersection of these two disciplines relies on the patrimonies accumulated in the last century. The historian Lucien Febvre was one of the most eminent modern theoreticians of geographical thought. In fact, bringing the geographical environment into history became the centerpiece of the school of the *Annales,* with Lucien Febvre, Marc Bloch, and Fernand Braudel. As the school has developed, the patterns of external influences have changed, as can be seen in the work of Fernand Braudel. *The Mediterranean World* (1949) makes geography central, beginning with a discussion of the Mediterranean's mountains, plains, plateaux, isth-

THE FATE OF THE FORMAL DISCIPLINES 95

muses, peninsulas, and islands, whereas his more recent *Civilization and Capitalism* (1979) draws instead from economic history, economic anthropology, and social history. This is a pattern found in geography more generally, not just in geographical history; the discipline is becoming increasingly oriented towards the social sciences and away from geology.

Sociologists and geographers have met not so much in terms of vast "interdisciplinary" work but in a series of individual fields such as urban studies. In the history of this hybrid, important work came from sociologists in the subfields of "human ecology" (Robert E. Park, Ernest W. Burgess, Louis Wirth, A. H. Hawley, O. D. Duncan, Foley, W. Firey, and L. F. Schnore), geographers influenced by sociologists (Harris, Platt, Edward Ullman), and scholars in both disciplines working on spatial statistics (Duncan, Cuzzort and Duncan, Berry and Marble, Chorley and Haggett, and others). Once a hybrid, "urban studies" is now a department of its own at many large universities.

Urban studies, as a discipline, includes subfields which overlap specialties in sociology, geography, and anthropology. It also encompasses architecture, which itself covers engineering (building design and methods), the natural sciences (climatology, energy conservation), the social sciences (socio-physical research), the humanities (history of architecture) and some hybrids of its own (urban planning). The great architect of today is a contemporary renaissance man. Some architects remodeling cities, building airports, cultural or commercial centers are among the most famous in the land, from Rotterdam to Brasilia to Osaka. Their fame is based on abilities which span engineering, the natural sciences, the social sciences, the humanities, as well as urban planning proper.

Urban studies has also been influenced by economics and economic geography. This latter hybrid has made its major contribution in the area of location theories for agricultural, industrial, and commercial activities. Communication seems to be much better with geographers and even sociologists than with economists, partly because the inductive nature of much of the work made it difficult to integrate into deductive economic theory. One exception may be Hotelling's spatial location result, applied by Anthony Downs to political science and the "location" of political parties on a left-right spectrum. From there, multidimensional spatial models of parties and voting have been important for the field of public choice, and Downs' model has worked itself back into economics through this door.

However, the flow goes more easily in the opposite direction, from economics to geography. The importation of economic ideas into geography was an important inspiration in the "new geography" movement of the 1950s and 1960s, led by Edward Ullman and others. Of course, the often extreme assumptions of rationality in such models do have their limitations, leading other geographers to borrow from psychology. These later researchers have tended to focus on how people perceive their geographical environment, and how these perceptions shape choices of location and the uses of space.

Anthropology, too, has joined geography. The subfield of cultural geography draws mostly from cultural anthropology. Geographers have the most to learn from anthropologists working in the areas of social organization, cultural areas, and the processes of cultural change. In exchange, cultural geographers can teach their anthropological colleagues much about settlement patterns, land use, land tenure, and cultural ecology. (Mikesell 1969: 230)

Geography's main contacts with political science have taken place in two subfields, international relations and electoral behavior studies. "Geopolitics" died a quick death after its German advocates were exposed as apologists for expansionary foreign policies, and after Halford Mackinder's famous "heartland theory" was undercut by technological developments in land and sea power. More recent applications of geography have not suffered from these problems, and have been used in studies of regional interaction, for instance. Karl W. Deutsch's classic study of nationalism, *Nationalism and Social Communication* (1953) rests on cybernetic decision-theory and communication density in a spatial context. While Deutsch did not stress the geographic component of his work, it had implications for such studies as Bruce Russett's *International Regions* (1967), Ernst Haas's *The Uniting of Europe* (1968), and subsequent research.

Research on electoral behavior also borrows from geography, but more often as an organizing concept (i.e., used in maps) than as a causal variable (see Laponce 1983). French electoral geographers, headed by André Siegfried, François Goguel and Alain Lancelot—to mention only one from each generation—have for a long time based their research on maps. André Siegfried, for instance, was able to show that granitic soils were associated with conservative political views in France, while limestone formations were not; the differences in soil quality and the potential for productive farming are the intervening variables between these two apparently unrelated features of the country. However, this geographical approach in electoral studies has been challenged recently by an ecological analysis of aggregate data, where geography simply disappears in favor of a sociological reordering of the territorial units. (Dogan and Derivry 1988)

Other political scientists have drawn from aspects of geography in conjunction with history and sociology. Stein Rokkan has suggested

THE FATE OF THE FORMAL DISCIPLINES 97

(1975) a conceptual framework for comparative political analysis, drawing largely from sociology and geography. He weaves together Parsonian pattern variables, the sequence of various kinds of "crises," and the typically Scandinavian notion of center-periphery relations into a geographical schema built around the main Hansa-Rhine-Italy trade routes, a country's distance from Rome, and whether a state faces seaward or is landbound. While complex, the scheme is very suggestive, not only because it can clarify the different political outcomes in the states of modern Europe, but also help us understand why many once-powerful states have since disappeared, such as Scotland, Wales, Brittany, Bohemia, Bavaria, and Aragon.

As a result of all these trends, there is today an incredible fragmentation which has made geography span large areas in both the natural and social sciences, with a general tendency to drift from the former to the latter. "From being students of the world as the habitat of human societies, geographers have turned to the societies themselves and their artifacts, the cities. Most geographers have become social scientists and are classified as such in universities." (Hare 1988: 46) This should not surprise us.

Like the other disciplines, interaction with the outside has kept geography on the move. "Many geographers have developed their method and penetrated other disciplines to such a degree that they became specialists . . . of another discipline (geology, hydrology, ethnology) or at least of one sector of these disciplines." (Brunet 1982: 390) Such emigration naturally leaves the old core of the discipline empty. At a symposium on the social sciences in Paris in 1982, a geographer asked, "With the progress of the other social sciences, what remains proper to geography? A residual part, or a boring nomenclature? . . . Does geography still have its own domain, or is it a relic . . . of an old division of labor? Has geography an identity and, if so, of what is it made?" (Brunet 1982: 383, 402) As is true for the other social sciences, we would suggest that its identity, if any, be found in a federative ideal, not in disciplinary unity.

PSYCHOLOGY

Psychology is torn between the social and natural sciences. Its origins are in philosophy, while psychiatry began as an offshoot of medicine and neurobiology. A genealogical tree of the field as a whole might begin with neuropsychology and psychobiology, which gave birth to psychogenetics and psychopharmacology. It covers a wide range of subfields today, including clinical psychology, cognitive psychology, developmental psychology, behavioral psychology, psychometrics, person-

98   PART THREE

ality, physiological psychology, social psychology, animal behavior, group behavior, political psychology, psycholinguistics, psychopathology, ethology, behavioral pharmacology, endocrinology, and neuropsychology. Social psychology is a well-established discipline of its own today; psycholinguistics enriches both psychology and linguistics; zoopsychology attracts as many zoologists as psychologists. Lawrence Kimpton unwittingly testified to both the fragmentation and the cross-fertilization in the discipline when he noted that, "in our psychology department we have agreed that there is biopsychology and social psychology, but nobody can describe to my satisfaction the difference between a biopsychologist and a biologist or can tell me what social psychology is." (Kimpton 1956: 348–349) As a discipline is penetrated by others, the attempt to delineate clear boundaries is futile.

Some of the remarkable diversity of the discipline can be seen in a brief history of one subfield, comparative psychology, whose advances have come in response to successive infusions from outside psychology. Darwin's theory of evolution first gave impetus to the field, by insisting that the human mind is not necessarily different in kind from that of other animals. British naturalists were the first to pursue the implications of this line of thought. G. J. Romanes, who coined the term "comparative psychology," was a pioneer in the field, studying the structure and function of nervous systems in jellyfish, starfish, and sea-urchins at a time when some still doubted that these animals had nervous systems. His popular writings can fairly be criticized for anthropomorphizing animals, but his work was important. C. Lloyd Morgan did his early work on the pecking abilities of newly hatched fowls, a study which led him to develop the idea of the method of learning by "trial and error." L. T. Hobhouse, another early comparative psychologist who wrote the book *Mind in Evolution,* was a philosopher and sociologist for whom the study of animal behavior was only one episode in his career. Comparative psychology was also central to the Soviet school of reflexology founded by Sechenov but which is most famous for Pavlov and his dogs. This second wave of comparative psychology was led by experimental psychologists, not biologists, and animals were usually not studied as individual species but as proxies for humans. The school's emphasis of reflex and conditioning systematically downplayed the role of instinct in favor of environment.

The third wave of comparative psychology reacted against this, relying on ethology and in particular the work of the zoologists Konrad Lorenz and N. Tinbergen. It led to a reassertion of the role of instinct and of the importance of studying animals in natural settings. Furthermore, the school argued, animals do not merely respond to stimuli in a certain way, but actually seek out particular forms of stimulation.

THE FATE OF THE FORMAL DISCIPLINES

Ethology opened in turn to physiological psychology. E. von Holst demonstrated that the locomotory activity of fish was controlled centrally, and was not a simple chain of reflexes dependent on sensory stimulation. He and U. von St. Paul later showed that stimulating specific points in the brain of chickens could elicit complete sequences of actions, giving further support to theories stressing the autonomous role played by the nervous system. In this, their work carries on the tradition of comparative psychology, which has consistently relied on fields outside psychology for advance, from biology to zoology to physiology.

Physiology has formed other hybrids with psychology. In a recent review, W. G. Hall and R. W. Oppenheim stated that "we consider the field of developmental psychobiology to be a subfield of the parent disciplines of developmental biology, on the one hand, and developmental psychology, on the other." (Hall and Oppenheim 1987: 93) There were many pioneers, from many fields: J. B. Watson, K. Lashley, F. Beach, L. Carmichael, C. L. and C. J. Herrick, George Coghill, W. Windle, Z. Y. Kuo, T. C. Schneirla, A. Gesell, M. McGraw, Jean Piaget, and others. Developmental psychobiology is now one of the largest subfields in the social sciences.

Recent innovations in developmental psychology have also depended on disciplines outside psychology, particularly as some have studied adult development. Developmental psychology, as it has moved from the study of childhood to include adulthood has gained on many fronts, and "assumptions about intellectual maturity are being challenged by new interdisciplinary perspectives on adult cognition." (Datan, Rodeheaver, and Hughes 1987: 168)

Interestingly, the original core of the discipline of psychology—the study of thought—was empty for many years as researchers spun off in many directions. Oden states the problem succinctly: "Thinking, broadly defined, is nearly all of psychology; narrowly defined it seems to be none of it." (Oden 1987: 203) Specialization has led not to the study of "thought," but of perception, memory, Bayesian decisionmaking, Gestalt approaches to problem solving, language comprehension, and other components of thought. More recently, some other disciplines have helped psychology return to this core topic. This invasion began during World War II with cybernetic theories of human behavior, which made it possible for behavioral psychologists to abandon a narrow focus on reflex and to reintroduce goal-oriented (teleological) behavior into their analysis.

Later, computer science also helped fill the void in thinking about thinking. A. Newell, J. Shaw, and Herbert Simon used computers to simulate the human use of heuristics to solve problems. They tested cognitive theory with these simulations and explored the question of which heuristics are most important for problem solving. Further modern study of thought mechanisms is largely traceable to Ross Quillian's development of a theory of the semantic network. A striking example of our thesis, "Although often thought of as originally being a piece of computer science, . . . Quillian's theory was actually part of the work done toward his degree in psychology under the guidance of Herbert Simon." (Oden 1987: 204) Herbert Simon is himself a remarkable hybrid and can also be claimed by the subfield of public administration in political science, to say nothing of economics, where he won the Nobel prize. Besides "thought" *per se,* computers have also stimulated thinking about information processing. The hybrid of psychology and computer science, artificial intelligence, is now a separate field, but it remains in contact with cognitive psychology.

Cognitive science, a related hybrid field, draws from psychology, linguistics, computer science, neuroscience and philosophy. The field asks how language is acquired and used, what processes are important in human perception and memory, how humans solve problems and how reason works, as well as looking at the biological foundation for these processes and the ways in which aging or neurological damage can affect them. This hybrid field has grown in recent years in large part out of advances in neighboring fields, especially computer science, linguistics, and mathematics. Technological advances in non-invasive brain imaging have also been important, enabling researchers to study these processes in action.

The field provides a good example of how hybrids become organized: a Cognitive Science Society was formed, and has published the journal *Cognitive Science* for the past thirteen years. A series of related journals have sprung up only in the past few years, including *Machine Learning, Cognitive Neuropsychology, Cognitive Neuroscience, Mind and Language, Connection Science, Neural Networks,* and others.

Besides filling previous gaps, the field benefits from differences among these discipines in methodology. As an illustration of the variety found, psychologists' laboratory experiments, linguists' study of speaker intuition, computer scientists' examination of programming successes and failures, and developmental linguists' study of children's speech errors all contribute to advances in the field. (Stillings *et al.* 1987)

Sociology and psychology have interacted to form what is also a distinct formal discipline today, social psychology. Social psychology looks at a wide range of behavior. Socialization can determine factors such as values, needs, and expectations which influence perception. Psychological development obviously conditions socialization. Personality can affect group interaction, and social interaction can affect

THE FATE OF THE FORMAL DISCIPLINES 101

personality. The field contrasts both with behavioral psychology's emphasis on stimulus and response, and economists' analysis of decision-making in terms of formal logic and rationality. It can be used to stimulate advance in either.

Others look at the interaction of sociological variables and mental health. This issue is a complex one: the death of a loved one, for instance, can lead to depression, while divorce may be either the result or the cause of depression. Review essays by G. Caplan, J. Cassel, and S. Cobb in the mid 1970s each suggested that the presence of social support systems and networks can protect people from the deleterious effects of stress on mental health, and this helped stimulate research in the area. Elsewhere in psychology, a new hybrid field called psychoneuroimmunology is breaking down Descartes' mind-body distinction and the tradition of Western thought which followed it. Scholars in this area study the relationships between social and psychological variables and physical health, giving special attention to the immune system. The field was spawned by an accidental discovery by the psychologist Robert Ader and the immunologist Nicholas Cohen that rats could be conditioned to suppress their immune system in a manner analogous to Pavlov's dogs. Biofeedback techniques, by which a patient trains her body to suppress pain, decrease heartbeat, and so on, is an important application of this area of research.

The diversity of the interconnections of psychology and the outside is remarkable. Linguistics intersects in several fields, because the study of language as a system of information processing is relevant to cognitive psychology, while language acquisition and second language learning are both part of psychological learning theory. Political psychologists have studied political leaders using personality theory, topics in mass behavior such as belief systems, attitudes, socialization, and the media, and issues in international relations from the perspective of theories of cognition and decisionmaking. (Sears 1987) While Americans in the field of political psychology have tended to focus on the psychological determinants of political behavior, Europeans such as the scholars of the Frankfurt School have been more interested in how politics, and especially political economy, influence the psychological development of the individual. (Deutsch 1983)

Psychology also includes the subfield of organizational behavior, which "is the confluence of individual, group, and organizational studies flowing from industrial organizational (I/O) psychology and organization and management theory (OMT) with headwaters in psychology (social, psychometrics, sociology (organizational, work, and occupational), and management (scientific, human relations)." (Schneider 1985: 574) The field as a whole studies role stress, job satisfaction, socialization to work, turnover and absenteeism, leadership and management, demographic cohorts, group structure, intergroup relations, and organizational climate and culture, all in the context of large modern organizations. Many members of the field are found in American schools of business, where they are often marginal to the concerns of most other faculty. Most business schools talk the language of "dollars," while the field of organizational behavior "speaks the foreign language of motivation, leadership, job satisfaction, environmental turbulence, and so on." (Schneider 1985: 574) Furthermore, the multiplicity of external influences on the field means that it generally lacks any unifying framework or approach to the study of its topic.

As a result of hybridization in this field and others, it now seems that one may combine the word "psychology" with the name of any other formal discipline and find a specialty of that title already in existence. Each of these has grown in contact with other specialties.

POLITICAL SCIENCE

The field of political science encompasses subfields of international relations, political theory, comparative politics, national politics, public policy, and public organization. They are not perfect fits; as Emmerich points out with respect to one of these subfields, "In the structure of intellectual organization, public administration has come to have a strong affinity for political science, even though in some institutions it is allied with studies of law and with studies of business administration." (Emmerich 1956: 385) Each classification is as arbitrary as the next.

Dividing the discipline by topics, even cross-fertilized ones, is in many ways misleading. Most of these subfields admit of specialization in political sociology, political psychology, political economy, or political anthropology, among others; area studies are of course a further division. Typically, there is relatively little scholarly exchange between the student of the American Congress and the specialist of Middle Eastern politics, between the political philosopher and the expert in statistical analysis or mathematical modelling, between the Africanist and the expert in East-West strategic studies. But most of them are likely to entertain substantial relations with scholars in neighboring disciplines, such as historians of the Middle East, African ethnologists, statistical sociologists, or a colleague in the department of philosophy. The relative absence of a common methodological stock contributes to the fragmentation of the discipline and the cross-fertilization of these fragments by others.

THE FATE OF THE FORMAL DISCIPLINES

As a result of cross-fertilization and hybridization, the field of political theory has had a varied history. Influences have come from all over the disciplinary map, and include scholars such as Jürgen Habermas, John Rawls, Robert Nozick, Martin Heidegger, Michel Foucault, H. G. Gadamer, György Lukács, Antonio Gramsci, Louis Althusser, Thomas Kuhn, and Karl Popper. By the 1970s, "Political theory was no longer centered in the discipline of political science, and political science no longer defined the issues in the literature of Political Theory." (Gunnell 1983: 28) Political theorists were influenced by the philosophy of science and epistemological concerns quite separate from substantive political issues. Much of political theory today is in fact the study of the history of political philosophy.

The subfield of public law, perhaps the second oldest in the discipline, has also pulled political scientists off in the direction of other social sciences. "Political science research on criminal courts, for instance, owes much to work by sociologists" such as Abraham S. Blumberg's *Criminal Justice* (1967). (Baum 1983: 196) Others have been influenced by anthropological research on dispute resolution, although the influence is limited because political science tends to focus on a different level of analysis, primarily appellate court decisions and the relations between policymakers and jurists. Such differences in focus are of course natural even where communication is relatively easy.

The major stimulus to hybridization and advance has been the postwar behavioral revolution. Between the wars, the field progressed relatively little, with a few exceptions such as the work done at Chicago in the 1930s. That research drew from several other disciplines, and in fact political science was but one of the many innovative exchanges there: "Chicago's greatest achievement was the true interdisciplinary cooperation it achieved in the social sciences." (Jensen 1969: 236) Subsequent specialization and fragmentation throughout the social sciences was to make this broad cooperation impossible, and contributions came from narrower areas.

Although the behavioral revolution stimulated the creation of many subfields in political science, William Riker could still write at the beginning of the 1960s that the process was incomplete:

There is considerable intellectual ferment among political scientists today owing to the fact that the traditional method of their discipline seem to have wound up in a cul-de-sac. These traditional methods—i.e., history writing, the description of institutions, and legal analysis—have been thoroughly exploited in the last two generations and now it seems to many (including myself) that they can produce only wisdom and neither science nor knowledge. And while wisdom is certainly useful in the affairs of men, such a result is a failure to live up to the promise in the name political *science.* (Riker 1962: viii)

Another forceful indictment of pre-behavioralist American political science is David Easton's chapter on "The Condition of American Political Science" in his *Framework for Political Analysis,* which stresses the need for theoretical approaches to politics. Easton goes so far as to argue that one central tenet of the behavioralist revolution in political science was that "political research can ignore the findings of other disciplines only at the peril of weakening the validity and undermining the generality of its own results." (Easton 1965: 7) Because of such concerns, innovators looked abroad for inspiration. B. R. Berelson, P. F. Lazarsfeld, and W. N. McPhee applied social psychology to politics in their book *Voting* (1954); Karl W. Deutsch applied communications theory to politics in his *Nationalism and Social Communication* (1953); and David B. Truman used sociological theories of the group in his theory of *The Governmental Process* (1951). As a result of this and other innovative work, the field as a whole has since expanded towards other disciplines, especially sociology and economics, to a lesser but still important degree psychology and social psychology, and some have sought cross-fertilization in anthropology and other formal disciplines.

There is a marked pattern to the cross-fertilization of political science. In the 1950s and 1960s, sociology was the major cross-fertilizer of political science, making such important contributions as group theory, political socialization, social cleavages, and systems theory. In the 1970s and 1980s, economics has been the major cross-fertilizer of political science, especially in theories of public goods and collective action, game theory, social choice, and international trade theory. Psychology has been a constant exporter to political science, but at a lower level. In the 1950s and 1960s, its major contributions came from personality theory and the study of values; in the 1970s and 1980s, social psychology and cognitive psychology have been the dominant cross-fertilizers.

One major reason for all this cross-fertilization is that political science has the advantage of being a policy-oriented discipline almost by definition, making it open to many eclectic practitioners attempting to solve policy problems. Heckhausen argues that this is typical of problem-solving fields: "Medicine is a case in point. The seeming necessities of practice have piled up a hodge-podge of multi-disciplinary curricula over the centuries." (Heckhausen 1972: 86) Although this eclecticism may be a major weakness underlying the problems many political scientists have in communicating with one another, it may also be a strength, an early form of hybridization.

SOCIOLOGY

Sociology has also fragmented to an extraordinary degree, but was an imperialist discipline at one stage of its expansion. August Comte ranked sociology second only to philosophy, and under the influence of Max Weber, Émile Durkheim, and Talcott Parsons, among others, sociology became the queen of the social sciences. In one form or another, their work invaded each of the other formal disciplines in social sciences.

Sociology has been buffeted by four waves in the last half century, from psychology, anthropology, political science, and economics; throughout these waves it has also enjoyed on-again, off-again cooperation with history (see Chapter 21). Interaction with psychology is in large part responsible for the development of current standards of inquiry in sociology by insisting on behavioral research, introducing key concepts such as values and socialization, and contributing methods such as survey research and statistical analysis. Anthropology's contributions came largely in the realm of theory, especially structural-functionalism. Political science, in contrast, changed the perspectives of many sociologists who began to ask more questions about power, especially in the 1960s. More recently, disappointing results in the efforts to explain how people's values differ have led many sociologists towards economic methods, which largely assume that values do not differ from one person to the next.

There is no longer any field which could be called sociology without an adjective. Greenstein is correct that "There are few if any 'pure' sociologists or psychologists who meet our abstract disciplinary definitional criteria." (Greenstein 1969: 164) As early as two generations ago, a dean of social sciences at the University of Chicago considered abolishing the field altogether, as James Miller points out, for "there was nearly a complete overlap between almost any course given in sociology and some course given in economics, political science, psychology, geography, history, or anthropology. Such a field would inevitably have internal tensions unless it was unified by a strong theoretical approach that was generally accepted." (in Deutsch, Markovits, Platt 1986: 55) At the same time, Talcott Parsons attempted to construct such a theory, and to keep the discipline unified. To do so, he "exaggerated the internal unity of the discipline; such descriptions, if applied today, would appear almost ludicrous." (Smelser 1988: 12) It is not clear how much more appropriate they were at the time.

Today, in the International Sociological Association, there is still a research committee on "Theory of Sociology," but otherwise this imperialistic discipline has expanded in all directions, as can be seen in the list of ISA research committees. There are sociologies of education, law, science, religion, medicine, values, knowledge, politics, economics, family, leisure, sports, deviance, communication, alienation, agriculture, organizations, imperialism, mental health, migration, gender, youth, and the arts, as well as committees on rural sociology, urban sociology, military sociology, comparative sociology, sociolinguistics, social psychology, sociocybernetics, social ecology, and others. No one talks today of sociology in general, except for administrative or teaching purposes. As the list suggests, the matrix of sociology has expanded into specialized subfields. Some, after invading a neighboring subfield, have "gone native," and a cultural gulf separates them from their former compatriots. One glance at the list shows the extent of overlapping between sociology and the other social sciences.

The term "sociology" really makes little sense today, although it is used as a label for a large group of people doing very different things. In an overview of the discipline, Neil Smelser predicts that "While there are obvious occupational career reasons for individuals who have been trained as sociologists, the likelihood that that name will be denotative of an identifiable field will be diminished; it is likely that commitment to the discipline in general will diminish, and that smaller groups will seek their interaction and identification in suborganizations that are inside (for example special sections) or outside (for instance, a society for public choice) the American Sociological Association." (Smelser 1988: 13) Actually, even those formally inside the discipline are for the most part already intimately connected with the outside. Of the fifty recognized specialties in the American Sociological Association's 1986 *Guide to Graduate Study in Sociology,* 41 are cross-disciplinary and only 9 could be considered in the core of sociology proper. Among these core specialties are such fields as the theory, methodology, and history of sociology, sociological practice, collective behavior, and stratification. The others are to various degrees interwoven with specialties in other disciplines, including all other social sciences as well as biology, medicine, mathematics, and music. Comparative sociology and comparative politics have had a fertile relationship, especially in the honing of techniques of comparing relatively small numbers of cases. Criminology depends not only on sociology and jurisprudence but on the psychological studies of deviance, and more recently economic models of crime have added to the debate. Industrial sociology is in close contact with industrial relations in economics and with an increasing number of political scientists interested in the role of trade unions in national politics. The sociological study of religion benefits not only from religious studies but also anthropology; rural sociology interacts with social geography, anthro-

THE FATE OF THE FORMAL DISCIPLINES

pological peasant studies, historians, and some political scientists. Those who study socialization come into contact with social psychologists, cultural anthropologists, and political scientists. Sociology meets linguistics in sociolinguistics, international relations in the sociology of world conflict, urban studies in urban sociology, and demography in the sociology of aging.

Sociology has also formed a hybrid with the discipline of education, a practice-oriented field like business administration or psychiatry. Education interacts with many other social sciences, in fact, and it has only a subject matter to hold the field together. Its major subfields encompass educational psychology, the philosophy of education, history of education, sociology of education, anthropology of education, and administrative and policy studies. Here, too, the subject matter becomes fragmented in contact with other formal disciplines.

There are many other divisions in sociology, inevitably so: "It is difficult to imagine a single paradigm applying to the range of problems and levels of analysis in sociology." (Turner 1988: 51) Raymond Boudon (1988) argues that there are several different approaches in sociological research which may coexist even if they are incompatible with one another. He distinguishes three separate methodological choices, each a binary choice, generating eight basic approaches in sociological research. Such intellectual pluralism effectively denies the discipline a core, and probably unity as well. Some choices are intimately connected to outside disciplines: approaches based on the decision to study social actors as rational will interact with economics, while those studying irrational behavior will rely on psychology and social psychology.

Other cleavages also divide the discipline. One cannot, it seems, belong both to the Marxist school and the Weberian tradition of sociology. The two are apparently exclusive, and have been since their origins, as evidenced by the fact that Weber himself cites Marx only twice; in spite of his efforts, Günther Roth has not succeeded in building a bridge between these two giants. Similarly, Durkheim did not refer to Marx and did not communicate with his contemporary Max Weber. Freudian sociologists are distinct from all, and in fact Freud himself referred to none of these others. Although Parsons found some inspiration in Weber, there is nonetheless an abyss between them. This history led Paul Veyne to argue that "to write the history of sociology, from Comte and Durkheim to Weber, Parsons and Lazarsfeld is not to write the history of a discipline but that of a word. From one of these authors to the next there is no continuity of foundation, of scope, of purpose, or of method." (Veyne 1971: 191) The followers of all of these giants have difficulty communicating, and ideological and political disagreements exacerbate the cleavages. Ideological differences can easily be deplored, but if a dialogue is established between them, the clash of perspectives can be beneficial to the cause of science, forcing each to argue its position more persuasively.

In other cases, the development of a new perspective can have implications for a number of subfields in the discipline. This is often a case of self-fertilization more than cross-fertilization. Neil Smelser describes one such case: "Beginning with the Simmel-inspired critique by Coser, the Marxian critique by Mills, and the Weberian critique by Dahrendorf, the conflict perspective burgeoned into dozens of avenues and affected subfield after subfield of sociology, including sociological theory, industrial sociology, the sociology of gender, the sociology of education, and deviance." (Smelser 1988: 11) Most of these have affected other formal disciplines as well. A single innovation can send ripples throughout the discipline and beyond.

Sociology's hybridization has of course given birth to many new areas of research and knowledge. Yet Boudon and Bourricaud (1982) have asked why the rise of sociology was followed by such a rapid decline; we view the process instead as dispersion at the peripheries and decline only at the core. Today, sociologists continue to fight in foreign lands, so much that the center of the discipline is, with the exceptions of a few dozen scholars such as Raymond Boudon, Goldthorpe, and Jeffrey Alexander, deserted. The core of sociology is as empty as the Italian peninsula in the late Roman Empire, which had all its troops on the frontiers. It is not inconceivable that sociology will in the future experience the same fate as philosophy: its progeny will abandon the maternal home with the ambition to build new academic fortresses. The incoherent diversity of sociology appears more clearly in comparison with disciplines with identifiable cores, such as linguistics and economics.

LINGUISTICS

Linguistics is an ancient discipline, traceable to the ancient Sanskrit and Greek grammarians. It was also one of the first to propose verifiable laws of social behavior. The first such laws were built upon William Jones' demonstration in 1787 that Sanskrit, Greek, and Latin shared a common ancestor and Frederick Schlegl's addition of the languages of India, Persia, Greece, Italy, and Germany to the family in 1808. With such raw material, Francis Bopp, William Humboldt, Jacob Grimm, and Eugene Burnouf developed a genealogical classification of languages and began work on the lawlike derivation of one language from its earlier forms. Generally speaking, these laws are still accepted today.

THE FATE OF THE FORMAL DISCIPLINES 109

Notwithstanding its age, linguistics is surprisingly coherent. Linguists must know a core of subfields, from which they choose a specialization without completely losing touch with the others: phonetics, phonemics, morphology, morphophonemics, semantics, syntax, and pragmatics. Of course, they do interact with other disciplines as well. Working out from this core, linguists intersect with acoustics, anthropology, artificial intelligence, formal logic, mathematics, psychology, and sociology. Sociolinguistics, for instance, examines the effects of class, geographical mobility, settlement patterns and other sociological factors on language usage and dialects.

Psycholinguistics studies the psychological reality of linguistic categories, the process of speech creation and comprehension, as well as aspects of cognition relevant to language. Other topics include comparative psycholinguistics, bilingualism, content analysis, associative processes in verbal behavior, the dimensions of meaning, style in language, aphasia, and language universals. The field received its initial impetus from a seminar of the Social Science Research Council in 1951, which led to the founding of a Committee on Linguistics and Psychology comprised of psychologists John Carroll, James Jenkins, George Miller, and Charles Osgood, and linguists Joseph Greenberg, Floyd Lounsbury, and Thomas Sebeok. It received further stimulus from A. R. Diebold's 1954 review of the field and its research problems written for the SSRC. In this first decade, the structural linguistics of Bloomfield, Fries, Hockett, and Pike dominated the nascent field. The field did not really explode until after George Miller's application of Chomsky's transformational rules to psychology, and this is usually taken as the real founding of the research frontier in psycholinguistics.

The breadth of the discipline can be remarkable: "linguistics is becoming a discipline that is concurrently a natural science, a branch of the humanities, and a social science." (Parsons 1965: 54) Its center, however, remains relatively coherent, and a subfield such as historical linguistics will draw from most of its siblings in any significant work. Scholars of syntax cannot avoid confronting semantics, morphology and even phonology, among other sibling subfields. All linguists know, for instance, that syntax cannot explain why the sentence, "Colorless green ideas sleep furiously," is "ungrammatical"; the answer obviously lies in the sister field of semantics, and not necessarily outside the discipline in psychology or logic. Such issues have helped contribute to current interest in semantics among scholars of syntax or morphology.

In such a coherent discipline, self-fertilization is possible among subfields, as it is with some plants. Frequently it is developments inside one subfield of linguistics which stimulate innovation elsewhere in the discipline. Noam Chomsky's pathbreaking *Syntactic Structures* (1957) led to a kind of imperialism of syntax within the discipline, a dominance which has only been seriously eroded in the last decade or so. Syntax has had an impact on generative phonology, exemplified by M. Halle's *The Sound Pattern of Russian* (1959), P. Postal's *Aspects of Phonological Theory* (1961), and the classic *The Sound Pattern of English* (1968) by Chomsky and Halle. More recently, issues of semantics and pragmatics have tended to come to the fore. Hybrid fields such as sociolinguistics or psycholinguistics are often the first to absorb and exploit the innovations of the core subfields. Other disciplines, too, frequently adopt linguistics innovations and methods, as did Floyd Lounsbury's and Ward Goodenough's semantic analyses of kinship systems in anthropology.

Linguists have benefitted from their relatively strong cores. For one thing, communication is much easier among the various specialties. To some degree, the existence of a core also allows for specialization by topic, while building on shared methods, concepts, approaches, and theories. Of course, there is also a price to pay for this coherence.

Cores can leave shocking gaps. The gaps in linguistics become most obvious when one examines historical linguistics: we still have only a rudimentary idea why languages change. In fact, one of the subfield's oldest observations, Grimm's law (as modified by Verner) remains a descriptive generalization, correlating original Indo-European consonants and their reflexes in common Germanic. Why any language group should play musical chairs with its entire consonantal system remains a mystery. On a larger scale, we may pose questions about the outcomes of clashes between two languages, asking why most British Celts abandoned their languages in favor of the dominant Anglo-Saxon in the low middle ages, while the Anglo-Saxons did not adopt the dominant Norman French after 1066; Norman French, for its part, was borrowed by the dominant Scandinavians from the subordinate Frenchmen of Normandy—but we do not know why. The reasons behind these different choices of languages have important effects on the subsequent development of whatever language is chosen, as for instance the partial creolization of English and Norman French stimulated the radical changes from Old English to Middle English, from Beowulf to Chaucer. Yet the methods of historical linguists, like that of most linguists, are very poorly suited to ask these questions.

ECONOMICS

Like linguistics, economics has a well-defined core of the discipline. All economists must have training in money and finance, macroeconomics, the core topics of microeconomics (theories of production, demand,

THE FATE OF THE FORMAL DISCIPLINES

exchange, and distribution), and a background in applied mathematics. For the most part, they borrow only from mathematics and statistics. Their divisions are driven by internal, not external forces. Economists may be classified as theorists or econometricians, and the communication between them is not always easy. The theorists, like medieval scholastics, build beautiful theories detached from reality. Econometricians, on the other hand, manipulate vast accumulations of data, ignoring the theories of the theorists, and which are ignored by the theorists in turn.

Alternatively, one can distinguish substantive subfields, but these, too, are driven from within the field: money and finance, industrial relations, international economics, economic development, law and economics, economic history, and comparative economic planning. Although internally driven, these subfields are—like those in linguistics—somewhat open to subfields of other disciplines, such as political science (industrial relations, economic development, economic policy), history (economic history), law (law and economics), and sociology (industrial relations). Industrial relations, for instance, interacts with labor law, personnel management, industrial sociology, industrial psychology, and industrial medicine. The most open of all has suffered at the hands of rival siblings; economic history, having tasted the fruit of historical knowledge, has been largely expelled from the garden.

Even if some of their subfields are open to the outside, economists do not usually work in hybrid fields. Instead, economists working at the border of disciplines typically take the methodology of their discipline and apply it to the subject matter of a bordering discipline—a very limited form of cross-disciplinary imperialism, but a powerful one nonetheless. This approach "has powered the imperialist expansion of economics into the traditional domains of sociology, political science, anthropology, law, and social biology—with more to come." (Hirshleifer 1985: 53) Gary Becker, for instance, has used economic methods to explain racial discrimination, crime, marriage, parental support of their children, suicide, and many other "sociological" phenomena.

The breadth of application can be remarkable. The economists George J. Stigler and Sam Peltzman, in research on law, economics, and political regulation, have developed a theory of "political support." Their model can explain public utilities, agricultural subsidies, self-regulation by doctors and lawyers, and many other forms of political intervention in markets. Their theory also shows a powerful ability to explain policy outcomes while abstracting from the political process. Others, such as Gary Becker, William Brock, Stephen Magee, and Leslie Young have begun to draw on the political science specialties of interest group behavior and party competition; the work of Brock,

Magee, and Young, in particular, shows potential for adding processural features to these kinds of models. In fact, political science has probably been the greatest object of the economic invasion. One hybrid specialty, public choice, is unrecognizable as either political science or economics. Poorly institutionalized, its practitioners can find academic homes in many different subfields of both disciplines, including political theory, comparative politics, public finance, or law and economics.

Economics, like linguistics, has sometimes shocking gaps. Economists are rightly proud of their imperialist expansion. Yet there are non-rational and non-economic variables which affect economic behavior, from the biological constraints on the human mind to the socialization process. Nobel laureate F. A. Hayek has even suggested that "nobody can be a great economist who is only an economist—and I am even tempted to add that the economist who is only an economist is likely to become a nuisance if not a positive danger." (Hayek 1956: 463) Hayek exemplifies this in his own work, and his polemic, *The Road to Serfdom,* draws heavily on democratic theory as well as economics. Another Nobel laureate, Herbert Simon, is claimed by several disciplines and draws from economics, psychology, political science, organization theory, and computer science; he has never held a position in a department of economics.

Besides the problem of irrationality, economic methods are relatively helpless in explaining discrete "events." This is in large part due to the fact that none of the economists' key concepts are observable or, even if observable, quantifiable; examples include utility, utility functions, supply functions, demand functions, economies of scale, and so on. What economics excels in is predicting the direction of change in some variables, given some change in another variable. Demand theory does not explain consumer tastes, but does explore the effects of changes in supply on the resulting equilibrium; Keynesian theory does not explain current demand, but explains and predicts how demand will increase or decrease in response to a given government policy.

While it has its limitations, the economic method has been both productive and imperialist. "This imperialistic impulse of one discipline is not unhealthy for the others; it obliges them to receive, accept and modify points of view and to use concepts, methods and techniques that have come from elsewhere. It reflects the impossibility of a specific definition of fields of phenomena and, paradoxically enough, of the unity of the scientific process." (Lichnerowicz 1972: 122) Economics simply needs to get as well as it gives.

We see, then, that the two most "imperialist" disciplines in the social sciences, economics and sociology, expand in completely different manners. Economists are a disciplined, well-organized Mongol horde which seeks to subjugate the indigenous populations across their borders.

THE FATE OF THE FORMAL DISCIPLINES

Sociologists, on the other hand, resemble the Germanic migrations: disorganized masses wandering aimlessly over an entire continent, ransacking some capitals before moving on, establishing only temporary kingdoms. Today, sociology is often the object of imperialism, because it is divided into ideological schools and methodological sects and unable or unwilling to resist the invaders on all sides. Economists, meanwhile, should remember that the Mongol empire of Genghis Khan divided into a series of khanates led by his descendants.

This review of the disciplines leads us to question the usefulness of existing patterns of university organization. We have no answers here, only questions. But suppose that, in some democratic country, all departments of sociology were eliminated, for whatever reason. This is not mere speculation. After the May 1968 crisis in France, the new minister of national education Edgar Faure (a professor of law) led a discussion about "what is to be done" about sociologists, well-known as political trouble-makers. Some suggested their dispersion, but others feared the virus would spread more easily that way. The solution agreed on was to concentrate and isolate some of them, bringing them together into a new university. This was a short-lived experiment, but suggests that our thought experiment is not absurd; so, too, does the early Reagan administration's reported efforts to eliminate all government funding for research in sociology. In fact, financial constraints may have the same effect: Washington University of St. Louis is gradually closing its sociology department, and Columbia University is phasing out both geography and linguistics (*New York Times,* 10 May 1989).

If the politicians had succeeded in eliminating sociology, what would have happened? As long as the other social sciences kept their complete freedom, sociological research would have continued as before, taking refuge in the other disciplines. Sociology's neighbors would likely have been delighted to welcome the newcomers. Thirty or forty new hybrids in these fields would soon result, paralleling the hybrid specialties which exist in sociology today. Only a very few subfields such as "Sociological Theories" or "History of Sociology" would have suffered. If anthropology, history, or political science were to be the victims, the same proliferation would happen in all neighboring disciplines. Demography has already been cut into pieces; philosophy is dispossessed, most of its tasks taken up elsewhere. The demise of economics, psychology, or linguistics would cause more difficulties, but not insurmountable ones. This capacity for adaptation and survival shows the artificial character of the borders between disciplines.

We are accustomed to the traditional disciplines, partly because of administrative divisions in universities, and partly because departments play a functional role in teaching. On the research front, however, such divisions are largely artificial today.

1989: 18) While some scholars irrationally reject mathematical approaches, others irrationally insist upon using such approaches for the study of all human behavior.

Remarkably, mathematical modelling seems to divide even the field of public choice, a hybrid of political science and economics characterized by a relatively high use of such models. Within this subfield, authors who cite works in the "verbal tradition" usually do not cite any of the classics of the mathematical tradition. Similarly, authors who cite the mathematical classics do not cite those in the verbal tradition. (Downing and Stafford 1981: 222–223) Such a lack of communication in the same subfield among authors using the same rational choice approach does not aid the scientific project.

Modelling has also left gaps. Economic models of inflation, for instance, exclude variables from outside their formal discipline. As Stanislav Andreski points out, economic theory "remains incapable of predicting such a *par excellence* economic phenomenon as inflation, because it excludes from its universe of discourse immensurable but causally crucial factors (such as the balance of political power), abandoning them to the step-motherly care of sociology or political science (with which most economists want nothing to do)." (Andreski 1972: 123) Inflationary expectations, for instance, presumably have psychological causes. In our terms, the solution is simple: these models will borrow from the appropriate subfields in sociology, psychology, and political science if they are really to understand inflation.

It is important to note that methodological borrowings rarely enrich the parent discipline. The use of mathematics by social scientists has contributed nothing to mathematics as a discipline, the psychogists' factor analysis excepted. Widespread borrowing of economic models by other social scientists, similarly, has done little for the economic method, and this is perhaps one of the greatest weaknesses of the economic paradigm. The irony in this is that the findings of applied economic theory in the other social sciences *could* be applied back to the parent discipline. However, because they apply the theory to "noneconomic" behavior, the work of these other social scientists is dismissed by most economists as irrelevant. Even economic anthropology's analysis of the role of status relationships on price is tossed aside as coming from "nonmarket" economies, excluded in practice if not by definition.

The cult of formalization in the economics profession also contributes to its insularity. For instance, although Herbert Simon won a Nobel prize in economics for his work on bounded rationality, a review of the leading economics journals would indicate relatively little application of this insight in theoretical work. There are many reasons for this: "satisficing" is less amenable to study through differential calculus than field of public choice; to voting, group preference, coalitions, and bargaining in political science. Social psychologists have done substantial experimental work based on game theory, and their results have had applications wherever game theory is used. Some sociologists and anthropologists have applied game theory to topics such as status systems and the sociology of conflict; it has also had many applications in military science. The future is likely to hold still more, and "the applications of game-theoretic reasoning to biology, sociobiology, demography, and multigenerational models of the economy may eventually be extremely fruitful." (Shubik 1982: 412)

The cross-disciplinary diffusion of statistics, mathematical models, and game theory is impressive. In a review of the use of mathematics in anthropology, Maurice Freedman lists works in economic anthropology, law, sociolinguistics, demography, genetics, and special studies in social ranking, acculturation, religion, divination, marriage and divorce, and ritual sponsorship, among others. (Freedman 1978: 199) Of course, not all formal models in the social sciences are derived from economics or mathematics, despite what some would have us believe. Transformational-generative grammar, for instance, resembles nothing so much as formal logic. Nonetheless, mathematical economics has been the fountainhead of the method.

Despite continuing progress in some areas, modelling has in other subfields reached what seems to be the limits of its innovative potential. Formal models of nuclear deterrence, which date to the late 1950s, have reached extraordinary levels of sophistication—which are even more remarkable if one considers that they have been developed without being able to refer to any cases of failed nuclear deterrence. It would be very difficult to innovate further without expanding the scope of the inquiry beyond the application of expected utility models to deterrence. John Steinbruner, among others, has shown one direction this could go, using decision theory and cybernetics.

Furthermore, modelling is not always appropriate. Even if a mathematical model may be the ultimate goal of many scientists, they must be careful not to identify models with reality—they are not reality. Social scientists must also be aware of their limitations as well as their assumptions. The distortion is analogous to that entailed in the use of natural languages, because mathematics is simply an artificial language. (Freedman 1978: 115) Each has its advantages and disadvantages.

Among the disadvantages from the standpoint of scholarly advance, mathematics may also prove divisive. Bertrand Russell never trusted mathematics after someone "proved" to him that $1 = 2$. Yet, the mathematical sophistication involved was minimal, and any algebra student should be able to find the flaw of the "proof." (see Rasmussen every political agent acts rationally to achieve goals with minimal use of scarce resources." (Hirshleifer 1985: 54) William Riker's *Theory of Political Coalitions* (1962) forced a similar rethinking of parliamentary coalitions, congressional log-rolling, and military alliances. Raymond Boudon's modelling has also opened new perspectives in several sociological subfields. While these models have attracted a substantial body of criticism, this is to a large degree the mark of their importance; one may disagree with them, but cannot ignore them.

Even less encompassing models have been useful. Bruce Bueno de Mesquita's *The War Trap* (1981), an expected utility model tested against the Singer-Small data set, demonstrates that positive expected utility is a necessary but not sufficient condition for war.

The rigor necessary for such modelling may have payoffs for work which relies on the logic of the analysis while forgoing the mathematical presentation. David Mayhew's *The Electoral Connection,* for instance, uses the assumption of rational pursuit of self-interest from Downs and others in order to explain the organization of Congress and various aspects of the behavior of congressmen. Along similar lines, Samuel Popkin's *The Rational Peasant* takes the logic of rational self-interest and the organization of collective action in order to understand peasant society in Southeast Asia over the course of the last century. In *Economic Imperialism* (1987), edited by Gerard Radnitzky and Peter Bernholz, the contributors "explore the potential of the economic approach to human behavior in various areas outside the traditional fields of economics." (Radnitzky and Bernholz 1987: viii) They apply the economic method to history, democracy, norms, law, the philosophy of science, the study of conflict, autocracy, and constitutions. Most rely on economic reasoning without using mathematical models.

Of course, these methods too have their critics. By examining the "rational" pursuit of culturally defined goals, "the constant danger of 'economic' theories is that they can come to 'explain' everything merely by redescribing it. They then fail to be of any use in predicting that one thing will happen rather than another." (Barry 1978: 33) Anthony Downs, for instance, had to fall back on "duty" and "habit" as explanations of why people vote despite the cost. Of course, those using verbal reasoning are often equally guilty of redescribing phenomena through jargon rather than actually explaining the behavior under investigation.

Game theory, another methodology stemming ultimately from mathematics, has been important throughout the social sciences. In a recent review of the literature, Martin Shubik discusses applications of game theory to oligopolistic competition and to general equilibrium models in economics; to welfare economics and public goods in the hybrid

Of course, statistical methods have been subject to many criticisms. Giovanni Sartori argues that the typical results are "trivial," because the method imposes an inappropriate narrowness. "Given the fact that one can always find socio-economic data, the field has largely developed as a by-product, as an outgrowth of the data." (Sartori 1969: 80) Yet, as the examples of Wright and Richardson show, sometimes the process of data collection can have important payoffs in conceptualization and the posing of questions in early phases of research. At other times the data are interesting in and of themselves and their explanation a fascinating problem.

Barrington Moore, more charitably, has argued that "although statistics can shed considerable light . . . there may also be a point at which quantitative evidence becomes inapplicable, where counting becomes the wrong procedure to use. In the analysis of qualitative changes from one type of social organization to another, let us say from feudalism to industrial capitalism, there may be an upper limit to the profitable use of statistical procedures." (Moore 1966: 519) Methods, like technological advances, can only go so far down the road of hybridization. Again, conceptualization and theorization may be complemented by a technique, but the technique cannot be substituted for this intellectual labor.

Formal mathematical models are another methodological advancement currently much in vogue. Its origins may be found in the application of a simple mathematical tool, differential calculus, to marginal analysis, the foundation of most economics today. The first work on economic theory to be expressed in mathematical language may have been Cournot's *Essai sur la theorie des richesses* (1838), although elementary mathematics had been used previously by such scholars as Condorcet, Canard, and Whewell. Cournot was much criticized, however, and his example was not followed until the Lausanne school of Walras and Pareto in the 1870s followed by Alfred Marshall's work in England; in the United States, Simon Newcomb, more well known as an astronomer, may also have been that country's first mathematical economist. From economics, modelling has spread to all the social sciences, to political science and sociology, to geography and anthropology. While not immune to the statistical virus, historians have so far resisted mathematical modelling.

Much fruitful modelling work has been done in other disciplines, particularly in political science. Anthony Downs' *Economic Theory of Democracy* (1957) presented a quite different view of party competition and individual voting behavior: "in the field of politics it was like a breath of fresh air when Anthony Downs boldly proposed as 'axioms' that men seek office solely for income, prestige, and power and that

134 PART FOUR

by political science, sociology, psychology, and marketing research. Formal methods were developed in economics but have spread to psychology, sociology, and political science. The participant-observer method, originally used in anthropology, has found applications in sociology, social psychology, political science, and organizational theory. Richard P. Fenno, for instance, has used this method to observe congressmen in committees and in their districts.

Advances in mathematical techniques have been essential to advances in the social sciences. The reasons are clear; as Plato wrote in his *Laws,* "arithmetic stirs up him who is by nature sleepy and dull, and makes him quick to learn, retentive and shrewd, and aided by art divine he makes progress quite beyond his natural powers."

Statistical methods are used in all social sciences. The use of statistics in demography goes back to men such as Adriaan Verhulst, Siméon Denis Poisson, Bortkiewich, Quételet, Wilhelm Lexis, and the Marquis de Laplace. After demography, economics was the next social science to use statistics, followed then by psychology. This latter importation began at the turn of the century, with Weber-Fechner's law, Spearman, and Thurstone; the Psychometric Society was founded in 1935. For a long time the application of mathematics to psychology remained isolated in psychometrics, but this has since changed. Furthermore, psychologists have even succeeded in exporting some statistical methods back to the mathematicians: factor analysis, developed by psychologists for their own purposes, was later taken up by statisticians.

In international relations, Quincy Wright was the first to study war systematically in quantitative terms, as leader of a project begun at the University of Chicago in 1926. This mammoth data collection project forced Wright and his colleagues to confront innumerable questions of conceptualization, categorization, and causality, and it relied on an army of co-workers from political science, economics, history, sociology, anthropology, geography, psychology, and philosophy. While little read today, his influence on the field of international relations is striking— much of the research on war, the questions asked, the conceptual framework, and many of the methods used go back to this project.

In economic anthropology, marriage has been open to mathematical treatment ever since André Weil's "Sur l'étude algébrique de certains types de lois de mariage (Système Murngin)" (1949) and Claude Lévi-Strauss's *Les structures élémentaires de la parenté* (1949). Here the methodological application was doubtless suggested by the observation that marriage is an exchange relationship, in some ways analogous to economic exchange; furthermore, in some societies brides are commodities.

conjunction with findings from archaeology and geology, stimulating the rise of historical-textual criticism.

Other fields could probably benefit from borrowing. Cyril Belshaw argues that social-cultural anthropology could gain by adopting comparative methods, among others, from sociologists and political scientists. As it now stands, "The field is dominated by strong ethnographic case studies and wide-ranging comparative enquiries." (Belshaw 1988: 195) In contrast, sociology and political science have had success in comparisons of the "middle range," neither global nor single case. Historians and economists could probably heed the same advice.

Sometimes a scholar can take a single powerful methodology, hone the tool as an innovative methodologist, and become an innovative generalist by applying it to several concrete problems. Such a scientist is probably the closest we come to a modern Leonardo da Vinci. A notable example is Lewis F. Richardson:

> His bibliography in the *Obituary Notices of Fellows of the Royal Society* lists twenty-nine papers on meteorology, twenty-seven on war causation, nine on approximate solutions, eight on scientific instruments, seven on quantitative mental estimates (including one on telephone acoustics still cited after nearly fifty years), six on the "dynamics of intellection," and four on other aspects of psychology. He had a varied and distinguished career as a chemist, physicist, and meteorologist in industry, government, and academic institutions. His forte was the application of mathematics; his first classic was *Weather Prediction by Numerical Process* (1922), a scheme of weather prediction thirty years in advance of the high-speed computers required to apply it. (Wilkinson 1980: 3)

Others are less encompassing methodological imperialists. Arthur Bentley was an economist who attempted to apply economic methods and reasoning to the subject matter of other disciplines including political science (1908), sociology (1926), mathematics (1932), psychology (1935), and logic and epistemology. Hermann von Helmholtz was an early psychologist and sensory physiologist, whose "successes resulted from his unusual mathematical and mechanical abilities. . . ." (Beck 1968: 345) He also wrote papers on anatomy, medicine, and physics, the intellectual source of his mathematical virtuosity.

Many methodological exchanges are important. Paul Diesing (1971) has classified social science methodologies into four main groups, the experimental method, the survey method, the participant-observer method, and formal methods. Each has migrated from discipline to discipline. The experimental method was developed in psychology but has since spread to social psychology. The survey method was developed more topics in the social sciences than there are methods for studying them; some methods will therefore be applicable to a number of topics.

Notwithstanding the potential for exchange, to some degree methodology is what divides the social sciences. An interdisciplinary team investigating mental illness concluded that "major divergences often *seemed* to be conceptual or theoretical, but the basic differences were methodological, not conceptual." (Simmons and Davis 1957: 298) For example, participants from one discipline wanted to choose cases on the basis of their intrinsic interest while others were more concerned with obtaining a representative sample. One can imagine problems of this sort in the social sciences; for example, one comparative political scientist who prefers to study a few cases intensively, another who prefers large samples and statistical analyses, and a third who clusters countries around a concept. (see Dogan and Pelassy 1984, Part 3) In other cases, differences in methodology have isolated a subfield from others: mathematical economics has had a great deal of difficulty interacting with nonmathematical fields on the outside because of its methodological suppositions.

Some fields are driven by methodological innovations brought in from the outside. When voting studies were limited to aggregates, "sociological" variables such as race, ethnicity, urbanization, and class necessarily dominated. With advances in interview surveys, the inclusion of psychological variables became possible. Innovative reinterpretations of formerly held theories in demographic history, too, are generally the product of methodological innovation: "One shows that the methods by which earlier historians arrived at crucial conclusions were faulty and that other methods produce substantially different conclusions." (Tilly 1981: 25) Since scholars cannot create historical data—in contrast to the creation of survey data, for instance—new approaches to old data are essential.

This was the case in one of the first important innovations in history, the method of historical criticism. It dates to the works of Papebroek (b. 1628), Jean Mabillon (b. 1632), Richard Simon (1638–1712), and Spinoza (1632–1677), in a milieu influenced by Descartes' recent *Discours de la Methode*. The original applications of the method were made in several different fields, such as diplomacy (Mabillon's *De Re Diplomatica,* 1681), theology (Simon's *Histoire critique du vieux testament,* 1678, and *Histoire critique du 'Nouveau testament,'* 1683), and philosophy more generally (Spinoza's *Tractatus Theologico-Politicus,* 1670). From then, critical techniques have been an essential part of the historian's toolkit. In fact, they were so well refined by historians that they were re-borrowed by theologians in the 19th century, in

12
BORROWING METHODS

Many social scientists face methodological issues, which often present more important difficulties than similar problems in the natural sciences; as Poincaré once observed, natural scientists discuss their results and social scientists their methods. Like concepts, methods form a lasting part of a patrimony, and once invented, a method can be applied by others to their own problems. Furthermore, important methodological works are of broad applicability, a phenomenon labelled "transdisciplinarity" by one group of scholars. (Apostel *et al.* 1972) Some of the most illuminating pages on methodology in the social sciences, in fact for all sciences, were written by a biologist, Claude Bernard, in his *Introduction à la medecine experimentale.* He discusses the process of scientific reasoning and the methods useful for conceptualizing problems in a manner useful for all the sciences.

Methods are central to the patrimony, and form an essential component of any scientist's training. In a sense methods are more important than ideas in the advancement of science, even if they get less recognition. In sociology, for instance, Paul Lazarsfeld is less cited than Talcott Parsons today, but his methodological advances remain, while the field may move beyond Parsons' ideas. In economics, the method of marginal analysis are greater than any of its applications, although its originators are less frequently cited than other contemporary economists.

The exchange of methods is an important aspect of cross-fertilization, so much so that "The transdisciplinarity of analytical tools even leads to the bold but erroneous expectation that disciplines sharing the same analytical tools might develop an intrinsic interdisciplinarity." (Heckhausen 1972: 87) Clearly, in light of our argument about the need for narrowness, such breadth is unattainable. Nonetheless, methods devised by one subfield are very often of use for another. After all, there are

Borrowing a concept does not make a specialization a hybrid—yet. However, such borrowing is an important part of the process, stimulating innovation in the new subfield. These concepts also facilitate the future exchange of theories among neighboring subfields and encourage their eventual hybridization.

DIFFUSION OF CONCEPTS ACROSS DISCIPLINES

Other concepts have retained a stronger semantic core during their peregrinations, while nonetheless stimulating innovation. We see this in the successive extensions of the concept of "ecology," as described by Phillip Hauser: "Ecology was a neologism in a natural science context less than a century ago. Studies labeled 'ecological' were restricted to 'plant ecology' in the nineteenth century. They were extended to include 'animal ecology' in the first part of this century and, then, to include 'human ecology' only in the last three or four decades. Moreover, the term 'human ecology' has been used in disciplines other than sociology, especially in biology and in geography." (Hauser 1956: 229) Yet none of these uses of the term change it very much. Certainly it is recognizably the same in each of these subfields.

Others do change in meaning but without extraordinary variations. The concept of "status" comes originally from law, referring to a set of legally enforceable capacities and limitations. Sir Henry Sumner Maine, a scholar of jurisprudence, developed the distinction between status and contract to aid his comparative research in anthropology and history; in the process, he was also the first to formulate the concept of ideal polar types made famous by Max Weber. Weber developed these concepts further for sociology, whence it spread to anthropology and political science. The concept is central to many subfields in the social sciences.

The twists and turns of conceptual trading are sometimes surprising. "Values," for instance, was originally an economic term with a narrow, technical meaning. However, in the 1920s it began to take on shadings from some psychological terms such as preferences and motives and from sociological terms such as interests. This opened Pandora's box and the concept took on related meanings: attitudes, needs, sentiments, dispositions, cathexes, valences, ethics, ideologies, mores, norms, aspirations, obligations, rights, and sanctions. From there, anthropology and political science borrowed the concept and adapted it to their particular concerns.

It is difficult to predict which concepts are likely to be productive for what other subfields. Even distant subfields may find conceptual intercourse productive; one interesting example is "the well-known convergence between the concepts of entropy in physics and in the theory of information. At a first glance there would seem to be nothing less likely to create a link between disciplines so far removed from one another as thermodynamics and linguistics." (Piaget 1970a: 40) Other surprises were in store, and the development of entropy in the theory of information has proven to be useful for the study of the codification of genetic information in DNA. How the specialists of each of these fields discovered this common ground is an interesting question.

as a unity distinct from its parts, and this has spread to research on affectivity and social psychology. It is, however, quite different from Marx's initial formulation of structures which both engender and are changed by class relationships. Both uses of the term are different from statisticians' concept of a "latent structure" to explore some properties of data; yet this latter concept, mutated almost beyond recognition, appears in analyses of interest groups, where it is used to ask how latent distributions of interests are or are not translated into manifest groups. All these changes in meaning have stimulated innovation; unfortunately, by giving the same concept different meanings, they may hinder communication.

A similar problem can be seen in the concept of a "system." The concept was first developed in biology, as a way to organize life and organic systems as phenomena not reducible to their constituent chemistry. Homeostasis, a related concept, also comes from biology. From there, however, these concepts have been borrowed by many, including sociologists (Talcott Parsons), anthropologists (Malinowski, Radcliffe-Brown), and political scientists studying domestic politics (David Easton, Gabriel Almond) as well as international relations (Kenneth Waltz, Morton Kaplan, Richard Rosecrance). Immanuel Wallerstein has since endeavored to construct a theory of the world-system which encompasses both domestic and international politics and which draws from several formal disciplines, including sociology, history, political science, and Marxian political economy. Each successive adaptation and reformulation of this concept has proven to be important as the concept has been borrowed from one subfield to another. In field after field, borrowing the concept has provoked questions of a given system's stability or instability, like other conceptual borrowings stimulating new questions. In his book *A Framework for Political Analysis* (1965), David Easton attributes the inspiration for his systems approach to the study of communication, and not to the formulations then current in sociology or economics. Further influences came from a group at the University of Chicago's Committee on Behavioral Sciences, which included Easton from political science, Donald T. Campbell, Donald W. Fiske, and James G. Miller from psychology, Robert Crane from history, Ralph W. Gerard from neurophysiology, Henrietta Herbolsheimer from internal medicine, Jacob Marschak from economics, Richard L. Meier from planning, John R. Platt from physics, Anatol Rapoport from mathematical biology, Roger Sperry from biology, and Sherwood Washburn from anthropology. In this group, participants found common ground in the perspective of systems analysis. However, it is doubtful that all used the term in the same way.

DIFFUSION OF CONCEPTS ACROSS DISCIPLINES

Interestingly, "The word is never . . . used in a friendly sense." (Braudel 1979: 236) Originally, the term refers to men of money, not to the narrower technical concept of an owner of the means of production; again, the modern technical meaning dates to Marx. These concepts were developed in a more scholarly fashion during the eighteenth century, and still more in the nineteenth. In fact, "capitalism" dates only to this period. Louis Blanc, in his polemic with Claude Frédéric Bastiat, gave it its new meaning in 1850, "the appropriation of capital by some to the exclusion of others." Proudhon used it in 1861, but the word was still unknown to Marx in 1867; Marxists did not begin to use the word until after Werner Sombart had published his *Der moderne Kapitalismus* (1902). (Braudel 1979: 237) In a very different area of knowledge, the concept and the initial theory of cybernetics comes from the mathematician Norbert Wiener's efforts in World War II to design equipment which could track a target, aim and fire a gun, and correct for its own errors in subsequent firing. With Julian Bigelow, he then realized that the kinds of information processing and feedback loops necessary for this task might resemble processing systems in the human brain. His book *Cybernetics* (1948) discussed these ideas with relation to neurophysiology, logic, computer science, psychology, and sociology.

Generally speaking, conceptual development exploded in the 1930s, particularly at the University of Chicago. Stimulated by the emigration of many Europeans to the United States, the postwar era unleashed a torrent. The flood of concepts developed by these scholars poured from one discipline to another, stimulating cross-fertilization. "Functionalism" came from biology to anthropology, and from anthropology to sociology and political science. Talcott Parsons and Gabriel Almond each innovated in part by importing the concept and some of its associated theories into their own discipline. The concept of "public opinion" has spread from history to political science to sociology and social psychology, and it is indispensible in some specialities of these latter disciplines.

Some concepts are of importance for all social sciences. There is no discipline which lacks the concept of "structure," for instance. The earliest use of the concept may have been Herbert Spencer in 1858, but its first productive use was in political economy, Marx's exploration of economic structures and Engels' later elaboration of social structures. The concept was then borrowed by sociologists such as Emile Durkheim, linguists such as de Saussure, and anthropologists such as Radcliffe-Brown, Murdock, and Claude Lévi-Strauss, and it has from there worked its way into behavioral political science. Of course, each subfield remakes the concept in its own image as it cross-fertilizes one topic after another. Gestalt psychology, for instance, stresses structure scientists—"totalitarianism" being, perhaps, the most recent example. A large number of fields have exported two or three concepts to political science, including biology, game theory, mathematics, social psychology, statistics, and theology. Political science is not particularly good at developing its own concepts, with only nine indigenous productions—the same number philosophy has exported to political science. Borrowing concepts is not inevitable: economics, for instance, uses mostly endogenous concepts such as utility, price, wage, rate of return, or reaction path.

This count is not based on etymologies, but the concepts' development in social science. "Role," for instance, obviously comes from the stage, but Max Weber gave the word a radically different meaning, making it a sociological concept. From there, it has spread into most social sciences, including anthropology, political science, and psychology. "Revolution" comes from Copernicus, but was first applied to political events by Louis XIV; journalists and then social scientists adapted and developed the concept from there. This political use of the term served as a basis for the analogy drawn by the economist Arnold Toynbee (uncle of the historian Arnold J. Toynbee), when he coined the term "industrial revolution" in his book of that title in 1884. "Socialization" originated in psychology, as a result of work by Sigmund Freud and Ivan Pavlov. It was exploited in the 1930s by anthropologists such as Alfred Kroeber, Bronislaw Malinowski, and Margaret Mead. In the same decade, the political scientist Charles Merriam borrowed the concept and applied it to the specific problems of political socialization. "Modernization," on the other hand, comes from economics but has been hybridized with sociological concepts such as *Gesellschaft*. The concept is also important for political science—as one example among many, it is central to Samuel P. Huntington's *Political Order in Changing Societies* (1968).

Some concepts are of ancient lineage. Aristotle's concept of a "constitution" *(politeia)*, the concepts generated by his typology of six political systems, and his discussion of the concept of power are all of great importance. No one improved on these concepts over the course of many centuries, until some were more fully developed by judicial theorists and by Machiavelli.

Many important concepts arose in the realm of practical affairs in response to new phenomena. "Capital" emerged in Italy no later than 1211, in the sense of funds, a sum of money, or a stock of merchandise. Shades of the modern meaning begin to appear in the 1700s, in Forbounais, Quesnay, Morellet, and especially in Turgot; Karl Marx finally honed it to its present sense, that of a means of production. (Braudel 1979: 232–234) "Capitalist" dates only to the mid 1600s.

The reformation of a concept's meanings often induces the reformulation of other concepts or methods. As the example of "rent" suggests, it can also change the way we classify behavior. Such rethinking often uncovers past errors and suggests new lines of thought, stimulating innovation.

A similar process is the use of analogies, often by means of borrowed concepts. As David Easton notes, "analogy and metaphor have more than once served as the source of new insights and fundamental transformations in thought." (Easton 1965: 2) Such analogies are difficult to classify. Alfred Sauvy, a mathematician-demographer-economist and founder of the French Institute for Demographic Studies, coined the term "Third World" (*tiers monde*) in 1952, by analogy to the *ancien regime's* third estate. Engineering contributed the concept of feedback to psychology, where it was used to explore the extent to which actions rely on "intrinsic" feedback (such as feeling one's limbs touch something) or "extrinsic" feedback (watching where one's limbs are, for instance); understanding feedback is useful for designing prosthetics, for helping the blind or otherwise handicapped, and is important for the study of learning process, especially the process by which people develop skills such as playing the piano. "Charisma" can trace its origins to theology, especially to the epistles of St. Paul, from where Max Weber adapted it to categorize nonreligious leaders of a certain type. "Evolution" began in family tree models of linguistic change, and suggested for some biologists a family tree model of speciation, exploited most notably by the two Darwins. From there it has spread to all social sciences.

Notwithstanding the potential breadth of analogy, concepts are by their nature of limited applicability. Whereas the same methodology may perhaps be applied to many subjects, applying the same concept to many subjects creates nonsense. Concepts are therefore not only central to a patrimony, but a vocabulary of concepts defines in some sense a specialized subfield.

It would be interesting to determine the direction and volume of the flow of concepts between each of the disciplines, but the task would be a herculean one. Instead, we have examined, as an example, the pattern of borrowing for all those concepts in the *International Encyclopedia of the Social Sciences* which are relevant to political science. For political science, sociology appears to be the most productive developer of concepts, with twenty-two listings in our inventory. Anthropology, economics (twelve each), and psychology are also major conceptual suppliers. Law has exported eight concepts to political science, while journalistic accounts of current events have managed to develop five concepts sufficiently well for immediate adaptation by social

Both kinds of novel concepts can stimulate innovation when borrowed. These concepts may or may not be of direct applicability, but the attempt to apply them is always likely to provide insights. Because scholars are socialized into a specific discipline, most of us labor under various kinds of conceptual blinders, which vary from one discipline to the next. By putting on the conceptual blinders of another discipline in order to examine one's own, or by looking at a discipline from outside, without these blinders, one has a greater opportunity to innovate. Concepts may serve as different kinds of glasses through which we can examine the world.

Any concept developed for some new phenomenon by one discipline may have implications for others. "Matriarchy," taken from ethnology, has obvious applications to the sociology of the family, history, historical demography, archaeology, and many other fields. Simply having such a concept in one's inventory may change the way a scholar views the role of gender in society. "Dependency," coined by developmental economists with the United Nations Economic Commission on Latin America, was quickly applied to several historical studies, and it has since spread to political science and other fields. The concept forced economists and others to confront questions such as the consequences of English-Portuguese trade, lauded by David Ricardo but now understood as a classic example of how dependence can inhibit economic development. An important measure of "dependence," the Hirshman index of trade concentration, came from a study of the political use of trade relations in interwar Europe, while the principle behind the index is useful for measuring the concentration of any variable. Similarly, the Gini index of inequality, formulated by the demographer-turned-economist Corrado Gini, is of great importance for various subfields of sociology, economics, and political science; as a tool it is a useful indicator of the unevenness of a given distribution for any variable. It enables researchers to answer questions about inequality with greater confidence.

When borrowed, a given concept must be recast to adapt it to its new subject matter. A borrowed concept will retain many or most of its semantic components, but will lose some and gain others. "Rent," for instance, originally referred to the returns on a factor of production. Through the course of its development in economics, it added a semantic feature which made its meaning more precise, the returns on a fixed factor. For technical reasons, the term "rent" changed its meaning again, to include "noneconomic" returns, and it has entered political science in this form. As a political concept, "rent-seeking" refers to many kinds of behavior, from interest group lobbying to institutionalized corruption.

11
THE DIFFUSION OF CONCEPTS ACROSS DISCIPLINES

Concepts are perhaps the basic element in each field's patrimony, and each has a history. First, any concept must be coined. When conceived, its meaning may be imprecise or of limited usefulness for research. In the second stage, scholars develop the concept for scientific use. Obviously, a term may exist both as a scientific concept and as a part of everyday speech, but it will often have different meanings in the two contexts: "rent" means one thing to a landlord, another to an economist; "to socialize" is intransitive in colloquial English, but is a transitive verb with a quite different meaning in sociology. Once developed and given a specific meaning, concepts can be used by any scholar, and that scholar's use of the term should be easily understood by all other scholars in the field. Because they are so fundamental, they play an important role in building bridges between disciplines and in hybridization of subfields.

There are two sources of new concepts. First, scientists may discover a hitherto-unknown object or phenomenon. The natural sciences provide hundreds of examples, including quarks, mesons, greenhouse effect, quasars, americanium, and DNA. The social sciences also make such outright discoveries, such as valence and ergativity in languages or elasticity and "consumer's surplus" in economics, all of which are phenomena not recognized prior to scientific research in these areas. The second, and primary source of concepts in the social sciences is the recategorization of previously known objects. Examples of this recategorization include "postindustrial" values, "bureaucratic-authoritarian" political systems, "motivated bias" in psychology, or "socialization." This, too, occurs in the natural sciences, in cases such as electromagnetism.

PART FOUR

THE INTERPENETRATION OF DISCIPLINES: THE PROCESSES OF HYBRIDIZATION

There are many different ways in which scientific specialties can influence one another. Any aspect of science can serve as the subject of exchange: concepts, methdologies, discoveries, theories, or perspectives.

These diverse components of the scientific project vary in the breadth of their applicability. Methods and theories are generally more exportable, since their advocates often attempt to apply them to as many social phenomena as possible. Concepts and discoveries are usually of much narrower range.

For each case, bringing something new into a subfield usually changes the nature of debate in that field. New concepts or methods often suggest new questions; new theories and concepts often call attention to phenomena previously overlooked. In each case, science advances.

These tools of the trade reach fruition in the work of individual scholars, who may migrate from one field to another. They can also be found in research communities, which are often reflected in academic journals. In many cases, a new journal at the intersection of two disciplines stimulates the growth of a new hybrid.

WHY INTERDISCIPLINARITY IS A FALSE NOTION

Narrowness is important, given the wealth of findings in all the social sciences today. The last person able to master all the social sciences of his day was probably Max Weber, who felt as much at home with a study of the contemporary German Social Democrats as he did with the Protestant Reformation, the agrarian history of Rome, trading companies in the Middle Ages, or the Hebrew prophets. He could draw as easily from political economy as from history, sociology, theology, philosophy, law, and *Staatswissenschaft*. No one can repeat this breadth today; in fact, even Max Weber would be kept busy enough trying to stay current with the secondary literature about him. In the first half of the 1970s, there were about one hundred books and articles published every year which dealt with Max Weber (see Seyfarth and Schmidt 1977). Faced with such an explosion in the relevant literature, in all fields, the modern scholar must specialize.

Some try to get around the problem by arguing, as does Jack Hirshleifer, that "There is only one social science." (Hirshleifer 1985: 53) Like most economists, he sees his discipline at the center of it, "the universal grammar of social science." We do not see any such universal grammar in social science, but a variety of dialects and language types. There are languages of structure, of choice, of evolution, of action, of function, of interaction, of power. In fact, Hirshleifer too recognizes the need for economists to learn other languages, to become aware of the limitations of what has to date been their "tunnel vision." We agree.

However, it is first necessary to train budding economists in the language of their discipline first, to make them economists before they are hybrids. For teaching purposes, for the transfer of knowledge to the next generation, unidisciplinarity seems inevitable because basic training is necessary before specialized expertise can be achieved. Once that level of expertise is reached, however, these scholars should widen their horizons in the direction of neighboring disciplines. The resulting cross-fertilization of one subfield by a related one will generally improve any scholar's research.

In the social sciences, then, the team strategy is open to question. It is true that some large teams, such as the *European Values Study* (1981), the *American Soldier* group (Stouffer *et al.*), the *International Study of Values in Politics* (Phillip Jacobs *et al.*), and Quincy Wright's causes-of-war project at the University of Chicago in the 1930s, have been major innovators. These are all data-oriented research, and a team may be necessary to handle the volume of field research required. On the other hand, such large teams are very unusual in projects which do not require this kind of research.

A different kind of "team," the scholarly conference, can also be innovative if there is good follow-through; Seymour Martin Lipset and Stein Rokkan's *Party Systems and Voter Alignments* is one example. Of course, this book relies on the single-author case studies and the dual-author introduction which unites them. The usual pattern of such conferences, even when they result in a book, is quite different. The group may have difficulty communicating, and the volume may include innovative chapters but may not be innovative as a unified whole. As Stanislaw Andreski correctly points out, "getting together into inter-disciplinary colloquia specialists who know nothing about each others' fields cannot produce any substantive results." (Andreski 1972: 68)

Why do group collaborations find it difficult to innovate? Scholarly collaboration can be very difficult when faced with a multiplicity of frameworks, perspectives, concepts, and theories. One example should make the problem clear. Some time ago, one of us heard a series of lectures on arms control given by a team of seventeen scholars, including political scientists, historians, jurists, and physicists; one could imagine still other disciplines being brought to bear on the topic. The seventeen specialists each presented a particular point of view in the hope that this would stimulate in the minds of their listeners a synthesis which they had been unable to achieve themselves. Of course, there is no good reason why the listener should succeed where the specialists have failed, and such an approach risks becoming a tower of Babel. What each specialist needs is not only knowledge of his own specialty and of the common topic, but also some familiarity with the relevant portions of related fields. This familiarity helps make communication a two-way affair, as each scholar can speak to her extradisciplinary colleagues in their own "language."

If innovation is more likely for one or at most two authors, then the reintegration of material from two or more disciplines must take place on a manageable scale. Although a scholar cannot master two disciplines, she can nevertheless hope to master a few specialties from two or more disciplines.

WHY INTERDISCIPLINARITY IS A FALSE NOTION

today and still retain the depth needed for scientific advance; we can never have another Leonardo da Vinci.

Since individual interdisciplinarity is almost impossible today, are interdisciplinary research teams the solution? Pierre de Bie advocates this approach, arguing that the complexity of the real world demands multidisciplinarity. He suggests multidisciplinary collaboration among scholars, which should be formalized: "Team work can only be fruitful if it is institutionalized." (de Bie 1970: 620) Yet institutionalization is anything but a cure-all—without focus, innovation is virtually impossible. As a result, "Scholarly history is replete with examples of the very limited success or the outright failure of massive experiments in inter-disciplinary teams." (Belshaw 1988: 21) While de Bie recommends focusing on practical problems so as to stimulate innovative interactions among related specialties, this solution limits the social sciences to questions whose answers are foreseen to have practical application. Not all applications can be foreseen, and there is also a place for abstract theory.

If simple juxtaposition is avoided, collaboration between scholars belonging to different disciplines can be a creative form of hybridization. In most cases, the productive collaboration involves only two authors, rarely three or more; it seems that two is company and three a crowd. Karl Marx and Friedrich Engels are probably the famous team of all. Game theory resulted from the joint efforts of the mathematician John von Neumann and the economist Oskar Morgenstern. Robert Dahl and the economist Charles Lindblom opened lines up between political science and economics. The anthropologist Robert Textor and the statistician turned political scientist Arthur Banks dichotomized a long series of variables which proved to be useful for comparative analysis in its day. Noam Chomsky and M. Halle's *The Sound Pattern of English* is a classic in generative phonology, while Milton Friedman and Anna Schwartz's *Monetary History of the United States* is the classic monetarist interpretation of American economic history. Collaborative work is becoming more frequent, as in the natural sciences, where team work in a single laboratory is a major form of cross-fertilization. Even so, most major innovations in the social sciences remain the product of only one or two minds. While difficult to prove, we suspect that authorship by more than two scholars almost always reduces a work's degree of innovation. This is aparently true for a large group of American sociologists, for according to one citation study, "among authors who are cited frequently, their single-authored works are most visible. . . ." (Chubin 1973: 189) Further studies, separating works with one, two, or more authors, would be interesting.

116   PART THREE

course they would like to be able to use all the tools available to them
in this task, but this is easier said than done. Marc Bloch observes
that

> very few scholars can boast that they are equally well equipped to read
> critically a medieval charter, to explain correctly the etymology of place-
> names, to date unerringly the ruins of dwellings of the prehistoristic,
> Celtic, or Gallo-Roman periods, and to analyze the plant life proper to
> a pasture, a field, or a moor. Without all these, however, how could one
> pretend to describe the history of land use? . . . We have no other
> remedy than to substitute, in place of the multiple skills of a single man,
> the pooling of the techniques, practiced by different scholars, but all
> tending to throw light upon a specific subject. (Bloch 1954: 68–69)

This is, of course, specialization-into-hybridization through borrowing
from other fields. Historians are especially dependent upon specialists
from the outside. Yet true hybridization is not a catch-all, and hybrids
are not jacks of all trades. They are specialized. Fernand Braudel's
three-volume *Civilization and Capitalism,* for instance, suffers from
overload; although the core arguments are truly hybrid there is much
extraneous—albeit fascinating—material along the way. He tends towards encyclopedism, and this sometimes obscures important arguments.

Specialization remains important, for it gives focus. "Each discipline
throws light on a set of variables precisely because other factors are
assumed to be external, distal, and equal." (Sartori 1969: 66) Such an
analytical simplification is important at first to clarify and explore
certain causal relationships. The different kinds of causal arguments
developed by the various disciplines can best be exploited by blending
them carefully in an attempt to capture the wealth of factors in the
real world. "One might say that each of the specialties within social
science is a lobbyist for the significance of one or the other organizational segments of the society. . . ." (Greer 1969: 56)

Of course, assuming these factors away does not necessarily lead to
innovation; at some point, they must be judiciously reintroduced. The
complexity of the real world requires not just the addition of more and
more variables, but the better understanding of already-identified variables. This requires first specialization. Encyclopedic coverage is by no
means a virtue.

It is for these reasons that we believe "interdisciplinarity" is usually
a poor research strategy, because it implies fairly thorough knowledge
of two or more entire disciplines. No one can master two disciplines

10

WHY INTERDISCIPLINARITY IS A FALSE NOTION

One may imagine a researcher facing three different strategies, conceived of as ideal types: pure specialization, utopian "interdisciplinarity," and hybridization. As this essay shows, each strategy has led to significant scientific advance in the past. However, innovative social scientists are increasingly turning away from the first two strategies: specialization is self-destructive, exposing its own weaknesses as it advances, while true interdisciplinarity is impossible today because of the extent of specialization.

Let us look to important historical events, often taken as cases which demand "interdisciplinary" research. Major historical events clearly encompass several scientific disciplines. The collapse of the Roman Empire, the rise of Islam, the Industrial Revolution in the West, the population explosion in Asia and Africa, the mushrooming of giant cities in Latin America, or the continued economic decline of Britain, all obviously require compound explanations which may range from geology to agronomics, from bacteriology to any of the social sciences.

To deal with this multicausality, it is very common to suggest "interdisciplinary" strategies; in fact, everyone seems to approve of interdisciplinary research. We do not. First, the very fact that major historical events—and minor ones as well—encompass several disciplines does not imply that we must take all of the relevant variables into account simultaneously. To do so would deny the value of analytical classification and of specialization. This approach leads to superficiality, for if a scholar does not exclude some factors he makes it impossible to understand that which is truly important.

Historians, in attempting to reconstruct an "event," rather than an analytical issue, are especially prone to overbroad multicausality. Of is maximization; it also pulls the rug out from most comparative statics because an individual may remain satisfied with a given course of action even as the parameters underlying that choice change. We must keep in mind that methodologies can divide as well as unite communities.

13
THE IMPACT OF TECHNOLOGY

There are many forms of cross-disciplinary influence, many different ways in which scholars combine specialties from different formal disciplines. Some are paths which lead in different directions, some are sudden but temporary, others are stages down the road to hybridization.

Technology, for instance, is an important kind of cross-disciplinary influence. Most technological advances are applied first to one discipline, and spread rapidly to others. The influence of technological advance is usually sudden and massive, but further application does not usually lead to hybridization. The telescope and the microscope are the most important classical cases of technological innovation stimulating scientific innovation; the radio telescope and the electron microscope are further extensions of the principle. Some more modern technological advances in the natural sciences would include seismographs, satellites, gene splicing, and hundreds other examples.

The same occurs in the social sciences. Archaeology, for instance, uses a wide range of scientific technologies as tools. Marine archaeology has only really become possible in recent decades, thanks to advanced underwater technology. Such advances have made possible such spectacular finds as the excavation of the Roskilde Fjord viking ships and the raising of the Wasa in Stockholm harbor. Aerial photography, also a product of technology, has been important for many fields: aerial views have shown the pattern of land distribution in older times and the ecology of contemporary giant cities; similar efforts have located many temples of ancient Cambodia, many Mayan pyramids, and huge Incan drawings of animals in the Nazca plain. Tape recorders have played a critical role in the analysis of tone-based languages and vocal inflections, to say nothing of oral history. Video cameras are important documentary tools in the analysis of nonverbal communication, small group psychology, linguistic discourse patterns, and the documentation of ritual in cultural anthropology, among other fields.

In all the social sciences, the computer is obviously the most important technology spawning innovative applications today. One surprising application comes from ethnomusicology, where a "particularly important development in the use of machines has been the attempt objectively to reduce musical sound to visual form" through machines called "melographs." (Freedman 1978: 61) Applications of the computer, even if we exclude statistical work, are older than most people realize: in 1953, Torsten Hägerstrand's *Innovation Diffusion as a Spatial Process* used computer simulation to reproduce experimentally the process of technological diffusion in southern Sweden. As an idea of the breadth of application even twenty years ago, a special issue of the *International Social Science Journal* in 1971 on the "use of computers in the social sciences," included articles on the application of computers to survey research, ethnography, archaeology, sociological simulation, experimental psychology, and the analysis of myths.

Some technological advances occur through serendipity, "the gift of finding valuable or agreeable things not sought for." Galileo used to polish concave lenses for Sforza, duke of Ferrara, who offered them to astigmatic ambassadors; so Galileo built his telescope. Cathode ray equipment, developed for other purposes, led to the discovery of X-rays. The electron microscope helped biochemistry open the road to cell biology, a new field which results from a double technological development. Since almost all technological advances come from outside the social sciences, their applicability is almost inherently serendipitous.

14
THE CROSS-DISCIPLINARY
REPERCUSSIONS OF FINDINGS

All sciences seek to make discoveries about the world, and these findings are essential to the patrimony of the field. Discoveries are eternal additions to the patrimony, whereas theories are continuously challenged. Even the most successful theories, such as Newton's, are ultimately modified or replaced. They end up in the cemeteries of books.

Discoveries are much more frequent and significant in the natural sciences than in the social sciences. In the experimental subfields of the natural sciences, certain discoveries can even be anticipated, setting off a race between rival scientists to be the first to verify the existence of a suspected object or phenomenon. Such races are very rare in most of the social sciences, where new interpretations are the most visible form of advance.

In both the natural sciences and the social sciences, new findings are a frequent form of interaction among specialties. Like concepts, findings are by their nature of narrower applicability than methods or theories. They have specific real-world referents, and do not easily extend beyond a certain limit. Nonetheless, like concepts, discoveries are important pathways to cross-fertilization.

New findings may make it possible to see things previously overlooked. These discoveries, almost by definition, are made in areas not studied, that is, at or beyond the margins of a field. When discovered, important findings can draw scholars into a hybrid. The economics of the gift, explored first in Bronislaw Malinowski's discussion of the *kula* theme and then given its primary emphasis by Marcel Mauss' classic "Essai sur le don" (1923–1924), is the basic stimulus behind what is today economic anthropology. Another anthropological hybrid, political anthropology, owes its initial development to the work of M. Fortes and E. E. Evans-Pritchard in *African Political Systems* (1940). This book led to a large number of ethnographic descriptions of "primitive" political systems as well as many attempts at better conceptualization and theorization about these systems (see Easton 1959): David Apter's *Ghana in Transition* and *The Political Kingdom in Uganda* are two noteworthy examples. Before this "discovery" of politics in stateless societies, political anthropology would have been impossible.

Social psychology, too, received its primary impetus from a series of important findings. Psychologists discovered that stimuli are not absolute but are conditioned by the contexts in which they are located: colors, for instance, are perceived differently depending on the background color; rats run mazes differently depending on where the windows in a room are. When studying more "real world" psychological behavior, too, social context was demonstrably important. This work by the psychologists then resonated with various observations by sociologists and anthropologists; Malinowski, for instance, had noticed that while Trobriand Islanders are able to see resemblences between fathers and sons, they do not see such resemblances between the sons and the daughters. From such cuttings was a productive hybrid made, psychological anthropology, including for instance N. H. Segall, D. T. Campbell, and M. J. Herskovits' *The Influence of Culture on Visual Perception* (1966)—a joint project of anthropologists and psychologists.

Some such discoveries are simply serendipitous, found but not looked for. The natural sciences provide many examples of this, such as Galvani's discovery of electrical activity in living tissue, Oersted's discovery of the relation between electricity and magnetism, and Claude Bernard's discovery of the nervous system control of blood circulation. Serendipitous discovery is far less common in the social sciences, but does occur. The brothers Grimm were linguists collecting data on German dialects, whose decision to collect folktales was methodological, an attempt to find "purer" linguistic forms as preserved in traditional stories. Yet their collection served as the basis for a new discipline, folklore studies, and was soon widely imitated, as by Asbjørnson and Moe in Norway. In all such cases, we should remember Pasteur's dictum that "chance only favors the prepared mind." Specialization does play a role.

Besides creating fields, discoveries can enrich existing specialties. Findings from one discipline may disprove theories current in another; they may also confirm them, giving scholars greater confidence in these theories. Such juxtaposition of the findings of two specialties can, in the words of Muzafer and Carolyn Sherif, serve as a "validity check." After all, if two subfields each try to understand the same phenomenon, the explanations should not be incompatible. Hybrid subfields do over-

CROSS-DISCIPLINARY REPERCUSSIONS OF FINDINGS

lap in their areas of interest. With greater opportunities for "validity checks," scholars may have greater confidence in their hypotheses and theories.

Robin M. Hogarth and Melvin W. Reder have suggested a useful analogy for this process: "one may have reason to be confident in the accuracy of a medical diagnosis if two physicians agree. However, confidence is liable to be far greater if one knows that the physicians have quite different backgrounds and training. . . ." (Hogarth and Reder 1986: 18) In this sense, then, the exchange of findings advances science because it increases the accuracy of our understanding of the world.

In other cases, findings are less obviously beneficial, destroying accepted theory without suggesting any better alternative. This problem has stimulated work in the philosophy of science, which has tried to understand how scientists may rationally continue to accept even such "disproven" theories. The phenomenon occurs constantly. Sociological, historical, and cross-cultural research has in recent years increasingly called into question Piaget's theory of child development, as has findings from adult development processes (Datan, Rodeheaver, and Hughes 1987: 156–157), but such work has not developed a better theory. The same can be said of transformational grammar in linguistics, which does not yet have a coherent replacement. In fact, it is fair to say that most theories in the social sciences have been disconfirmed, but many are still current because they are better than nothing and because there is a wide range of behavior which they do in fact explain.

15
THE INFLUENCE OF THEORIES

Science often begins by developing a set of concepts with which to organize a given field of study, and then also a collection of methods with which to approach this area. Next, scientists begin to collect data on their subject and to make discoveries. As this work progresses, or even before it begins, scientists soon start to make hypotheses and to create theories which explain what they have found.

Just as we have found for the other components of each field's patrimony, another common kind of influence is the exchange of theories among specialties. There are good reasons why the borrowing of theories can be innovative. Theories from other disciplines are similar to methodologies in so far as they can be used by anyone once the difficult process of invention and initial elaboration is completed. As Stephen L. Wasby points out for the case of political science, "political scientists have found that their colleagues in sister disciplines have already developed and tested frames of reference which have seemed promising." (Wasby 1970: 86) As examples, Wasby suggests functional approaches from political anthropology, ecological theories from geography, personality and perception theories from psychology, and role theory, demographic variables, and structural-functionalism from sociology. Another remarkable case in political science is the literature on voting behavior. In a review, Kinder argues that there have been five main approaches to the study of this topic: personality, self-interest, group identification, values, and inferences from history. (Kinder 1983: 402–412) We cannot help but notice not only that each corresponds to some outside discipline—psychology, economics, social psychology, sociology, and history, respectively—but also that the most innovative early works in each of these approaches were in fact closely linked to that discipline.

The theories of one discipline may prove to be new explanations of phenomena studied in other fields. It is difficult to predict which theories will apply to what subjects. The ancients would have been surprised that the same laws of gravity and motion which apply to a falling apple also describe the motion of stars and planets. Until this century, people would not have believed that the same "base" instincts driving animal behavior also drive human behavior—including that of the "better classes."

The reasons why the exchange of theories can be innovative have been explored theoretically. Wassily Leontief (1948) has proposed a model of science in which the various disciplines each include an explanation of part of reality. Scientific progress consists of refining each discipline's theories so that they exclude successively more logical possibilities which are not actually found in reality. Ideally, all disciplines would converge to a point which would represent the event to be explained. His schema suggests that one can approach the truth by working at the intersections of disciplines. If each discipline possess part of the truth, then those theories unique to one discipline must be incorrect for they necessarily exclude that which is correct in the theories of the others. Understanding and developing theories where disciplines overlap helps exclude successively more invalid theories. Here, too, interaction can serve as a validity check.

These exchanges of theories can be observed at work. Two subfields may each suggest theories which attempt to explain a given phenomenon, or which explain some aspect of it. Frequently, scholars aware of both theories will try to synthesize the two and this new theory may be innovative indeed, and of broader application than either parent. Great men in the history of science were able to achieve vast cross-disciplinary syntheses of existing knowledge which, by recasting what was previously "known," had the effect of undermining previous work. Some large-scale syntheses become "holistic" theories, which are able to encompass many subfields from a number of formal disciplines; Toynbee's theory of history is a notable example. The implications of these holistic theories are often revolutionary, even if ultimately untenable. Their danger lies in that they tend to become unidimensional and therefore require synthesis with other causal factors; Mancur Olson's *Rise and Decline of Nations,* for instance, can easily be criticized as exaggerated even if intriguing.

Alternatively, the confrontation of theories may disprove one while confirming the other. The classical dispute between purely supply-side and demand-side theories of prices have been largely resolved in favor of the latter, leading to the rejection of the labor theory of value held by Ricardo and Marx. Again science moves forward, since our confi-

THE INFLUENCE OF THEORIES

dence in the victorious theory is now greater than before. The success of the second theory suggests that it may be more robust than previously thought, and may lead researchers to apply it to a wider subject area.

On the other hand, the confrontation of two theories may disprove them both. This creates a theoretical void, and innovators may rush in to fill the gap. As a result, sometimes the borrowing of a theory stimulates the creation of a hybrid. The rapid growth in psycholinguistics dates to a paper by George Miller in the *American Psychologist* (1962), in which he suggested that several of the major features of Chomsky's transformational grammar (deep and surface structure, transformational complexity, grammaticality) had experimentally verifiable psychological reality. While the theory has been much attacked, the subfield of psycholinguistics thus created lives on, and has gone on to make many other findings about language comprehension and memory.

This process would include theories of both broad and narrow range. Some theories are of surprisingly broad applicability, and have been borrowed by a number of other fields. Nonlinear dynamics ("chaos theory"), developed in physics, fluid dynamics, and meteorology, has an application in cardiology, in understanding the dynamics of fibrillation during and after major surgery—a potentially dangerous condition. The theory depends upon sophisticated mathematics and powerful computers, and explores the ways in which disorder is ordered. Since disorder appears in the social sciences as well as in the natural sciences, it may have applications here as well, although we are aware of none to date. It would not be the first time that novel mathematical theories would find application in the social sciences, of course; James Cassing and Arye L. Hillman, for instance, have recently found an application of so-called "catastrophe theory" in the dynamic response of industries to tariff protection.

Also quite broad, psychological theories have been important for most of the social sciences. Géza Róheim, for instance, brought Freudian theory to anthropology; "the dual nature of his training made it possible for him to do pioneering work as the first psychoanalytic anthropologist." (Muensterberger and Domhoff 1968: 544) Psychoanalytic theory was imported into the United States in the 1920s and 1930s by men from several formal disciplines, including Alfred L. Kroeber, Bronislaw Malinowski, and Edward Sapir in anthropology, William F. Ogburn in sociology, and Charles E. Merriam in political science. Furthermore, such hybrids were among the most important of those who extended Freud's work. Other developers of the theory were driven to break with their psychoanalytic colleagues: "the implications of the inner transformations of psychoanalysis are often more clearly seen in the positions taken by 'defectors' from the 'core' than by those who

150   PART FOUR

remained organizationally faithful." (Lasswell 1956: 89) Many scholars, rather than extending the original theory, have simply applied it. Alexander and Juliette George, for instance, used Freudian psychology to understand the behavior of a political leader in *Woodrow Wilson and Colonel House*. Subsequent psychological theory has also had applications in political science; Robert Jervis, for instance, applied cognitive psychology to international relations in *Perception and Misperception in International Politics* (1976). Similarly, Glenn Paige applied decisionmaking theory to his analysis in *The Korean Decision* (1968). At the intersections of three formal disciplines, political scientist Deborah Welch Larson used psychological theories to attempt to resolve some historiographical debates over the *Origins of Containment* in postwar U.S. foreign policy.

Psychological theories have been important for many fields. Franz Alexander, trained in medicine and physiology, and then active in psychoanalysis, coauthored a book on criminal personalities with the lawyer Hugo Staub. Besides criminology he was also attracted to the application of psychoanalysis to medicine, and he was a founding editor of *Psychosomatic Medicine*. Carl I. Hovland was a leading psychologist best known for his research on social communication and individual attitudes. The citation for the Distinguished Scientific Contribution Award he received from the American Psychological Association reads in part that "he has done much to isolate the major factors at work when an individual is confronted with the complex informational input of a persuasive argument. By judicious use of psychological theory, he has been able to relate this area of social psychology to basic investigations of the higher mental processes." (cited in Janis 1968: 527) Such recombinations of aspects of communications theory, psychology, and social psychology are the hallmark of the hybrid.

In other cases, psychology has imported theories from the outside. There are many examples, and their work may be quite influential for others. Edward L. Thorndike, often identified as America's most productive psychologist, was greatly influenced by Darwin and his work helped make psychology more "genetic." Besides drawing on such aspects of biology, he was also a leader in the use of quantification in the "new psychology" of the early twentieth century, and his *An Introduction to the Theory of Mental and Social Measurements* (1904) is the first influential handbook of the field. Clearly Darwin's theory affected others in the social sciences as well. John Lubbock, biologist and anthropologist, was one of Charles Darwin's few proteges, and he applied Darwin's theory in an effort to develop a theory of cultural evolution which had great impact upon English anthropology.

THE INFLUENCE OF THEORIES

The interactions of theories may be seen in many fields. W. I. Thomas was a sociologist and social psychologist who was interested especially in the interplay of biological and sociocultural factors in human behavior. These concerns appeared first in a series of paper on the sociology of sex, but they were also evident in the "Methodological Note" of his collaboration with Florian Znaniecki, *The Polish Peasant in Europe and America* (1918–1920), which discussed theories of personality development, social change, social organization, and attitudes and values. He was also greatly influenced by the biology of Jacques Loeb, H. S. Jennings, C. M. Child, and A. J. Carlson, the psychology of Ivan Pavlov and J. B. Watson, and the psychiatry of Sigmund Freud, Adolf Meyer, and Harry Stack Sullivan. Achille Loria used agronomy and demography to understand political economy, arguing that differences in land productivity and population densities determine different historical forms of subjugation such as slavery, feudalism, and the varieties of capitalism. His emphasis on the importance of free land in American history influenced Frederick Jackson Turner's theory of the role played by the frontier in the United States.

Sometimes borrowed theories from one discipline will resonate with different theories from a third discipline in an unpredictable manner. The anthropological study of law in societies which lack judicial institutions has been driven afield in some surprising directions. The concept of "ordered anarchy" in Evans-Pritchard's classic, *The Nuer* (1940), bears an interesting relation to the pattern of international law in an anarchic international system, a parallelism noted by Hans Kelsen and others. It bears potential relevance to game-theoretic analyses of cooperation in international relations. Such studies are currently much in vogue but have not drawn from anthropology at all.

There is a potential danger in the borrowing of theories, the problem of "lags," or the borrowing of outdated theories. Many political sociologists, as they began to study "third world" politics in the 1960s, relied on structural-functionalism even as it was increasingly rejected by the field of social anthropology. Examining why the parent field had rejected its progeny would have helped these political sociologists avoid many subsequent criticisms. Even so, they were probably better off than the social anthropologists, who could have borrowed from political sociology but did not. Anthropological questions about local power elites, for instance, could have made useful reference to works by Robert Dahl, Nelson Polsby, and Floyd Hunter, but almost none did. (Weingrod 1967: 128–131) Those who would borrow need some specialization in the source of their theories, and should stay current in the literature from which they borrow.

Hypotheses and theories are also subject to diminishing returns in the end. While they become part of the patrimony of one discipline, or even of several social sciences, they cease to be innovative. A hypothesis rarely serves as innovative after having been broadly diffused. The theory of evolution, for example, is too old to stimulate new explorations in biology and kindred sciences. Biological research no longer finds any inspiration in Darwinism but in specific hypotheses on heredity, cytology, and other new subfields. It is for this reason that contemporary scholars in biopolitics and biosociology often succumb to criticisms that they have only rediscovered social Darwinism; to innovate, scholars in these potential hybrids borrow from biological research closer to the research frontier, including that which is currently controversial in biology. It seems, in fact, that there is a need for controversy to stimulate advance. Areas of consensus rapidly become sterile, even though once important additions to the patrimony.

Some dismiss this borrowing as mere imitation. This is mistaken, for imitation requires imagination. There are many theories and concepts from which one could take inspiration—choosing the right one is not easy, and refining it for its new application requires much thought. It is by stimulating thought, rather than slavish imitation, that the diffusion of concepts leads to innovation across scientific subfields. For instance, as Willigan and Lynch noted with respect to one subfield, "Rather than being a sign of immaturity or weakness . . . This multidisciplinary and increasingly interdisciplinary style of research is responsible for the intellectual vitality and growth of historical demography." (Willigan and Lynch 1982: xii) The same is true of many other fields.

16
PERSPECTIVES, PARADIGMS, AND PRAXIS

Most people are used to thinking in terms of disciplines which study certain subjects, such as politics, economics, or the mind. However, subject matter is not the only—or even the primary—criterion distinguishing the social sciences. Mancur Olson correctly points out that "the basic differences between the social sciences involve not the subjects they study, but rather preconceptions they have inherited, the methods they use, and the conclusions they reach." (Olson 1969: 139–140) Taken as a whole, such intangibles make for the unique perspective of each discipline.

Different perspectives make it possible to see new phenomena, or new aspects of old phenomena. What could be more difficult than being innovative in the interpretation of sacred texts? Nevertheless, the perspective of another discipline can help. By treating Moses as a political leader, David Rapoport and Aaron Wildavsky were able to reinterpret some passages. While they are political scientists, their work cites primarily historians, theologians and classicists, and they rarely cite their disiplinary colleagues. Other innovators in the study of sacred texts have also looked beyond their discipline. Theologians such as Leonardo Boff, engaged in practical political work, have reinvigorated the study of the Israelite exodus by interpreting it both as political emancipation and as theological liberation. Other liberation theologians have used Marxist political economy to cross-fertilize studies of both the Old and New Testaments. Concerning Islam, Sir William Muir, Alfred Guillaume, and Maxim Rodinson, each writing about Mohammed as a politico-military leader, have placed themselves at the intersection of various subfields of history, theology, geography, sociology, anthropology, and linguistics.

154 PART FOUR

The importance of different perspectives can be seen theoretically, with reference to the philosophy of science. Scientific activity can be divided into two kinds, "normal" science and "revolutionary" science. (Kuhn 1962) Normal science is what most scientists do most of the time. It takes place within a "paradigm," a given set of assumptions, methods, and questions. Normal science is important, for it is the theoretical and empirical development of the existing paradigm, and it is the major process by which science progresses. Through the work of normal scientists, progressively greater portions of social reality are more fully understood, and the implications of existing paradigms thoroughly fleshed out; "normal science" is by no means a pejorative term, as Kuhn has himself insisted. (see Kuhn 1970)

There obviously exist paradigms in the social sciences; microeconomic theory is the most prominent, but by no means the only example. Robert Keohane (1983) has argued that the study of international relations has a paradigm called "structural Realism." Linguistics, too, until fairly recently, may be said to have had something close to a Kuhnian paradigm. The discipline focused primarily on *langue*, not *parole*; little study was given to non-standard forms; it ignored pragmatics and other social uses of language; the units of analysis were phonemes, morphemes, deep structures, and the like, and the focus of attention was on transformational rules which could link these abstractions with actual grammatical utterances. Like any good paradigm, it also discovered anomalies and made attempts to solve the puzzles they presented. The paradigmatic assumption that the present indicative in independent clauses is the basic sentence structure across languages proved fruitful for comparative grammars and the study of basic word order, but had great difficulty explain anomalies such as verb placement rules in German. The problem is not in the data, as descriptive accounts of the rules for German verb placement are well-known, but it is difficult to place these rules into the context of the paradigm as a whole.

In the social sciences, paradigms are often not universally accepted even within the relevant subfield. This is why there was at first some dispute as to whether political science, for instance, was aparadigmatic, preparadigmatic, or multiparadigmatic. (see Truman 1965; Almond 1966; Beardsley 1974) The existence of several different "schools of thought" in a formal discipline does not make each of them any the less productive for those who share them. It would be fairly easy, for instance, to elaborate the "pluralist" paradigm which dominates most research on advanced democracies: people have "interests" derived from a mix of material motives, socialization, and personality; people act on their interests and form groups, including parties, subject to collec-

PERSPECTIVES, PARADIGMS, AND PRAXIS

tive action problems; these groups both compete with one another and cooperate in the pursuit of their goals; parties seek some mix of policy goals and continuation in office, and present profiles based on this mix; voters choose between parties on the basis of their interests and on the information at hand; and so on. Obviously much is left unexplained by these oversimplifications, such as the nature of the mixes involved, but its very statement in this form suggests the research programs many American political scientists in this area have pursued. Some early works, such as those by Charles Beard and Harold Laski, needed to assert that groups other than the state could be sovereign over important matters (Garson 1974); with that battle won, subsequent pluralists have explored questions such as: what is the relative importance of different factors for a person's interests (or values)? why are some types of groups more easily formed than others? why are some more powerful?

Paradigms point scholars in a given direction, suggesting what is and what is not important. Galilean physics suggested that falling stones were more important than falling feathers, and this focus was very important for the theory of gravitational attraction. The social sciences are no different. Scholars from different formal disciplines ask different questions even when studying the same event. Historians studying the origins of the Cold War, for instance, seek to identify the chain of events and the development of causal forces which led up to Soviet-American hostility. Many political scientists specialized in international relations, on the other hand, have asked which characteristics of the international power structure made such an outcome likely—bipolarity, hegemonic leadership, certain belief structures, and so on. Being well versed in both kinds of questions enables one to build on both—separating out necessary and sufficient conditions, for instance. This can lead to synthesis, but it can also lead to new questions and innovative extensions of the arguments of each subfield in its own terms.

Those who seek to apply science to real problems also ask different questions than theorists. Their perspective, too, is an important source of innovation. Agitation for calendar reform had a direct effect on Renaissance astrologers, making them face the inadequacy of their computations more directly. This ultimately led Copernicus to ask questions which had apparently heretical answers. In technical innovation, in the design of scientific instruments, 77 per cent of manufacturing innovations came from suggestions by product users (von Hippel 1988: 13), again suggesting the important role of the practical perspective. Similarly high figures are found in semiconductors and printed circuit boards and in pultrusion processes (fiber-reinforced plastics).

In the social sciences, one well-known center of problem-focused innovation is the RAND corporation. Some of its major innovations include the development of policy studies methodology, formal deterrence theory, refinements of arms race theories, Leites' theory of the operational code, and many others. Besides those who study war, those who study peace have also been innovative through a cross-disciplinary approach: "It is its applied character . . . that forces peace research to be interdisciplinary." (Boulding 1977: 602) Economists at the International Monetary Fund, the World Bank, the OECD, the Federal Reserve, and economic agencies in many countries have been leading researchers in a number of areas in both theory and practice.

The study of economic development and social modernization was given stimulus in all social sciences by the problems of the newly independent countries in the 1950s and 1960s. Anthropology, too, has benefitted from the perspectives of practical men: "the Netherlands government, through its involvement with Indonesia and *adat* law, employed an enormous corpus of anthropologically trained scholars to study and elucidate traditional concepts and methods." (Belshaw 1989: 13) This has produced data valuable for anthropology and comparative law. One last important example of problem-focused innovation, this time by a single scholar, is Gunnar Myrdal's *The American Dilemma,* the research for which was commissioned by the Carnegie Corporation as an outsider's "comprehensive study of the Negro in the United States." In all of these cases, the key to the innovation was the posing of new questions suggested by practical concerns.

While academics are probably prone to downplay this, there are many fields in which one should not neglect the practitioners. After all, Freud developed free association out of frustration with the therapeutic use of hypnosis. One important area of neuro-linguistics has been the study of speech disorders in medical patients, a tradition going at least back to Broca, the first to identify the part of the left hemisphere responsible for speech (now know as Broca's area). John Maynard Keynes' *General Theory of Money, Inflation and Employment* (1935), arguably the most influential book of the last half-century, was preceded by the writings of policymakers and party strategists who not only put his policy recommendations into practice before he had recommended them, but even developed some of the theoretical foundations of his argument. Ernst Wigforss, the Minster of Finance in Sweden in the 1930s, is perhaps the most notable example here.

Both the successes and the prospects for this kind of praxis-oriented theoretical innovation has encouraged Joseph Ben-David (1973) to advocate a "clinical-engineering" approach to all the social sciences; the focus is on problem-solving and an eclectic application of general

PERSPECTIVES, PARADIGMS, AND PRAXIS

principles to specific events and issues. He laments the tendency of many social scientists to fragment the study of individual events, instead of simply looking to whatever field is necessary to solve a problem. Recombining fields with a focus on narrow events and problems, testing them in their application, is the solution, he argues. Ben-David does not, however, discuss the role of those who develop the "general principles" which his clinical-engineers will draw from; some specialization in theory-building, with or without practical concerns, is doubtless essential.

Regardless of strategy, some care is of course required when using the problem-solving perspective. The consumers of applied social science are likely not to appreciate the researchers' disclaimers, *ceteris paribus* restrictions, and other nuances. As Joseph Ben-David notes, "typically, a social science idea or result is taken up by the policymakers with much enthusiasm but little understanding, and used in a way not justified by the actual findings." (Ben-David 1973: 43) This means that social scientists cannot simply "solve" a problem, but must be involved in implementation.

Besides changing the ways questions are asked, the interaction of paradigms also leads to innovation by setting two large bodies of theories and findings in opposition to one another. Paradigms are not only a set of questions but also a set of answers, making up a patrimony, as well as a given vocabulary of concepts and a certain toolbox of methods. What we have said of each of these pathways is true on a larger scale when all are brought together into a widely shared paradigm.

This is most clear in the case of theories and findings, and their interactions with one another. Paradigms are most threatened by anomalies (Lakatos 1970; Kuhn 1970), those phenomena which are inexplicable by any of the theories making up under the paradigm. Some of these anomalies become puzzles for "normal" scientists, who use them to push the old paradigm forward. At some point, however, the complications necessary to explain anomalies become too unwieldy, and the accumulation of anomalies leads to dissatisfaction with the existing paradigm. The system of spheres within spheres used to predict planetary motion grew too complicated, necessitating its elimination; Copernicus simply placed the sun at the center of the solar system, and by building on this insight constructed a new paradigm. Marxist historians have also been forced into intellectual gymnastics in order to retain their master's theory intact. More controversially, the increasingly complex world of transformational grammar is under major attack from functionalist theories of syntactic universals, which show signs of greater parsimony, better predictions, and more convincing causality.

A common source of anomalies is material generated in other disciplines, from outside the paradigm. Forcing a field's theories to confront new issues, in other fields, can at a minimum expand the boundaries of formal subdisciplines. More typically, the confrontation forces scholars to refine their theories, to synthesize them with other theories, or to abandon them altogether. If one finds oneself being forced to abandon existing paradigms, the borders of scientific disciplines are good places to look for new ones. Extradisciplinary explanations of anomalies may serve as some of the raw material for innovative development of new theories and even new paradigms.

Sometimes both external "anomalies" and the contributions of other disciplines play a role. For instance, Arend Lijphart suggests that the traditional paradigm of international relations came under attack in part because of the importation of new methods and approaches from other social sciences. The rival behavioralist approach was largely built on these other social sciences, as in the work of Morton Kaplan, Karl W. Deutsch, J. David Singer, Bruce Russett, and others.

Because of the productiveness of any successful paradigm, evidenced by the additions it has made to the patrimony, scholars are loath to abandon it unless there is an alternative at hand. Chomsky's followers in linguistics are unlikely to abandon transformational-generative grammar until a new, potentially more productive paradigm is presented them. Even if not accepted, however, the existence of rival theories is essential for progress: "The history of science has been and should be a history of competing research programmes (or, if you wish, 'paradigms'), but it has not been and must not become a succession of periods of normal science: the sooner competition starts, the better for progress." (Lakatos 1970: 155, original in italics) On the other hand, the competition between rival programs requires that some scientists work solely within one paradigm in order to articulate it to its fullest.

If scientists grow dissatisfied with current paradigms, other subdisciplines can provide the new material with which to construct alternatives. They are a source of theories, many of which have been tested and found useful. New perspectives and new approaches are both likely to come from the outside.

Something of the same sort happens in technological innovation, as Gilfillan notes, "cardinal inventions are due to men outside the occupation affected, and the minor, perfective inventions to insiders." (Gilfillan 1935/1963: 88) These "perfective" inventions are analogous to Kuhnian "normal science," and the "cardinal" inventions vaguely similar to "revolutionary" science. The process we describe seems general.

Contraposing different perspectives can greatly illuminate a subject. Brian Barry's *Sociologists, Economists and Democracy* (1970) is a good example of this. He reviews two "ideal type" approaches to the question of democratic stability, the economic approach and the sociological approach. Economic approaches are deductive, axiomatic, and often mathematical; sociological approaches are discursive, organismic, and literary. Playing classics off against each other, such as Harry Eckstein's study of Norwegian democracy and Anthony Downs' economic theory of democracy, Barry suggests future lines of research. Each has both its strengths and its weaknesses, and they should be able to complement each other in future work.

Another example is the difference in perspectives of a legal scholar and an anthropologist. "For the anthropologist, a suit brought in court is the culmination of a perhaps long and complex suit or grievance; it is played out within an arena where more is involved than the application of rules to be found in writing; it may lead on to a sequel that no court interests itself in." (Freedman 1978: 44) Juxtaposing these perspectives may help us better understand the social role of law. In fact, setting against one another just the many competing pardigms within anthropology itself—structuralism and social-exchange theories, neo-Marxism and functionalism, social ecology and biological determinism—can help move the various fields of the discipline forward.

Different perspectives are not, however, an unmixed blessing. In some cases, they may make communication more difficult, since the differences in training may blind each side to the reasons why the other discipline asks what may seem to be naive questions. Mikesell, giving the example of the interaction between geography and sociology, rightly suspects the existence of a more general phenomenon:

> The relation between geography and sociology seems to illustrate a general principle. When scholars trained in different fields recognize their commitment to a common substantive issue, the communication barriers created by independent academic status tend to disappear or at least be reduced. . . . However, this does not mean that members of a particular discipline will have an accurate overall impression of the interests or traditions of their neighbors. (Mikesell 1969: 233)

Much is shared, but both subfields will nonetheless enter into the relationship with a series of concerns deriving from their training and socialization in a different field. Cultural geographers may be very interested in how man reshapes geography, a question which cultural anthropologists may find uninteresting. It is these differences even within a shared field which help drive science forward.

Despite the difficulties, the interaction of different perspectives is most valuable indeed. As Karl Popper points out, "The difficulty of discussion between people brought up in different frameworks is to be admitted. But nothing is more fruitful than such a discussion; than the culture clash which has stimulated some of the greatest intellectual revolutions." (Popper 1970: 57)

17
HYBRIDIZATION OF ACADEMIC JOURNALS

In all social sciences, subfields are linked to one another not only within disciplinary boundaries but across them. We see this specialization and hybridization in the multiplication of specialized journals, each with limited circulation but a faithful following. How many read each issue of the *Journal of Craniofacial Genetics and Developmental Biology*? It is likely to be valuable indeed for those in the field, who may have no other forum. There are 10,000 scientific periodicals in biology, if we include regular research reports issued by important laboratories. Depending on the definition we use, there may be 300–500 journals relevant to the scholar in any formal social science discipline. In the last decade, ten or so such journals were launched every year. The extent of this specialization is impressive, as can be seen in a sample of those journals listed in the *Social Sciences Citation Index* whose titles begin with the words "Journal of." This is but a small fraction of the total, yet simply by referring to their titles one can see much. It is also likely to be an unbiased sample.

Some valiantly attempt to be "general" journals, such as the *Journal of Psychology*. One wonders what it covers. Much more common are those which attempt to survey a broad specialty, such as the *Journal of Abnormal Psychology*, the *Journal of Pragmatics*, or the *Journal of Strategic Studies*. At least one of these has found the task so difficult that it fragmented into sub-specialties: the *Journal of Experimental Psychology* is now four journals, subtitled *General, Animal Behavior Process, Human Perception and Performance*, and *Learning Memory and Cognition*.

It is true that some journals are specialized without penetrating other disciplines. *Electoral Studies*, for instance, remains entirely political in its substantive focus although it is of course open to methods from other social sciences. The *Journal of Economic Theory* is analogously specialized in economics. Other specialized journals obviously build bridges between classical disciplines: *Comparative Studies in Society and History; Politics and Society; Economy and Society; History and Theory; Society and Theory; Philosophy and Public Affairs; Science and Society; Journal of Law and Economics;* and the journal *Les Annales,* which synthesizes history and geography. Sometimes the name is deceptive: *International Organization,* for instance, bridges traditional studies in international organization with more recent approaches to international political economy.

A major focus for interaction among social scientists from different disciplines who study the law has been journals such as the *Law and Society Review, Law and Policy Quarterly,* and *Judicature;* while the first two are by intent multidisciplinary, the third has only gradually become receptive to social science research. As hybridization occurs, such monodisciplinary journals do come under attack, in this case successfully. In the subfield of public choice, *Public Choice* is an intentionally hybrid journal, while the more highly mathematical work in the subfield appears in economic journals such as *Econometrica* and the *Journal of Economic Theory.* However, the lead journal in political science, the *American Political Science Review,* publishes many more articles in this subfield than does its equivalent journal in economics, the *American Economic Review.* These patterns demonstrate how truly hybrid such a subfield is.

Such journals are very useful for stimulating interaction. Economists writing in a journal read by sociologists will come equipped with quite different patrimony than will their readers. By citing leading works from their patrimony, economists distill the research front for sociologists, who can then be better informed of progress being made outside their own disciplines.

Recognizing this, some try to stimulate hybridization, and are self-consciously multidisciplinary problem-focused journals, such as the *Journal of Peace Research* or the *Journal of Conflict Resolution.* By staying focused while also being open to influence from specialties from a number of disciplines, these journals are likely to be successful loci of cross-fertilization. Others address hybrid fields, such as the *Journal of Economic History,* the *Journal of Clinical Psychopharmocology,* the *Journal of Genetic Psychology,* the *Journal of Historical Geography,* the *Journal of Historical Geography,* the *Journal of Political and Military Sociology,* the *Journal of Psycholinguistic Research,* or the *Journal of Social History.* Others attempt to form methodological hybrids, journals which are organized on the basis of the use of a given

HYBRIDIZATION OF ACADEMIC JOURNALS

methodology in a certain subfield. Examples include the *Journal of Mathematical Sociology* and the *Journal of Optimization Theory and Application.*

The twin phenomena of fragmentation and hybridization are by no means limited to Anglo-Saxon scholarship. Among the German journals cited it the *Social Sciences Citation Index* which begin with the word *"Zeitschrift"* we find—in psychology alone—a *Zeitschrift für Entwicklungspsychologie und pädagogische Psychologie,* a *Zeitschrift für Experimentelle und angewandte Psychologie,* a *Zeitschrift für Psychosomatische Medizin und Psychoanalyse,* and a *Zeitschrift für Tierpsychologie.* Similar examples could be found in all languages of scholarship, such as the Scandinavian *Nordisk tidskrift för politisk ökonomi.*

The proliferation of journals is a function not just of the supply of scholars but of the demand for their product. Publishing a journal is time consuming and expensive; no one wants to edit, or be on the editorial board of, a journal their colleagues do not read. Even if we admit that a fair number of journals consist of communication among scholars in stagnant subfields, of relevance only to one another, there must nonetheless be a huge amount of innovative research in the rest. Not all is earth-shattering, it is true, but it adds to the stock of scientific knowledge. It also serves as the raw material for future work.

The proliferation of journals is both cause and effect of specialization. The problem of inadequate specialization can be seen, writ large, in the "official" journals, those which are nominally supposed to be of interest to all practitioners in the formal discipline. There are very few truly general-interest journals today. Some previously general journals have, in effect, become media for a minority of the formal discipline. The *American Political Science Review,* for instance, had in recent years so emphasized sophisticated quantitative and formal methods that most of its articles were uninteresting or inaccessible to a majority of political scientists. Some scholars complain that most articles were probably read by only a few hundred of the *APSR*'s total subscription of 15,000. While this might be exaggerated, and there are definitely generational differences in the reading patterns, it does point to a serious problem for the survival of general journals. Certainly if the APSA offered each member the choice of a subscription to one of the top ten journals of the field, instead of giving everyone *APSR,* its circulation would decline dramatically. In fact, there is survey evidence that professional opinion of the *APSR* is unusually polarized: "while for the large body of political scientists the *APSR* is without doubt the premier journal, a significant minority of the profession is exceptionally critical of the articles which it publishes." (Giles, Mizell, and Patterson

1989: 616) As a result, the *APSR* receives only the fifth highest average ranking of all journals in political science, although it receives a far higher percentage of the highest ranking than any other—(20 percent rank it 10 on a scale of one to ten). Of course, it is difficult to see how such a journal could remain general enough and sufficiently methodologically heterogeneous for the entire community of political scientists. What we say about *APSR* could be said also of the *American Sociological Review* and the official journals of other classical disciplines.

Journals are growing exponentially throughout all sciences, and the *World List of Scientific Journals* now approaches 100,000 such titles. These are both specialized and hybrid. Because one of the barriers to exchange across disciplines is a lack of knowledge about developments in other specialties, computer access to journals will be an essential component to cross fertilization of these tens of thousands of scientific fragments. The hybridization of journals will expand still further as a result of what is known as "electronic publishing." These journals are not printed, but are stored in a computer with public access; individual articles can be printed on demand. This will enable small and dispersed scholarly communities to communicate better.

18
THE BALANCE OF TRADE
BETWEEN DISCIPLINES

The patterns of borrowing and lending across disciplines are obviously of high interest, although probably impossible to quantify in any way which takes into account the relative innovativeness of the various flows. Michael Intriligator (1985) has reviewed some of the major flows betwen the social sciences, which go in all directions. Economics has exported game theory and social choice theory to political science; structural models to sociology; utility theory and decision theory to psychology. Political science has exported organization theory to economics, theories of the balance of power to sociology, and the concept of power to psychology. Sociology gave bureaucracy theory to economics, social systems to political science, and anomie to psychology. Psychology, for its part, developed factor analysis for economics, survey research for political science, and cognitive dissonance for sociology. Interestingly, "Among the most fruitful developments in the advance of the behavioral sciences are those for which there are 'whirlpool effects,' in which an idea developed in one behavioral science is applied or extended in another and then that extension is used or further developed in the original science." (Intriligator 1985: 8) Game theory and organizational theory in economics and political science, and anomie and cognitive dissonance theory in psychology and sociology are some important examples. Intriligator does not include anthropology or linguistics in his overview, but these social sciences are no less involved in the interchange. Anthropology's theory of functional equivalence, for instance, has been applied to political science, sociology, and linguistics.

The relative weight of the exchange is also of interest. J. A. Laponce (1980, 1983) has done pioneering work in this direction, examining patterns of exporting and importing in academic journals. In the 1930s, political science was mostly introspective, borrowing almost exclusively from law when it borrowed at all; in the 1950s, it borrowed from sociology and history and to a lesser extent from philosophy; in the 1970s economics, psychology, and mathematics became prominent sources of imports into political science. Political science is second only to sociology as an importer from sister social sciences, although closely followed by anthropology. While geography and history are intermediate-level importers, psychology and economics import very little. Economics and psychology are major exporters, however, as are both sociology and political science—but these last two export mostly to one another. If one expands the picture to include imports from disciplines outside the social sciences, anthropology is the leading importer, borrowing from "science," zoology, linguistics, biology, and medicine; geography borrows from "science" and engineering, while psychology is a moderate importer from "science" and medicine. Political science appears closed to the natural sciences, which is hardly surprising if one considers the relative scarcity of successful work in "bio-politics" up to this point. Clearly there is much room for innovation in this subfield.

Further research on these patterns of exchange would be interesting. There are data suggesting, for instance, that political science is remarkably dependent on the outside for its innovations. Because the innovative works of today become models of scholarship and set the research agendas for future young scholars, one can usefully survey lasting innovations by looking at what graduate students are taught today. Dean E. McHenry, Jr., (1988) has analyzed the syllabi of introductory graduate courses in comparative politics at thirty-two American universities, and his list of the most widely taught topics is revealing. Of the twenty-one most frequently taught topics, fifteen are hybrids— eight of the top ten. These include development (developmental economics), political culture (political anthropology), elites (political sociology), dependency (international economics), group theory (various subfields of sociology), functionalism (comparative anthropology), systems theory (biology via sociology and anthropology) and class (social stratification). Only comparative methods and political parties are unique to political science among the top ten—although many of the works read under the auspices of "comparative methods" are doubtless equally useful for comparative anthropology or comparative sociology. After the top ten, two topics come ultimately from anthropology (consociationalism, clientelism), and others from history (historical evolution), sociology (military sociology), or from hybrids (revolution and violence from sociology and history). It is no wonder that dissertation committees include members from other departments. At many universities, this is even compulsory.

Political science is not the only discipline with a large trade deficit. Paul Claval (1988) argues that geography has been less successful as an exporter than as an importer; Cyril Belshaw (1989) holds that the same is true of anthropology. What explains these patterns? A major reason for this pattern is the different principles upon which the various social sciences are based. Economics is set apart by a strong methodological and theoretical core, and both methods and theories are easily imperialist. At the other end of the spectrum, ethnography is traditionally organized around discoveries, the description of unstudied societies. Not surprisingly, then, economics has had a greater effect on anthropology than vice versa. We would hesitate to set this forth as a rigid rule—as we have shown, concepts and empirical findings also stimulate innovation across disciplinary borders—but it is generally true that disciplines with methodological and theoretical cores export more than they import.

PART FIVE

GALLERY OF HYBRIDS: CREATIVE MARGINALS

No matter what the disciplinary patterns, no matter which pathways are taken, hybridization is ultimately incarnate in individual scholars. We must examine this incarnation to understand the process in full.

The task is somewhat easier because the phenomena we discuss are recent in historical terms. Most social sciences are less than one century old. In many countries, their official existence is measured in a few decades. As we go backwards in time, we encounter more and more generalists on the front of the stage: it is not meaningful to speak of Aristotle as a hybrid, to take an extreme example. The epitome of the generalists are the encyclopedists of the late 18th century, but this breed had nearly become extinct by 1900.

Many 19th century scholars are less general than the encyclopedists, but still neither specialist nor hybrid. John Stuart Mill is fully a philosopher, fully an economist, and fully a political scientist. There are at least three Karl Marxes: philosopher, political economist, and sociologist; the same can be said of Friedrich Engels. Yet Mill and Marx were not universals: they were not psychologists, linguists, geographers, or anthropologists.

The date of transition varies from field to field. Because hybrids combine parts of two or three disciplines, we should expect them to be even more difficult to categorize. Max Weber is a hybrid looked at from the well-developed field of history, but a generalist from the perspective of an infant sociology. Such cases make any typology difficult, but not impossible, as we discuss in the following section.

19
THREE IDEAL TYPES
OF SOCIAL SCIENTISTS

We would like to be able to show how the most innovative hybrid scholars came to cross the borders of their original discipline, but this is probably not possible. We have already discussed the difficulty, if not the impossibility, of determining which scholars are the most innovative in the social sciences. The question of obtaining accurate personal histories only compounds the problem. In the next section, we will explore this problem further and suggest some approximations.

There does exist something close to a survey of the most innovative deceased scholars. There are close to one thousand scholars who have biographical articles in the *International Encyclopedia of the Social Sciences* (1968). To find the hybrids, we have studied the biographies of those scholars who died between 1850 and 1963. We excluded those before 1850 so as to minimize the number of generalists and encyclopedists: Descartes, Montaigne, Locke, Vico. These 1,000 names are the best list we have, even if it does not include contemporary scholars. We do not believe that the *Encyclopedia* includes all of the major innovators in the social sciences—and some of those included may not belong there. Furthermore, there are very different degrees of coverage given the various disciplines: geographers are underrepresented, psychoanalysts overrepresented. Nevertheless, the selection was made by competent teams of scholars under the leadership of David L. Sills and is the best available source.

Among the scholars mentioned in the *Encyclopedia,* the diversity is so great that any attempt at classification risks being arbitrary. The problem grows more severe as one scales the peak, approaching the most innovative of all. The scholars at the summit are so different

172 PART FIVE

from one another that they are unclassifiable. In many cases, they play a unique sociological role as well as an intellectual one:

> A Freud, a Fermi and a Delbrück play a charismatic role in science. They excite intellectual enthusiasm among others who ascribe exceptional qualities to them. . . . Often in their later years, or after their death, this personal influence becomes routinized in the fashion described by Max Weber for other fields of human activity. Charisma becomes institutionalized, in the form of schools of thought and research establishments. (Merton 1973: 453)

They are undeniably important, but this typology will not encompass them.

At a slightly lower level of elevation, it is possible to construct a typology, if a somewhat unsatisfying one. This is a typology of ideal types; no single scholar exemplifies a single type perfectly. For this reason, the classifications are in some cases arbitrary. There are three basic types of scholars: the pioneer, the builder, and the hybrid.

The pioneer is the scholar who expands the territory of a given discipline, who pushes forward the frontier of his or her discipline. This expansion moves into *terra incognita,* into an area about which science was ignorant. The pioneer does not encounter resistance from other disciplines, but conquers empty territories and annexes them. Pioneers do not really cross the borders of their formal discipline: they push that frontier outwards towards other disciplines, covering in most cases a no-man's-land. Even if closely associated with one discipline, their marginality means that each could be appropriated by more than one modern discipline. In fact, many of them never held university chairs in their fields: Adam Smith, Sigmund Freud, David Ricardo. The great historian of the Roman Empire, Edward Gibbon, had little formal education and never held an academic position.

The time of their appearance varies, but the pioneers are the first generation of specialists. They are marginals in the sense that they explore the boundaries of their growing field, claiming new ground in the direction of other fields. They gain by being footloose.

After the pioneers come the builders, who follow in the footsteps of these frontiersmen. The role of the builders is to develop the land discovered by the pioneers. They exploit the same territory, developing the subject area of their discipline to the fullest.

Builders are scholars who specialize in a discipline which has already been defined by the pioneers, and they are important innovators in the maturing discipline. They may discover regularities and causal relations through empirical research, create theories, develop concepts and meth-

THREE IDEAL TYPES OF SOCIAL SCIENTISTS

ods, or establish disciplinary organizations and journals. Many are revered as classics. Yet they are monodisciplinary scholars, who make important contributions to a given discipline using only the tools of that discipline. Their work may be of interest outside their field, but they do not themselves cross the borders of the territory in which they work.

With time, all surface gold is collected, and the builders are obliged to exploit the territory more intensively, digging beneath the surface, discovering veins of ore. Once developed, there is less room for further research, and the paradox of density sets in. The lode is exhausted, too expensive to pursue further. Then comes the time for the new generation, the hybrid scholars, who combine knowledge from a number of fields.

The hybrid scholar is a border crosser, who penetrates territory held by another discipline or who establishes a province carved out of the territory of two or more disciplines. The hybrid scholar's research takes place at the periphery of two or more formal disciplines, not their core; it also occurs only along a specific part of the periphery, not the entire frontier. The hybrid scholar does not work in a no-man's-land. He borrows from his neighbors, and what he creates may be borrowed by both parent disciplines in turn.

It is a geologic fact that gold is almost always found in conjunction with other ores, and the hybrids make a point of developing these other minerals. Furthermore, while the land may be fully exploited for one end, hybrids look at the same territory with new perspectives, and they see new uses for it. Some become assayers, buying the gold of the territory in order to profit by selling it to the outside; others are merchants who bring the produce of other territories to the miners. Still others may ignore the gold entirely, seeing in the region opportunities to apply methods of farming they bring with them. This is the new generation of scholarship, and it is in this phase we find the progress of the social sciences today.

Hybrids are, in a sense, pioneers at the intersection of two disciplines, and they may give rise to a second generation of builders within the hybrid field. It should not surprise us that some hybrid fields are old by now. Social psychology and economic history are much older than psychological anthropology or sociolinguistics. Different fields are in different phases of growth and decline. Some develop in a spiral, such as political economy.

It is not easy to define clear criteria for their growth, because disciplinary boundaries have changed over time. Ethnography and cultural anthropology, economic geography and political geography, are examples of fields which became separated only recently. Because institutional growth lags behind intellectual growth, some giant hybrids never held chairs in their discipline. Max Weber was never a professor of sociology, but of legal history, then economics, and finally *Staatswissenschaft*. At a lower level of elevation, Woodrow Wilson received his degree in history but his first appointment was in jurisprudence and he is known today as a political scientist (and politician).

As both the metaphor and the examples suggest, hybrids are naturally a diverse lot. Hybridization is not usually a combination of two equal parts. Usually, one component dominates; hybridization does not exclude dependency. Economic history is mostly history, while demographic history is mostly demography. Social psychology is divided between those who are mostly psychologists and those who are mostly sociologists. Economic anthropology and political anthropology are both anchored in anthropology, and are not well understood in the other parent discipline. On the other hand, psycholinguistics is an even mix of the two parts.

We see these unequal combinations in a variety of scholars. Rather than continue with the classification, we will prefer to explore the variety of individual intellectual histories of innovative scholars. Before moving on, however, we should note that our placement of these ideal types into an ideal sequence should not be taken too rigidly. The pattern varies from discipline to discipline, and its rhythm was different in Europe and in the United States. However, as it is true overall that there is no more empty territory between the social sciences, it follows that the future lies with hybridization. Scholars will not be satisfied with borders which butt up against one another, but will make them overlap.

20
INTELLECTUAL MIGRATION
ACROSS DISCIPLINES

We would like to know the personal histories of frontier scholars better. Personal histories can help illuminate the process of hybridization to some extent. Thorstein Veblen, for instance, was handicapped in college because English was his second language; as the son of immigrants, he felt marginal to both American and Norwegian society. He later analyzed such cultural marginality as a stimulus to intellectual creativity, especially among Jews. In fact, it is interesting to observe in our list of hybrids a relatively high proportion of scholars born in Jewish or Quaker families, especially those who emigrated from Europe to the United States. At the turn of the century in the major Western countries less than two percent of the population was Jewish, for instance; but among the scholars in the *International Encyclopedia of the Social Sciences,* the proportion is between 10 and 12 percent. It is also interesting to note as an aside that a relatively high proportion of the social scientists mentioned in the *Encyclopedia* are sons of ministers or teachers. This source of upward mobility has been observed in other domains, such as politics.

Often the life of a social scientist can help explain his intellectual interests. Robert Michels was a cosmopolitan, born in Köln of German-French-Belgian background, and he studied in England, at the Sorbonne, in Munich, Leipzig, and Halle. His disillusionment with the Social Democratic Party obviously influenced his sociological theory on oligarchy. Gaetano Mosca's Sicilian background may account for his critical view of the democratic game and the parliamentary system. Karl von Clausewitz was dismissed from the Prussian army in the Seven Years' War for being unable to substantiate his title, and later became one of Scharnhorst's collaborators in attempting to change the class-based military establishment into an effective fighting force. His classic *On War* was in part a criticism of that inefficient institution. Thomas Kuhn was writing his doctoral dissertation in theoretical physics when his chance involvement with an experimental college course in physics for the non-scientist exposed him to the history of science, convincing him that his previous understanding of the nature of science had little to do with the actual history of scientific advance. From the study of the history and philosophy of science thus initiated came a book on intellectual paradigms.

Other personal histories reveal an interesting and consistent pattern of creativity, in each case built on the combination of two or more subfields. Such scholars are attracted to gap after gap. This remarkable kind of hybrid, the "sequential hybrid," tackles a number of formal disciplines throughout their intellectual career. What is more, such scholars also manage to develop hybrid approaches to everything they study. What drives their intellectual evolution is often a mystery. Charles Cooley began as a political economist and sociologist, and his thesis "The Theory of Transportation" (1894) was a pioneering work in human ecology. He soon shifted gears, however, and became interested in psychology, especially in the psychological ramifications of sociological phenomena. Through works such as *Human Nature and the Social Order* (1902), *Social Organization* (1909), and *Social Process* (1918), he came to argue that all social interaction takes place in the human mind and must be understood from that perspective, a position which was of greatest interest for the not-yet-existent field of social psychology.

Another remarkable case is Gustave Le Bon, who researched three broad areas in successive phases of his career: anthropology and archaeology, theoretical and experimental natural science, and then social psychology. His work in the natural sciences was diverse: he invented recording instruments, analyzed cranial capacity, blacklight, intra-atomic energy, and tobacco smoke, and he published a photographic method of making plans and maps as well as a treatise on training horses. It is by no means clear what holds these interests together other than curiosity. He then moved into social psychology, bringing his earlier work with him; his biographer in the *Encyclopedia* notes that when Le Bon dealt with pedagogy and politics, he carefully applied to people what he had learned about horses.

In such cases the sequential's migration from one discipline to another clearly affects the character of his work. Johan Huizinga studied first Dutch language and literature before taking a degree in comparative philology and writing a thesis on Sanskrit. He then moved towards history, where he pioneered the use of literature, the visual arts, and

INTELLECTUAL MIGRATION

philology as historical data. Focus on these sources fit hand in glove with his growing interest in social history and intellectual history. His "De taak der cultuurgeschiedenis" ("The Task of Cultural History," 1929) strongly advocated borrowing concepts, theories, and questions from the social sciences as well as arguing that studies of the law, philosophy, music, literature, and the fine arts all belong under the roof of history. Taking such advice to heart, he was himself influenced by sociologists such as Max Weber and Ernst Troeltsch and the anthropologist Marcel Mauss.

Sequentials may travel a relatively narrow path. Cesare Lombroso held successive professorships at Turin of legal medicine and public hygiene (1876), psychiatry and clinical psychiatry (1896), and criminal anthropology (1906). He wrote on the nervous system, genius, and pellagra, but is best known as an early student of criminology. His most famous work was *L'uomo delinquente* (1876), and his medical background led him, not surprisingly, to stress the innate and biological determinants of criminal behavior (although his estimate of this variable's importance steadily declined throughout his career).

Sequentials are almost by definition marginal to each of the fields they approach, and their innovativeness may not be recognized. Antoine Augustin Cournot began life as a natural scientist, writing his main thesis in mechanics and a supplementary thesis in astronomy. Some of his work attracted the attention of the great mathematician Siméon Denis Poisson, who saw to it that Cournot was appointed to a chair in mathematical analysis. His next research interest was probability analysis, after which he applied mathematics to economics. He was the first to apply the concept of a mathematical function to economics, inventing demand functions, supply functions, and others. His work was unappreciated for decades in economics, although it has since been resurrected and he is recognized in the concept of a "Cournot equilibrium." Lacking a real intellectual home, and unappreciated by scholars in the field in which he made his most lasting contributions, Cournot was truly a creative marginal.

Some, like Cournot, we could also call "hybrid marginals," creative scholars whose work at the intersection of many subfields leaves them essentially without a home. Like prophets, they often may have no honor in their own fields but exercise their influence in those more distant. Examples would include Sigmund Freud, Arnold J. Toynbee, Jean Piaget, Herbert Marcuse, Wilhelm Reich, and Immanuel Wallerstein. Marcuse's psychology and Toynbee's history are of more interest to the sociologist than to their disciplinary colleagues; Wallerstein's sociology is of interest more to political scientists than to sociologists; Freud was rejected by his colleagues in psychology and medicine, but

178 PART FIVE

his work has obviously been important for many fields. Because of this marginality in their nominal discipline, some scholars are more famous in an adopted field than in their discipline; among economists, for instance, this is true of Mancur Olson, Albert Hirshman, Thomas Schelling, Anthony Downs, and others. The reverse also occurs, and it is possible for non-economists to obtain fame in that discipline, as did Herbert Simon in economics. Because the fame of hybrid scholars may be in "foreign" disciplines, many of the most famous scholars do not belong to the most famous universities.

In many cases, an innovator's major contributions comes in a side interest, not in their formal discipline. Wilhelm Launhardt was a transportation engineer by training and profession, and held a position as professor of highway, railroad, and bridge construction. He is remembered, however, as an economist. His engineering background influenced his choice of economic topics: transportation engineering economics and industrial location theory, as well as public utility (railroad) pricing and welfare economics. He was also one of the pioneers in applying mathematics to economic problems, an application for which his mathematical training as an engineer could not but have been helpful.

Some of these scholars could also be classified as "imperialists," another recurrent type of hybrid. Imperialist scholars see their discipline, or some method or theory within their discipline, as primary, and they invade the territory of other fields armed with the tools of their own. Setting aside contemporary scholars, one straightforward example is Alfred Thayer Mahan, an American naval officer who came to stress the role of the history of naval strategy and tactics upon political history and war in general.

At times the imperialists meet substantial resistance. Friedrich Ratzel was originally a geographer who wrote a number of regional texts, but he is most well-known for his application of geography and biology to anthropology in his books *Anthropogeographie* (1882–1891), *Politische Geographie* (1897), and *History of Mankind* (1885–1888). These works were controversial at the time for being too monocausal and deterministic, but this exaggerates his theory (Ratzel has also suffered from the fact that some of his ideas were later used by apologists of the Third Reich's need for *Lebensraum*). In other cases the resistance is less severe. Charles Babbage was a mathematician by trade, and did pioneering work on calculating machines and operations research. However, he also sought to apply mathematics, and did so in papers on physics, geology, astronomy, biology, archaeology, and life insurance.

Many, like Babbage, are appreciated in their day. Jules Dupuit was first a civil engineer and only gradually became an economist instead,

INTELLECTUAL MIGRATION

but his most important ideas were developed in the course of the transition from one to the other. His primary concern was developing a rigorous system of cost-benefit analysis. This concern led him to his major discovery, that benefits are not measured by the amount a customer actually pays but by the amount each customer would be willing to pay at a maximum—that is, benefits are represented by the entire area under the demand curve, which Marshall later called the "consumer's surplus." Robert MacIver, not easily pigeonholed as either political theorist, sociologist, or philosopher, worked in each area at different phases of his career. Alexander A. Goldenweiser was an anthropologist whose interests were so broad that in the course of his career he held appointments not only in anthropology, but also in psychology, sociology, and thought and culture. His curiosity led him to read extensively in many fields, although he made relatively little use of work from the research frontier of fields outside anthropology.

Perhaps the best measure of acceptance is when a scholar from one discipline is named president of the professional association of another. Several past presidents of the American Political Science Association come from other disciplines: Charles Beard (history); Seymour Martin Lipset (sociology), Phillip Converse (psychology), Charles Lindblom (economics), Harold Lasswell (law), Carl Friedrich (philosophy).

We may also take individuals in groups, as sometimes whole groups move from one discipline to another. The core group of the Reseach Committee on Political Sociology, affiliated to the International Political Science Association, was composed at its inception entirely of people who began their professional careers in departments of sociology, but who later focused most of their research in political science: Seymour Martin Lipset, Stein Rokkan, Raymond Aron, Morris Janowitz, Juan Linz, Giovanni Sartori, Samuel Eisenstadt, Gino Germani, Erik Allardt, Jerzy Wiatr, Mattei Dogan, and a few other hybrids. Many Europeans, having been trained as sociologists, economists, or historians, became active in politics; after failures in politics, they turned to political science: Rudolf Hilferding, Robert Michels, Andre Siegfried, Ralf Dahrendorf.

The entire first generation of scholars working in two typical subfields of political science, electoral behavior and elite recruitment, came from sociology, social psychology, history, law, and philosophy. This is true not simply because most European countries lacked formal departments of political science before World War II; in the United States, where political science did exist as a discipline, it did not have the methodological and conceptual tools with which to address these quintessentially political topics. Cross-fertilization was absolutely necessary. At the time, political science appears to have been the poor cousin of sociology. Even today, some scholars have a joint appointment or have recently moved from one department to another: Juan Linz, Seymour Martin Lipset, Giovanni Sartori, Reinhard Bendix, Philip Converse, Luciano Cavalli, Peter Flora, Manuel Castells, Theda Skocpol, Bruce Bueno de Mesquita, Michel Crozier, Mattei Dogan, and others.

Migration from one discipline to another is sometime facilitated by migration from one country to another. An entire phalanx of European sociologists and political scientists became well-known comparativists on the other side of the Atlantic: Arend Lijphart, Juan Linz, Karl W. Deutsch, Giovanni Sartori, Peter Merkl, Dankwart Rustow, Heinz Eulau, Günther Roth, Alfred Diamant, Jean Laponce, Rene Lemarchand, Otto Kirchheimer, Rudolf Heberle, Lewis Coser, and others. Still others, such as Lucian Pye and Fred Riggs, were born in China. Why should such migration stimulate cross-fertilization? Probably because having lived in more than one country forces one to be a comparativist, and "it is singly difficult to establish acceptable comparisons between countries and cultures without bringing in broader ranges of variables than those of only one discipline." (Rokkan 1979: 5) Forced to look to other disciplines, they are like bees seeking pollen.

Muzafer Sherif relates how his interest in the effects of social situations on psychological behavior was stimulated by his observation that the psychological generalizations taught him at Harvard in the 1930s were "so completely out of line with his own experience in a different culture, namely Turkey." (Sherif and Sherif 1969: 11) Coming from a different society made him much more aware of the cultural biases of psychological theory, and he became a leader in the formative years of social psychology.

Studying abroad can have a similar effect. As we have noted on several occasions, one sign of the arbitrariness of disciplinary boundaries is the existence of varying forms of organization from one country to another. The same thing happens in the development of subfields, and some builders innovate by bringing together the traditions and methods of subfields from different countries in the same formal discipline, or even in the same subfield. William James Ashley is an example, an economic historian of the English school which included Arnold Toynbee and Thorold Rogers. Yet he was unusual among English economic historians in that he had ties to German historical economists such as Gustav Schmoller. His innovations brought "English" deduction and "German" induction together in economic history.

Migration is not a necessary prerequisite for collective innovation at the border of disciplines. There are privileged locales in intellectual history, such as Periclean Athens, Renaissance Florence, prerevolutionary Paris; others, such as the American "founding fathers," appear to

INTELLECTUAL MIGRATION

have been very close to achieving this status. In these cases, an entire community is able to reach "critical mass," at which a group of innovative thinkers in a number of disciplines feed off one another's concepts, approaches, and theories, and strongly influence one another. What causes this explosion? How can there be such a concentration of talent and creativity in so many fields in one place at one time? We do not know. Cross-fertilization, however, is a part of the story.

The most recent example of this phenomenon is *fin de siecle* Vienna. (see Schorske 1961) There, innovation took place in the natural sciences, the social sciences, the humanities, as well as between them: Ernst Mach, a mathematician-physicist-philospher and sometimes economist, psychologist, and biologist, provided cross-fertilization for many innovators: his psychology had a direct impact on the aesthetic views of *Jung Wien*. Poet and dramatist Hugo von Hofmannsthal attended Mach's university lectures and recognized Mach's problems as somehow similar to his own, while novelist and philosopher Robert Musil, too, was very much in Mach's debt. Mach also influenced Hans Kelsen and his positivist theory of law, as well as the young physicist Albert Einstein. (Janik and Toulmin 1973: 133) Karl Kraus contributed his critique of language to Arnold Schoenberg, who applied it to a critique of musical forms of expression; the philosopher Ludwig Wittgenstein later borrowed Kraus' basic idea as the core of his own work. (Johnston 1972) Prewar Austria also gave birth to Austro-Marxism as well as to Paul Lazarsfeld, F. A. Hayek, Karl Polanyi, and Karl Popper. After World War I, however, the city was no more the capital of a great empire and lost much of its intelligentsia in the 1930s. It lies dormant today.

Despite the explosion in the number of intellectuals in the West, there have been no such privileged locales since World War I. Because of scientific fragmentation, stimulating intellectual climates today generally encompass several fields, but not all of them. There are many examples, centered at great universities and especially those metropolises which are blessed with more than one such university. Furthermore, the "invisible college" by which modern scholars communicate over distances makes the advantages of a single locale less necessary than before. Without air travel the field of comparative politics would have progressed more slowly.

Informal communication occurs not only between universities within a given discipline but across disciplines whether at the same university or not. It is not easy to confirm these patterns of communication in most cases, without conducting a survey of scholars. Sometimes acknowledgements at the beginning of books bring testimonies. In the preface to his classic *System and Process in International Politics* (1957),

Morton Kaplan acknowledges comments and assistance from seventeen scholars, five from political science, three from sociology, three from economics, two from psychology and social psychology, and four from other disciplines. The book reflects an author able to draw from certain areas of these other disciplines.

Although not our primary interest, we should conclude with a brief mention of the monodisciplinary scholars. We have already admitted that not all innovation takes place at the intersections of disciplines. The exceptions seem, however, to wander from one specialty to another within a single discipline. In political science, for example, Richard Neustadt has stayed largely within the borders of political science while traveling from one subfield to another. Kenneth Waltz and Nelson Polsby, George Burdeau and Jean Claude Colliard, Samuel Finer and David Butler, Klaus von Beyme and Renate Mayntz, Norberto Bobbio and Sabino Casesse, Richard Rose and Anthony King are a sample of the many political scientists who have been innovative while remaining firmly in their original discipline.

Other disciplines, too, produce innovative monodisiciplinary scholars. Meyer A. Girshick was a statistician whose major achievements lie in multivariate analysis. At the same time, he occasionally applied statistics, especially in a collaborative project examinining American agriculture which conducted one of the first major empirical studies of an econometric model. Toward the end of his life he also became interested in decision theory and game theory, coauthoring a series of papers with Blackwell, Rubin, Savage, or Arrow. There he treated several topics, including a study of Bayesian estimation procedures and a rigorous analysis of the concepts of sufficiency and invariance. Roland B. Dixon was an anthropologist, "a generalist at a time when such virtuosity was still possible in anthropology." (McKennan 1968: 242) Most of his writings pertain to cultural anthropology, but he also wrote a thesis and a few publications on the languages of the people he studied, and his *The Racial Theory of Man* (1923) draws heavily from physical anthropology and anthropometrics. At the same time, he can also be characterized as a minor importer; he had a long-standing interest in geography, and this awareness of the role of the natural environment in culture greatly affected his work.

Many contemporary monodisciplinary scholars are best characterized as wanderers. Wanderers are especially important among the more coherent disciplines. Can most of the more imaginative economists be easily pigeonholed into one subfield? Where would George Stigler or Paul Samuelson go? Even those with identifiable homes, such as Kenneth Arrow ("public choice"), Milton Friedman ("money and finance"), John Maynard Keynes ("macroeconomics"), Wasily Leontief ("input-

INTELLECTUAL MIGRATION

output analysis"), and James Buchanan ("public choice"), are broader than these labels make them seem. Some, such as the two in public choice, are in a sense hybrids. In linguistics, the other discipline with a strong core, the major innovators also seem to wander, as has Noam Chomsky, for instance. For these, as for the others, their work has been of such breadth that it has also gone on to cross-fertilize other disciplines. The monodisciplinary scholars nevertheless represent only a minority among the most innovative scholars. The majority are border crossers.

PART SIX

CROSSROADS: FOUR ILLUSTRATIONS

Up to this point, we have explored the processes of specialization, fragmentation, and hybridization in the social sciences as whole. We have not yet focused on concrete research areas to show how, in fact, hybridization encourages innovative research. It is to this task that we turn in this part.

In a review of the social sciences, it would be possible to list all the possible pairs of the dozen or so disciplines and to demonstrate the cross-fertilization among their specialized subfields. The topics thus generated, however, would fill volumes, as there are approximately one hundred such pairs. Because there are more subfields than disciplines, if we were to look at all possible combinations of subfields, the number would be far greater. It is only practical to be selective, and to choose illustrative cases.

One possible illustration is to construct a chain of hybrid fields, beginning with one discipline and returning to it again. Act 1 could perhaps be political science and economics; Act 2, economics and psychology. We could continue with psycholinguistics, linguistic anthropology, anthropology and geography, historical geography, and historical sociology; political sociology would complete the chain. All social sciences are brought together by this intercourse.

While it would be interesting to follow such a chain of interaction, we choose a different path which is more analytically based. All the forms of interaction we have discussed so far may or may not be reflected in a concrete scholarly community, that is, there are formal and informal recombinations. Because each discipline consists of a number of subfields, the interaction of two disciplines may result in a series of scholarly communities, which may or may not be loosely connected to one another; in other cases, the interaction of two disciplines produces only one point of intersection. These two dimensions determine four categories: formal hybrids versus loose interchange among fields, a single point of interaction between two disciplines or multiple interactions. There are dozens of examples of each type, and we cannot discuss them all. In the following part, we give one example of each.

Historical sociology is the broadest, and the most institutionalized, case. It consists of a wide range of subfields where different analytical fragments of history and sociology overlap. The life sciences have also interacted with the social sciences at many points, but most of these subfields are informal, not usually recognized by university administrations. Some of these combinations have been very controversial, reminding us that superficial recombination of subfields is undesirable and that a more narrow hybridization, which takes advantage of the current state of the patrimony in both fields, is necessary. In contrast, international political economy is a single field which draws from several subfields of economics and political science; it is, however, beginning to fragment itself and may also create a series of connected fields. Like international political economy, economics and psychology have intersected in a relatively fixed area, but the results of this interchange have not created an independent subfield, either formal or informal; instead, there are a number of economists interested in how psychology affects economic behavior and a number of psychologists interested in applying their theories and findings to economics.

21
HISTORICAL SOCIOLOGY
AND SOCIOLOGICAL HISTORY

History and sociology have always been closely linked. Because each is so broad, and because they often examine the same phenomena, such ties are inevitable. As specialization has progressed, however, they have occasionally forgotten about one another. Their recurrent rediscoveries have been much more than cyclical fads; by building on steadily expanding patrimonies, they have repeatedly overlapped.

As soon as their disciplines had begun to fragment in the previous century, innovative historians and sociologists reached out towards one another. In the United States, Frederick Jackson Turner's study of the American frontier was one marriage of sociology and history. Some Germans also bucked prevailing trends, such as Otto Hintze and Eckart Kehr, although both are more well-known as a result of recent revivals than they were to their contemporaries. These scholars were historians, a fifth column supporting the invasion of the sociologists which was to come in the late 1950s, including Robert Bellah's *Tokugawa Religion* (1959) and Seymour Martin Lipset's *The First New Nation* (1963). These sociologists were soon joined by a new generation of historians, represented by Charles Tilly's *The Vendee* (1964), Barrington Moore's *Social Origins of Dictatorship and Democracy* (1966), and Charles Maier's *Recasting Bourgeois Europe*. Such interweavings of sociology and history continue up to the present day.

The result of this interaction has not been a single synthesis. Such breadth is patently impossible today; it is not clear that it ever was possible, although Karl Marx, Werner Sombart, and especially Max Weber all made notable efforts in that direction. "Historical sociology" is in fact a series of hybrids, not a single hybrid. The topics officially represented on the program of the 1979 meeting of the Social Science

188   PART SIX

History Association testify to this diversity, making room for theory, methods, labor history, social structure and mobility, family history, ethnicity, urban history, economic history, demography, international relations, electoral history, violence, and other topics. (Tilly 1981: 28–29) These are the real hybrid fields; nevertheless all these combinations raise several common issues which will enable us to speak at least of "historical sociologies."

It is not always easy to determine what distinguishes good history and good sociology, because both seek to understand society as a whole. In fact, "most sociologists and historians have no clear understanding of what historical sociology really is." (Aronson 1969: 294) Unlike economics, political science, or linguistics, the distinction is not based on subject matter. Nonetheless, the fragmentation does have its *raison d'être*, as "a matter of methodology and intent." (Knapp 1984: 34)

Many have attempted to clarify the differences between the two disciplines, with no two authors in agreement. (see Aron 1958; Boudon 1979; Lipset and Hofstadter, eds. 1968; Tilly 1981) The reason for the lack of consensus is clear: the remarkable diversity of the historical sociologies, to say nothing of the parent disciplines, makes any unidimensional characterization of the issue completely unsatisfactory.

More accurately, history and sociology as disciplines can be distinguished along several dimensions. Not all of these distinctions provide an accurate characterization of all historians or all sociologists, but taken as a whole they do clarify the differences between them. Each dimension can open an avenue for developing a truly hybrid historical sociology in a particular subfield. On the other hand, it is difficult to combine the two disciplines along *all* of these dimensions simultaneously. It is probably for this reason that Braudel concludes that, "Economics and history have been successfully united, but historical sociology does not yet exist." (Braudel 1979: 458) We would go further: what Braudel means by the term "historical sociology" cannot exist; neither, for that matter, does a simple "economic history" exist today.

If we are willing to be flexible about our portraits of these fields, we should begin with a cartoon. For a few scholars, the distinction is simple, even simplistic: historians study the past, and others do not. Marc Bloch relates the case of one of the more amusing examples: "A high-school teacher, who was very old when I was very young, once told us: 'Since 1830, there has been no more history. It is all politics.'" (Bloch 1954: 37) Of course, the critical date has changed since then, but it is still true today that an overwhelming majority of all political scientists seem to believe that politics began in 1945. Although a caricature, the prevalence of this belief helps account for the success of Barrington Moore's *Social Origins of Democracy and Dictatorship*

HISTORICAL SOCIOLOGY AND SOCIOLOGICAL HISTORY

(1966), which made a convincing case for the importance of history to the very current question of democratic stability; Reinhard Bendix's *Nation-Building and Citizenship* (1964) is a slightly earlier example of the same kind of success. Many other examples could be given: in order to understand social and political cleavages in central Italy today, you must go back to papal land ownership patterns in the 16th century. Such cleavages cannot be properly understood without reference to their origins and history.

More seriously, the difference between history and sociology has traditionally been described as that between the "idiographic" and the "nomothetic." Idiographs revel in the narration and interpretation of the historically unique; nomothetes seek law-like generalizations about human behavior. The distinction is trite and superfcal as applied to real historians and real sociologists, and if the terms are to have some value it is as ideal types. If the pure idiograph or the pure nomothete actually exist anywhere, we doubt they are taken any too seriously today, as either, when taken to an extreme, must ultimately be sterile; one classic example of the *extensio ad absurdum* of the historical method can be found in Charles Booth's monumental seventeen-volume *Life and Labour of the People in London,* which concludes that "things hang together in a perplexing tangle of causation beyond possibility of unravelment." (cited in Barraclough 1978: 289) This is not social science.

Clearly, no meaningful behavioral research can avoid mixing generalization and the study of unique persons, groups, societies, or events. If Booth neglected the first, many game theorists and others today ignore the second. The distinction between idiography and nomothesis parallels that between theory and data, and neither can survive without the other. Even so, specialization in the 19th century tended to divide the disciplines. Some historians persisted in idiography, helping drive a wedge between sociologists and historians, and causing early sociologists to hold historians in contempt. Auguste Comte, for instance, referred to the historians' "insignificant details so childishly collected by the irrational curiosity of the blind compilers of sterile anecdotes"; Spencer was only somewhat more generous when he stated that "the highest office which the historian can discharge is that of so narrating the lives of nations, as to furnish materials for a comparative sociology." (both cited in Burke 1980: 19) Spencer's view is alive and well, in reduced form. By producing anomalies for everyone else to try to explain, as Louis Gottschalk notes, "an important service the historian can render to social science is to test and to check the relative merit of the generalizations of others." (Gottschalk 1956: 448–449) As he

190 PART SIX

argues, historians can also go beyond this role, and this position is more flattering for historians than Spencer's.

The dialogue between the specific and the general is an important issue explored by many who discuss "historical sociology." Along these lines, Peter Burke (1980) isolates two different aspects of these contributions history can make to sociology, one negative and one positive. The negative contribution entails sculpting, picking away at the edifice constructed by others, by showing how a theory does not fit "their" society. This entails tests which are hazardous for any theory, but those which can survive are proven to be of greater value. The positive contribution involves building up, working out from the general to the particular in order to construct a revised general theory. This sculpting task is especially valuable because the sociologist's generalizations may appear vacuous to the historian, too often deservedly so. Fernand Braudel writes that "Sociologists and economists in the past and anthropologists today have unfortunately accustomed us to their almost total indifference to history. It does of course simplify their task." (Braudel 1979: 227)

At the same time, generalization is essential. Because of the inexhaustible wealth of detail in history, it must be constructed to be told. (Aron 1958: 35–36) Social science can be of assistance here. Most historical constructions focus on the individual in history, a kind of "methodological individualism" which Raymond Boudon (1979) argues may be conducive to the importation of game theory. The interaction of scholars from within these two formal disciplines thus improves the study of society as a whole. Other approaches are also possible, of course. Often with the aid of social science, successful historians avoid becoming what J. H. Hexter called the "Tunnel Historian," one who specializes in a particular narrow area and pursues his studies in a mole-like fashion without reference to other aspects of the country or period. At the same time, these historians retain "the discipline and wisdom of the narrative historian who has worked and lived with the concrete, unique, and individual. . . ." (Parker 1957: 111)

Historians can gain from such interaction even though—or because—many historians categorize their discipline as one of the humanities, not a social science. Some argue that what they seek in the study of any event is *verstehen*, not *erklären*. The reaction of German historicism against positivism divided history and the social sciences in large part along these lines, a cleavage followed by many subsequent historians. Such historians insist on asking event-oriented questions, not pattern or process-oriented questions, and they demand synthesis in the answers to these questions. This does present obstacles for hybrids. Charles Tilly argues that successful historical sociology must persuade profes-

HISTORICAL SOCIOLOGY AND SOCIOLOGICAL HISTORY

sional historians that it presents a new answer to a question historians are already asking. Mere hypothesis testing is not enough, which is why historians are not impressed by economists' derivation and estimation of a model from neoclassical theory. (Tilly 1981: 25) Peter Knapp is still more severe: "hypothesis testing does little to establish cumulative falsifiable theory, as historians are well aware. Rather, it leads to a proliferation of different interpretations." (Knapp 1984: 51) Again, synthesis and not proliferation is the goal. Yet the social sciences can and do produce new understandings even of well-studied topics. One hybrid area which has succeeded in this task is econometric research into the profitability of slavery, first by Alfred Conrad and John Meyer and then also by Robert Fogel, Stanley Engerman, Gavin Wright, and Richard Sutch. These scholars' work has proved to have important implications for historians examining a number of questions about the ante-bellum South and the viability of slavery.

When posed in this fashion, the social sciences' insistence on generalization can be helpful for historians. In the words of one sociologist-turned-historian, "Whatever else they do, the social sciences serve as a giant warehouse of causal theories and concepts involving causal analogies; the problem is to pick one's way through the junk to the solid merchandise." (Tilly 1981: 12) When one finds quality goods, a simple application of sociological theory to historical problems can be innovative. As an example, William Nisbet Chambers' *Political Parties in a New Nation* (1963) applied Max Weber's analysis of charismatic leaders in postrevolutionary situations to George Washington and the emergence of rational-legal authority in the United States. Other examples could be given in the same subfield, and social science theory has also helped drive the study of American history forward. "Ever since the late 1940s, the field of American political history had been in a state of quiet ferment, with numerous younger scholars—first individually and then in some cases collectively—engaged in a search for new concepts and new directions. Some began to borrow ideas from the social sciences and to break down the historical guild's long-standing resistance to that approach." (McCormick 1986: 90) For instance, research on American political history has benefitted from the use of methods and concepts from studies on contemporary voting behavior by political scientists.

The distinction between sociological generalization and the historically specific has other implications and can help us understand another distinction between the two formal disciplines, that between outcomes and sequences. Sociologists tend to look at events as isolated from one another, amenable to classification along many different dimensions; historians insist that any event must be looked at as part of a sequence of events. This also has implications for the degree of freedom a scholar enjoys. Raymond Aron (1958: 39) has argued that historians have greater freedom to characterize a period however they will, subject to empirical investigation; other social scientists are channelled into seeing that period through the lens of their discipline. An economist, for instance, may legitimately decide that the relationship of men to work interests him above all other topics, and may study that relationship in a given period without needing to argue that this was the fundamental characteristic of that age. Historians, in contrast, may contemplate the proper role of economic relations within their synthesis of the period. The historians are best suited to place this relationship in context.

Peter Knapp (1984) builds on this idea, suggesting that historians can help overcome the inattention to context of most social theory. He argues that one of the major problems of sociological theory is the implicit or explicit *ceteris paribus* clause. Since all other factors are never the same in the real world, such theories are repeatedly disconfirmed and often appear vacuous. "When sociologists (or political scientists, economists, or anthropologists) decide that concern with theory absolves them from concern with history, their product will not only be irrelevant historically, it will not even be adequate as theory." (Knapp 1984: 34) By opening theories up to allow variation in the *ceteris paribus,* theories can be applied to specific historical contexts. Historians, who are most familiar with the peculiarities of "their" period or country, have much to add to social theory in this regard. Besides enriching history, the historical sociologies should be able to enrich the various social sciences.

Contexts are always connected to one another. Events which occur in a given context creat a different context for subsequent events. As a result, historians tend to examine events in terms of those causal events which preceded them and those subsequent events which they helped cause in turn. For Bloch, the focus on sequence is the *raison d'être* of the historian: "Let us assume two consecutive periods taken out of the uninterrupted sequence of the ages. To what extent does the connection which the flow of time sets between them predominate, or fail to predominate, over the differences born out of that same flow?" (Bloch 1954: 28–29) Historians' attention to sequence has made important contributions to the other social sciences. Alexander Gerschenkron's *Economic Backwardness in Historical Perspective* (1962) is a classic demonstration of the importance of sequence in a process many economists had viewed as common to all societies. Britain's industrialization, he argues, fundamentally changed the nature of the challenge that other would-be industrializers faced; Germany, France, and the United States in turn changed the nature of the challenge for Russia and

HISTORICAL SOCIOLOGY AND SOCIOLOGICAL HISTORY

others. From Gerschenkron and other such sequence-sensitive works were large literatures spawned, including those on dependence, dependent development, and later, the world-system approach.

However, when constructing sequences, historians often postulate causal relationships as they go along. What some historians miss is that while the events concerned are presumably unique, the causal relationships presumably are not; the weakness of traditional historiography is the failure to recognize the generality of most causality. Most good historical sociology is sensitive to the uniqueness of the preceding events while comparing the causal relationships to other sequences of events or to some body of sociological theory.

A more general approach to causation is one contribution of the social sciences for the study of history. We know, for instance, that the problem of collective action recurs in all human societies, from Rousseau's stag hunt to modern trade unions. Examining this problem in the context of a unique event, as the economist Charles P. Kindleberger did for the case of international monetary policy in the aftermath of the Great Depression in *The World in Depression* (1973), does not mean that an economist cannot write good history. Part of what makes Kindleberger's work succeed is that the starting and end points of his story are historically unique situations studied as such, while the problems along the way are more general. Furthermore, the historical personages involved are to a greater or lesser degree themselves aware of the problem of collective action even as some of them work (in vain) to overcome it.

This distinction between unique events and general laws of causation was important for Max Weber, a truly hybrid historical sociologist. Weber begins with the observation that events are infinitely complex, that for instance, no physicist could accurately predict all the details of a falling leaf's descent. Nonetheless, leaves do fall in roughly the same way, and this a physicist can understand through theory. Gravity limits the number of objective possibilities inherent in a leaf's fall; however the inexhaustibly complex details of that path may never be understood. (Knapp 1984) Social sciences and their associated theories are well suited to examine the objective possibilities in any situation, just as historians are better able to elucidate the inexhaustible concrete to be found there.

These examples enable us to respond to a common view of what history is, held by many insular historians. Many deny that history can be a true social science, usually arguing that history is the study of historically unique events, about which generalization is impossible. Hybrids freely admit the uniqueness of historical events while insisting that causation is much more general and can be understood through science.

One straightforward means to hybridization is comparative history. Comparative sociologists and political scientists have developed comparative methods to an extent greater than have other social sciences. Being willing and able to use this method in history can make important contributions. The idea is not new, of course. Historians have been making implicit comparisons through their terminology for years. However, such implicit comparisons are analytically insufficient by themselves–categorizing agrarian systems into forms such as "wet rice agriculture" does not necessarily imply any developed comparison of such systems, although such categorization is an essential first step.

Historians have also made explicit comparisons of the "lessons of history" since the early days of the craft. Using such comparisons as a research strategy can be innovative. Günther Roth's *The Social Democrats in Imperial Germany* (1963) uses history to illustrate modern problems of development. *The Formation of National States in Western Europe* (1975), edited by Charles Tilly, uses history to explore state and nation-building, with obvious relevance to the "new" nations of Africa and Asia.

Arguments in favor of comparative history are not new. Already in 1898, in the early years of the fragmentation of the two disciplines, *L'Année sociologique* argued that "History could be a science only if it becomes comparative, because we can explain only when we compare. . . . Once there is comparison, history is indistinguishable from sociology." (cited in Besnard 1986: 28) Nor has this potential been forgotten since then; Val Lorwin (1965), another sociological historian, shares the view. Notwithstanding the potential, most historians have not "paid much attention to the methods and opportunities of explicit and more or less systematic comparative study." (Lorwin 1968: 107–108) It is difficult to understand why. It is always true that as disciplines fragment and specialize, the gaps they leave are sometimes shocking. Remarkably, the collection *L'Histoire et ses methodes* (Charles Samaran, ed., 1961) does not refer at all to Bloch's seminal "Pour un histoire comparée des societés européennes"; nor does H.P.R. Finberg's edited *Approaches to History* (1962) have a single chapter on comparative history.

Yet comparisons are invaluable. One of the first to take this path was the French school of the *Annales,* which developed an approach to social history that was both sociological and comparative. Marc Bloch was one of the most influential figures in the development of this school, both in his programmatic statement, "Pour une histoire comparée des societés européennes" (1928), and in his subsequent

HISTORICAL SOCIOLOGY AND SOCIOLOGICAL HISTORY

exemplar, *La societé feodale* (1939–1940). In no case need comparative history trample on historical reality, nor the details of context and sequence. Properly done, comparative history does much to enrich narrative.

Another important comparison can be seen in Norman Jacobs' *The Origins of Modern Capitalism and Eastern Asia* (1958), which compares the historical accretion of social structures in China and Japan in order to understand why one adapted capitalism much more successfully than the other. In the process of analyzing trade, property, politics, the division of labor, social stratification, kinship, inheritance, and religion, he also keeps an eye open for those features present in pre-capitalist Europe, which might help explain the rise of capitalism there.

Comparative history is useful for many topics. Seymour Martin Lipset has argued (i.e., 1968: 35–37) that it is very difficult to understand American history without comparison with Canada. While the two countries are similar in many ways, the lack of a revolution in the one alongside a revolutionary past in the other has a surprising number of implications for later developments of both societies and their political systems. More broadly, a comparison of the similarities and differences in the "frontier" of the United States, Canada, Australia, Brazil, and Argentina, can highlight the problems of Turner's thesis on the importance of the frontier experience for the United States. This comparison highlights those features that made the American experience different from that found on other frontiers, making possible a deeper understanding of how the frontier affected American history.

The comparative method is also a very useful way to unify general statements of causality and the uniqueness of historical events. Cahnman and Boskoff argue that it is impossible to assess the validity of any causal interpretation based on a single case, making a comparative approach absolutely necessary for useful explanation. (Cahnman and Boskoff 1964: 7) Geoffrey Barraclough notes the added advantage that comparative history overcomes "the fragmentation of specialized (and especially of national) history." (Barraclough 1978: 402) Examining similar causal processes in two or more specific contexts can greatly illuminate both the nature of the causal forces at work and improve our understanding of the events concerned.

Besides the comparative method, other methods also divide history and sociology. Historians often rely very heavily on primary sources to the exclusion of secondary sources. This emphasis arose in the second half of the 19th century as sociology and history grew apart. Leopold von Ranke, the most respected historian of his day, focused on narrative political history, buttressed by scientific study of documentary evidence. Social history, for which such documents were generally less available, inevitably fell by the wayside.

As this example shows, an insistence on primary sources may tend to limit a historian's breadth of vision. This emphasis minimizes the importance of the patrimony, of cumulative research. Among other things, this focus tends to impose a methodological division between sociology and history. Many historians seem to believe that an event cannot have occurred if they have not personally seen it documented in the relevant archives. For some topics this could be an enormous mistake—the twelfth century archives of the abbey of Sainte Germain des Près make no mention of women, although women did exist in Paris, of course. Social scientists studying historical periods, on the other hand, usually rely largely on secondary sources, but for some insular historians this is unjustifiable because one cannot "know" (*verstehen*) a period without immersion.

The insistence on primary documents does have the notable advantage of giving historians high standards of evidence. Use of the historians' evidential standards can lead to innovative sociology. Some social scientists took this as a challenge, and wrote social history using the kind of evidence historians demand. William I. Thomas and Florian Znaniecki's classic, *The Polish Peasant in Europe and America* (1918–1920), for instance, succeeded by using sociological approaches to the questions of social values and social change, making use of a body of documents usually the province of the historian: letters, newspapers, parish histories, and the like. Today, studies of adult development in developmental psychology have benefitted from a change in focus stemming from a change in data collection, moving away from experimentation and towards (auto)biography, diaries, literature, and clinical histories.

The historians' high standards can be learned by others. Many sociologists in the 1960s grew disappointed with the secondary literature of historians and began to learn primary source skills themselves. This coincided with the fragmentation of sociology, and the end of attempts to construct general theories of society. As sociologists left the speculative realm of general theories, and began to focus more on the concrete, on case studies, the historians' detailed factual knowledge and primary source skills proved invaluable. Any psychological approach to the study of important historical figures must be able to utilize primary sources, as did Elizabeth Marvick's *Louis XIII: Making of a King* (1986), for instance.

The reverse is also true: historians can benefit from a sociologist's approach to historical evidence. Content analysis, by allowing quantification of newspaper editorials, minister's sermons, baccaleaureat ex-

HISTORICAL SOCIOLOGY AND SOCIOLOGICAL HISTORY

aminations, and political speeches, can help confirm or disconfirm historians' subjective observations about what subjects most concerned the people of a given period. Sidney Aronson's *Status and Kinship in the Higher Civil Service* (1964) coded social background characteristics of higher civil servants in the John Adams, Thomas Jefferson, John Quincy Adams, and Andrew Jackson administrations, finding that the overwhelming majority of all such officials came from the socioeconomic elite. This calls into question contemporary views, since repeated by historians as a given, that Jackson had introduced a "spoils" system by having recruited officials on a different basis than previous administrations.

This brings us to quantification in history. Contrary to what is generally believed, historical sociology may or may not be based on quantified research. Nonetheless, quantification is such a ubiquitous part of most social sciences that it was easy for historians to misunderstand the nature of the beast. As Tilly points out, "In field after field, the leading edge of the change was some form of quantification. Because of that uniformity, many nonquantitative historians mistook the prow for the whole ship." (Tilly 1981: 34)

Quantified data is for most sociologists what primary sources are for historians. If some historians cannot resist quoting diaries, some sociologists are addicted to overquantification. Both kinds of evidence have their advantages and disadvantages, and each discipline can gain from making greater use of the kind of evidence most popular in the other. This does not always happen, often for reasons of training: Seymour Martin Lipset could still write in 1968 that "few historians, including those dealing with the modern period of American history, seem to have been aware of the uses of survey data for their problems." (Lipset 1968: 32) Fortunately, this situation has since changed, especially in American political history.

In addition to differences in method, history and sociology are often distinguished by their conceptual inventories. Burke (1980) suggests that there are a number of sociological concepts which historians can and do use to their advantage, such as structure, function, social role, kinship, socialization, deviance, social class and stratification, social mobility, modernization, patrons and clients, and factions. The breadth of such a list makes it clear that there is much room for hybridization of subfields across the disciplinary boundaries. Most of these concepts support their own speciality in sociology, and could probably support a hybrid subfield if cross-fertilized by history.

Social science concepts, along with methods and theories, are often an important component of any hybrid work even for a scholar solidly within history. As an example, Paul Kennedy's *The Rise and Fall of the Great Powers* is obviously the work of a historian, not a political scientist. Nonetheless, he makes use of many political science concepts and theories, to an extent unusual among historians. For instance, he uses not only the concept of power but the work of political scientists who have attempted to measure it. He also takes advantage of some theories of political scientists. Like systems-level political scientists, he argues that certain kinds of power configurations, or structures, make war more likely: for example, a multipolar system is different than a bipolar system, making a distinction rarely found among historians but common among political scientists. He also makes use of the theory of hegemonic stability from international political economy. Furthermore, the book is comparative, and anything but narrow. Kennedy shows what familiarity with the work of other social scientists can add to the writing of history. Judicious use of social science concepts can also be of great value in the writing of even more traditional history, with Eric Hobsbawm's *Industry and Empire* a noteworthy example.

Even all these differences do not exhaust the dimensions along which historians and sociologists may be distinguished. For a further characterization of the divisions between them, we should look at how practitioners specialize. For historians, almost all academic divisions are based on time, place, and subject: Modern French Intellectual History, Medieval European Legal History, Ancient Chinese Political History. Sociologists, on the other hand, divide themselves by social subsystem: industrial relations, criminality, human ecology, social stratification, leisure, family, religion, and so on. Most focus, at least implicitly, on modern society and especially the society in which the sociologist lives. Time and place is not central to their internal divisions and is usually ignored. Given these self-classifications, it becomes clear that what interests historians are questions of context (place) and sequence (time). Sociologists, on the other hand, usually hold sequence and context constant while beginning with the notion of role (family, labor, military, religion, politics, leisure).

This distinction is interesting when we compare the forms that history and sociology take in hybrids with a third discipline. Consider historical linguistics and sociolinguistics. In historical linguistics one studies a sequence of linguistic forms and the relationships between them, attempting to find the rules underlying these relationships. Sociolinguists study how social relationships such as role, status, and class affect speech and language. In a sense, the difference is that the historical linguist begins by describing the effects (linguistic change) and then looks for causes, while the sociolinguist begins with causes (role, status, class) and looks for their effects. By their very nature, identifying causes may require a greater degree of abstraction than is necessary to

HISTORICAL SOCIOLOGY AND SOCIOLOGICAL HISTORY 199

describe effects, and this may explain why many sociologists are so enamored of abstract theories.

As a second example, consider political history and political sociology. Political history is an old hybrid, traditional in many ways, which organizes and describes political events. Like historical linguistics, it too goes from effect to cause. Political sociology is quite different. In many cases, it ignores the ultimate political outcome (policy) in favor of understanding the processes of political behavior. Many political sociologists study political attitudes and values, electoral behavior, or political recruitment, all of which are important components of the process by which political decisions are made but which are not directly connected to those decisions. This second distinction, between a concern for outcomes in history and a greater focus on process in sociology, also appears in many areas. Bringing both together is another focal point of hybrids.

Some historians might not be convinced by our arguments about the usefulness of sociology for their discipline. They could respond that the study of history is by its very nature a task of synthesis, that is, recombination. What distinguishes one history from the next is not the extent of synthesis but the value of the historian's vision, or perspective. What historians do, according to these historians, is to bring together all material which bears on that vision regardless of its discipline of origin. Recombination exists but is commonplace, and really not the source of innovative history.

These historians make some valid points. Certainly it is true that no successful historian can postpone synthesis nearly as long as a good sociologist can. Nonetheless, we have two objections to this view, two ways in which the process of cross-fertilization changes—and improves—a historian's vision.

As we discussed in Chapter 16, clashing perspectives often lead to innovation. It is true that one historian's perspective may contend with another, but the extent of disagreement is likely to be greater between a historian and a sociologist. For one thing, virtually all historians arrive at their perspectives inductively, while other social sciences enjoy a mix of deductive and inductive approaches. Good economic history, for instance, brings the deductive power of economic theory down to earth in a way that can enrich both. Eli F. Heckscher is a good example, an economic historian who is still known as both historian and economist today, most known for his economic history of Sweden and for a theoretical contribution, the basis of the Heckscher-Ohlin model of the effects of international trade.

Second, historians do not—can not—bring as much as possible to bear on their vision from whatever source. Inevitably, some things are left out, and others are put in, and the mixes favored by historians have changed over the years. Take any number of histories of medieval England, for instance, and watch the changing fates of theological, philological, demographic, economic, political, and sociological evidence and approaches to the topic. Advances in the other social sciences are responsible for the trends first in one direction, then the next.

Of course, hybridization is not easy. Sidney Aronson reminds us that "historical sociology will require the historian who is oriented to traditional methods to drastically alter his approach. He will no longer be able to indulge his penchant for straight narrative." (Aronson 1969: 300) This kind of disciplinary inertia hampers efforts at hybridization. Certainly, changing perspectives and training through enforced inter-action would help break down barriers. Yet, as Sidney Aronson points out, it is very unlikely that any graduate department of history might give a full-time appointment to a sociologist in order to help train future generations of historians. (Aronson 1969: 293) The reverse is equally true, although Aronson notes that Columbia's sociology depart-ment did appoint a historian to its faculty in 1954 in order to encourage faculty and students to make greater use of history.

The hybrids will also have to endure the wrath of the traditional historians, who—a bit defensively, perhaps—can nonetheless make a stirring argument in favor of their method. For instance, Henry Ashby Turner, Jr., anticipating criticisms that he is a "vulgar factologist," in whose work "the larger picture is hopelessly lost in a mass of detail, the forest being obscured by the trees," produces the following preemp-tive counter-attack:

> Analysis must take place, it will be announced (by the critics), on a "higher plane" and be informed by conceptualization and theory. Such strictures have a superficial ring of profundity that will doubtless impress many. But the deficiencies of the body of historical writing produced by those who have relied on such formulas undercut the plausibility of these particular strictures. Objections of that sort have no validity unless it can be demonstrated by those who raise them that history can be written in the terms they propose without reliance on the impressionistic use of a smattering of evidence, without the misconstrual and omission of evidence, and without the use of fabricated or otherwise invalid evidence. (H. A. Turner 1985: 357–358)

Rather than have the theorists simply tell him he is wrong, Turner quite reasonably demands that they show him to be wrong. Sociological theorization, he insists, must not do injustice to any part of the wide range of evidence available, but must prove its ability to include that evidence while using it to move beyond mere narrative and into deeper levels of understanding. Meeting this challenge shows the intellectual tasks facing a good hybrid, one who can move beyond one perspective while encompassing that which remains behind.

22
JUNCTIONS BETWEEN THE SOCIAL SCIENCES AND LIFE SCIENCES

Not all hybrids are as mature as social geography or political sociology. Some are in early stages of courtship, and the marriage may or may not ever be consummated. Let us now turn to one such series of encounters, for the most part not yet instutionalized: the interaction of the social sciences and life sciences.

Because of the depth of specialization required for scientific advance, simple combination of formal disciplines can be superficial and unproductive. The interaction of biology and the social sciences shows both the potential for advance as well as illustrating the difficulties involved. If man is a social *animal,* biology is obviously relevant to social science. Psychology, which has always had close ties to biology, can therefore be considered as much a natural science as a social science. While man is a social animal, biological reductionists, who ignore the adjective, miss too much, as do their social science colleagues who forget the noun.

Separating that adjective from its noun means that specialization into the various sciences has left gaps between them. There are two basic models of human behavior, the traditional social science model based on social environments and rational behavior, and the biological model which stresses the animal side of man while ignoring cognition. (see Wiegele 1979: 20–26) Clearly both are incomplete.

Yet it has not always been easy to recombine them. Social Darwinism and its modern incarnation, popularized sociobiology, are not yet among the most productive hybrids. Losco and Baird, in a sympathetic review of the impact of sociobiology on political science, admitted that the impact "has so far been less than modest." (Losco and Baird 1982: 353) One can find sociobiologists who use the same alleged genetic imperatives to explain both polygamy and monogamy in human societies; clearly neither line of argument is yet persuasive.

Some sociobiologists and their allies overstate the importance of biology. Those who wish to use Darwinian theories should keep in mind how far modern evolutionary biology has come since Darwin. Instead of Darwinism's heavy reliance on random mutations, modern biologists are much more inclined to stress the mixing and cross-mixing of gene pools; they also analyze the effects of each organism's selection of environments to which it is adapted, rather than the selection of organisms by the environment. Social processes clearly shape the gene pool as well as being shaped by it. Modern-day Social Darwinists can be innovative only if they exploit the current state of the patrimony in biology. Biological reductionism is a serious—or at times comical—mistake.

Even if one were to admit that "nature" is more important than "nurture," the social context cannot be ignored. To take a striking, and experimentally verifiable example, bilingual Hungarian-Serbocroat children learn the Hungarian illative, elative, sublative, and superessive cases before they are able to use the single Serbocroat locative case, which covers essentially the same grammatical ideas. (Mikes 1967) Physiological or neurological constraints on language acquisition cannot, therefore, be specified without reference to the social context, the language being spoken. In this case, hybridization means examining the mutual interaction of physiology and the psychology of development, in conjunction with language acquisition and linguistic theory.

The reverse is also true: some social scientists tend to insist on wilful ignorance of biology and overstate the importance of "nurture," as in the famous example of Margaret Mead's argument that sexual behavior is culturally learned, not biologically determined. Derek Freeman has strongly attacked this proposition, in a thorough critique of Mead's data, methods, logic, and conclusions, reasserting the importance of biological factors. The truth presumably lies somewhere between the two extremes, and continued debate can help locate it more precisely.

To apply biology to social phenomena, one must form a true hybrid of specialties—not a vast synthesis of disciplines which is an oversimplification. Narrower topics and more specific hypotheses are essential. James Chowning Davies (1983) argues, as an example, that custom, habit, routine, and the like are most likely to have environmental or social causes, whereas acts which violate these customs *may* have biological bases. When placed in an uncommon situation of physical violence, for instance, instinct may override rationality and social norms.

JUNCTIONS BETWEEN SOCIAL AND LIFE SCIENCES

We agree that this kind of focused hybrid is the correct way to pose the problem of the encounter between biology and the social sciences.

Because of both the potential and the dangers, the success of biological hybrids varies considerably. Biology is relevant, for instance, to several topics in linguistics. The physiology of speech production is relevant to acoustic phonology; the cognitive elements of language can be studied with reference to the biological constraints of the brain; the biological foundations of language can be discovered from experience with split-brain operations (such as those used to treat some forms of severe epilepsy). E. H. Lenneberg, in the *Biological Foundations of Language* (1967), has proposed a "critical age" hypothesis that the ability to acquire a first language ends with the completion of the development of cerebral dominance, or lateralization, which occurs around puberty. This hypothesis has found its most direct test in observations of "Genie," an extraordinarily socially deprived child discovered at age thirteen, in a project by Curtiss, Fromkin, Krasher, Rigler and Rigler. Social deprivation, physiology, and language all interact in the study of such a case.

Others have suggested interesting applications of some biological theories. One biological maxim is that ontogeny recapitulates phylogeny, that is, the development of the individual organism repeats the evolution of its species, as in human fetal development. S. M. Ervin and W. R. Miller (1963) have proposed that the same may be true for language— that is, the observable sequences of child language development may repeat the unobservable processes of the origins of human language. If correct, this proposition can help solve a question which has been a subject of speculation from the time of the Greeks. Another interesting question in linguistics with ancient antecedents is the extent to which human language is unique. Studying animal language requires knowledge of linguistics and comparative psychology and physiology, and has interesting implications for many fields. Washoe, a chimpanzee which apparently learned American sign language with the proficiency of a young human child seems to have taught it to other chimpanzees, possibly creating a rudimentary chimpanzee speech community. Those who argue that language is essential for human culture may learn from this experiment.

The exchange operates in both directions between linguistics and biology (including physiology and medicine). Some areas of medicine and biology are expanding towards the social sciences and creating true hybrid fields, in which the social science makes significant contributions. In the area of neurolinguistics, "Clinical neurology, psychiatry, and neurosurgery historically have contributed more to the study of aphasia than any other disciplines, although recently there has been more of a balance between them and the fields of speech pathology, psychology, and linguistics." (Dingwall and Whitaker 1978: 212) Linguistic theory, for instance, is much more likely now to be used as the basis for clinical tests of the extent of speech disorders. In exchange, this data is very useful for linguistic theory and for understanding how language comprehension and production are organized in the brain.

One early flow from linguistics to biology proved to be extrordinarily important for both the life sciences and the social sciences. Erasmus Darwin was a physiologist, botanist, and poet, who was very interested in speech, language, and linguistic disorders. He learned of the "family tree" model of language change, and this influenced those elements of his *Zoonomia* that anticipated parts of the theory of evolution. His theories were important in turn for the naturalist Jean Baptiste de Lamarck, who first proposed that animals and plants adapt in response to changes in the environment and that such acquired characteristics are transmitted to their offspring. Both Lamarck and Erasmus Darwin were important for Darwin's grandson, Charles Darwin. Darwin's theory has another ancestor in the social sciences; he was influenced by Malthus, himself influenced by Adam Smith. Economics and demography, then, are also Darwin's intellectual ancestors.

Biology has had, and continues to have, a fruitful relationship with psychology. "Obviously, any profound psychological analysis whether it concerns perception, motivity, affectivity or even intelligence, must sooner or later refer to physiology. . . ." (Piaget 1972: 133) Konrad Lorenz's work into animal imprinting is of obvious relevance to child development and to socialization processes more generally. In fact, Lorenz's subfield of ethology, the search for regularities among intact animals in relatively natural settings, is also related to anthropology as well as psychology and its home field of biology. Developmental physiology and the psychology of development are interdependent, as is the study of conditioned reflexes in physiology and in psychology. This last example can highlight some of the complexities involved. Conditioned reflexes are obviously affected by the environment, and this environment may both itself change and cause the reflex to change. Examining the biological phenomenon without reference to the social environment is but one side of the coin. Some have also brought cybernetics to bear on this problem.

Comparative psychology (zoopsychology) has many advantages for the study of human behavior, theoretical and practical. Primatology, for instance, can add much to our understanding not least because the range of ethically acceptable experiments on non-human primates is wider than the comparable range for experiments on humans. Others suggest that any form of social organization found among all higher

JUNCTIONS BETWEEN SOCIAL AND LIFE SCIENCES

primates today may be presumed to have characterized the social order of early man as well. This may help shed light on important questions of prehistory, in conjunction with the archaeological record.

Comparative primatology is but one step away from a social science; it is therefore not surprising that anthropology, too, has met with biology. Freedman argues that anthropological interest in common human nature has recently been given impetus by developments within ethology. (Freedman 1978: 94) The exchange between these disciplines may also flow in the opposite direction: ethnobiology investigates the biological knowledge of indigenous peoples, and this hybrid with anthropology is of use to both medicine and pharmacology. As is well known, many drugs come from the pharmacological knowledge of "witch doctors" and other traditional healers.

Many examples of the importance of biology for other social sciences could be given. Alcoholism, for instance, is not just a sociological phenomenon, but a physiological one as well. Biology can also help ancient history and prehistory. It is possible, by analyzing the blood composition of contemporary populations, to make inferences about ancient migrations. Hemoglobin, rhesus factors, and porphyrines can testify before the grand jury of historians, archaeologists, anthropologists, and geographers about the ancient Khmer empire, the Vikings, the origins of the Ainu in Hokkaido and of native Americans. (Bernard 1986)

In political science, Douglas Madsen, building on the work of endocrinologists, has argued that human power seekers are biochemically different from the rest of the population, a difference associated with elevated levels of white blood seratonin. This is associated with various psychological traits such as extreme aggressiveness, easily aroused hostility, a sense of time urgency, and competitive achievement striving.

In general, biopolitics is a young hybrid, and so far its advances have been meager. In a recent bibliography of the field (Somit, Peterson, and Peer 1987), a large but declining number of items were still primarily concerned with arguing in favor of research into this hybrid; most of the substantive research was concentrated in sociobiology/ evolution/ethology, a very controversial area. Other research topics may prove more tenable. One which is receiving increasing attention is the theory of the state. Roger D. Masters has, in articles in *Daedalus* (1978) and *World Politics* (1983), explored the implications of evolutionary biology for political philosophy, and more specifically the theory and origins of the state. The question of the origin of the state obviously has relevance in other disciplines, such as anthropology or history. Such work shows how even apparently unrelated specialties can occasionally help one another.

Some economists have been much attracted to sociobiology. Jack Hirshleifer argues that biology can add much to economics, and in fact that "in pursuing their imperialist destinies, economics and sociobiology have arrived in different ways at what is ultimately the same master pattern of social theory." (Hirshleifer 1985: 66) Michael T. Ghiselin, following Hirshleifer, argues for a "general economy," based on the concepts of resources, scarcity, and competition, and the laws of nature governing them; this field would divide into "political economy" (traditional economics) and "natural economy" (traditional biology). The usefulness of this is overstated; we are very skeptical of "master disciplines" and find hybridization of specialties much more persuasive. Hirshleifer does point to conceptual parallelisms between economics and biology, such as species/industry, mutation/innovation, and evolution/progress. The convergence of these concepts is much more likely to be innovative than attempts at holistic sociobiology.

Others have sought to apply the evolutionary concept of punctuated equilibria to social institutions. Carl Gans (1987), in a review of the problems and promise of this application, argued that this can be useful as a metaphor, but the incongruence of the units of comparison and the different assumptions of each field do not yet promise a real application of biological theories of punctuated equilibria to social processes. As Hirshleifer also points out, both biology and economics are concerned with some similar problems, such as competition in an environment of scarcity. In such focused areas, innovation is possible, and Hirshleifer has himself done interesting work in the area of conflict, drawing on economics, biology, and political science. As we have insisted, such focus is essential for innovative hybrids.

One economic method, game theory, has proven to have applications for biology. For an overview of these applications, a good reference is Robert Axelrod's *The Evolution of Cooperation* (1984), which brings together several strands of game theory and tests them in a computer simulation. He then applies his findings to problems of international relations, social class and stratification, and in conjunction with the biologist William Hamilton, relates them to a number of problems in biology.

The life sciences and the social sciences may also impact the physical sciences. James Lovelock's controversial "Gaia" hypothesis suggests that life on Earth has created a self-regulating and self-perpetuating system which has the effect of maintaining certain physical constraints such as atmosphere and climate within acceptable limits. To take a simple example, consider the fact that animals burn oxygen and give off carbon dioxide as waste while plants consume carbon dioxide and give off oxygen; notwithstanding the potential for disequilibrium, the ratio be-

JUNCTIONS BETWEEN SOCIAL AND LIFE SCIENCES

tween oxygen and carbon dioxide in the atmosphere has remained stable for extremely long periods of time. Lovelock is also a good example of the variety of personal histories of hybrids, as his work initially stems from interplanetary atmospheric research for NASA.

As these bodies of research demonstrate, notwithstanding the obstacles, careful exchange between the life sciences and social sciences can help answer important questions. As further illustration, we briefly review two topics of global importance which have recently been the object of hybridization from biology broadly conceived. The two issues, imperialism and economic development, are of such magnitude both from a historical standpoint and as matters of contemporary politics, that we trust we will be forgiven a somewhat lengthy review of the topic. Because of the relative depth of the discussion, we wish to state that we do not entirely endorse the views of either Alfred W. Crosby's *Ecological Imperialism* (1986) or Andrew M. Kamarck's *The Tropics and Economic Development* (1976); we maintain only that they raise fascinating questions.

What these examples remind us is that the exchange of theories is frequently destructive before being cumulative. Theories are disproven, assumptions proven wrong-headed, whole perspectives thrown into doubt. Consider changes in theories of imperialism, a poorly defined term which is usually taken to mean the domination of one people over another. Theories of imperialism abound. The first such theory was proposed by none other than Thucydides in his history of the Peloponnesian War. In modern terminology, he attributes Athenian imperialism to changes in the distribution of power among the city-states. Such theories remained influential for centuries. A group of hybrid theorists called this into question by stressing the economic foundations of imperialism (more specifically, the economic foundations of the "new" imperialism of 1870–1914). First proposed by J. A. Hobson and then adopted by V. I. Lenin, these theories stress the economic reasons why capitalists invest overseas, and then examine why core governments set up colonial governments to protect their citizens' investments. Criticizing this theory, another hybrid, Joseph Schumpeter, proposed a sociological theory in his *The Sociology of Imperialism*.

Contemporary scholars have both built upon and sought to reconcile these theories. Johan Galtung's "Structural Theory of Imperialism" encompasses most of these ideas but adds cultural and scientific imperialism as well, and finds structural reasons for all of these varieties. Others, such as Benjamin Cohen's *The Question of Imperialism* (1973), reassert the primacy of one factor while integrating other theories as subsidiary forces in specific periods.

Another hybrid theory has the potential to destroy many of these other theories. In a recent book, Crosby suggests that the causes of imperialism are not just political, economic, and social, but biological. If correct, his argument seriously weakens these earlier explanations and requires the inclusion of biological variables. He begins with the observation that European flora and fauna have been at least as successful as European humans in several overseas regions. For him, the success of Europeans in conquering these areas is at least partially related to the ecological causes of the success of the other European biota: "Perhaps European humans have triumphed because of their superiority in arms, organization, and fanaticism, but what in heaven's name is the reason the sun never sets on the empire of the dandelion?" (Crosby 1986) Furthermore, the success of European fauna and flora helped the European humans succeed:

> If the Europeans had arrived in the New World and Australasia with twentieth-century technology in hand, but no animals, they would not have made as great a change as they did by arriving with horses, cattle, pigs, goats, sheep, asses, chickens, cats, and so forth. Because these animals are self-replicators, the efficiency and speed with which they can alter environments, even continental environments, are superior to those for any machine we have thus far devised. (Crosby 1986: 173)

Even those biota introduced unintentionally were of critical importance: weeds, parasites, and feral animals. The flow is curiously one-sided. For instance, by the mid 1800s, there were hundreds of British plants thriving wild in Australia, but not one Australian plant had been naturalized in Great Britain: although many plants were accidentally introduced from Britain to Australia, no Australian flora seem to have made the reverse voyage.

Climate is one part of the story. European settlement moved more slowly where the climate was not right, as on the Siberian taiga, South African veldt, and Brazilian sertão, and the Europeans conquered but did not Europeanize India, Indonesia, Malaysia, and East Africa. Yet surely some Australian plants could have survived naturally in Britain.

Immunology is another important variable. "It was their germs, not these imperialists themselves, for all their brutality and callousness, that were chiefly responsible for sweeping aside the indigenes and opening the Neo-Europes to demographic takeover." (Crosby 1986: 196) Amerindians and aborigines were wiped out by diseases. Many African peoples, on the other hand, have prospered in demographic terms since European contact, both at home and even in the New World, notwithstanding the awful living conditions for slaves. Eurasian-African agri-

JUNCTIONS BETWEEN SOCIAL AND LIFE SCIENCES

culture developed stronger immune systems in both man and beast, as well as more competitive fauna and flora. When settled cultivation began, it attracted weeds and vermin; villages also attracted "crowd diseases" such as venereal disease, which depend on some minimal concentration of humans. Villages also mean garbage and filth, attracting diseases such as typhoid or dysentery. Last but not least, domesticated animals are carriers of some diseases which can be transmitted from one species to another, such as cowpox/smallpox (cattle), distemper/measles (dogs), and influenza (pigs, horses). All these diseases meant, over time, higher immunity for the agriculturalists and for the peoples in contact with them. This lends credibility to "McNeill's law," that the "civilized" will generally conquer the "uncivilized," thanks to better immune systems. As Crosby suggests, the Old World man was a bit of a "superman":

> his fields were plagued with thistles and his granaries with rodents; he had sinuses that throbbed in wet weather, a recurring problem with dysentery, an enervating burden of worms, an impressive assortment of genetic and acquired adaptations to diseases anciently endemic to Old World civilizations, and an immune system of such experience and sophistication as to make him the template for all the humans who would be tempted or obliged to follow the path he pioneered. . . . (Crosby 1986: 34)

He suggests that the first case of successful "ecological imperialism" was, ironically enough, the original migration of Amerindians to the Americas, and of aborigenes to Australasia. In these new lands, there were no natural enemies of man, and in fact most native animals did not see man as an enemy. Man's hunting, man's animals, man's parasites, and the absence of parasites adopted to man, stimulated chain reactions in the ecospheres, such as the extinction of mammoths, moas, giant sloths, and North American camels and horses. The extinction of traditional prey also brought doom upon predators such as saber-toothed tigers. By thus making these lands "empty," man and his animals expanded quickly throughout the new lands.

However, the new inhabitants were quickly cut off from their homelands, and lost immunological contact with the Old World. The consequences were to be great; for instance, the most developed culture in North America, the Mississippi civilization, appears to have been wiped out by indirect contact with Europeans, who left diseases in Florida. This civilization's agriculture soon collapsed, opening up an ecological niche for the previously restricted buffalo. The effects of European diseases on the Mayans, Aztecs, and Incans are well known.

European imperialism may therefore have had biological roots. Furthermore, many theorists have suggested that "imperialism" is a major cause of "underdevelopment," another major topic in the social sciences. Yet, if imperialism is partly biological, might not the causes of underdevelopment be in large part climatological? Again, such an approach would be destrictive in its implications for many existing theories, but would be of great significance if correct.

In the 1950s and 1960s, economic theories of development became increasingly divorced from questions of climate. As always, fragmentation into separate fields, such as economics or climatology, is the core reason why there were gaps left between them. W. W. Rostow's famous stages of growth do not admit of any physical constraints on growth, and as a result his analysis has proven to be far too simplistic. Most countries have not and will not follow the model. In this case, the divide was in part a reaction against the simplistic theories of a few geographers such as Ellsworth Huntington, and in part it is a result of the difficulties in including climate in mathematical models of the economy. It is here that Michael Ghiselin's suggestions in the direction of unifying "political economy" and "natural economy" could perhaps be most helpful, for the subjects of the two subdisciplines are closely interconnected on this point.

Political theories of economic development are also too simplistic. Several such arguments appeared in 1981, discussing the problems of underdevelopment in Africa. The World Bank's *Accelerated Development in Sub-Saharan Africa* (1981), known as the "Berg Report," put the primary responsibility for underdevelopment on poor policy choices by African governments. The U.S. Department of Agriculture's *Food Problems and Prospects in Sub-Saharan Africa* (1981) reached a similar conclusion, although it did not emphasize the policy factor to the same extent as the former. In the same year, Robert Bates' *Markets and States in Tropical Africa* not only looked at the effects of these policy choices but also explained why African states persisted in following them. Even the Organization for African Unity had already admitted the serious effects of policy errors two years before, in "The Lagos Plan of Action," although these African leaders naturally focused on the colonial legacy in Africa and an adverse international economy as well.

Taken to an extreme, such "policy failure" arguments suggest that Third World leaders are for some reason less intelligent than other leaders. Obviously, this is an untenable conclusion. When explaining the failures in terms of economic policy, these political explanations ignore the obvious relation between temperate climates and the more successful "third world" countries of Argentina, Chile, Uruguay, south-

JUNCTIONS BETWEEN SOCIAL AND LIFE SCIENCES

ern Brazil, South Africa, Turkey, Hong Kong, and North and South Korea, for all their very different political structures. Ignoring this relationship overstates the role of policy.

On the other hand, no one-sided emphasis on climate is possible, either. Taiwan is tropical and a newly industrialized country. Furthermore, there are many pairs of neighboring countries, with similar climates, which vary greatly in their economic and political success: Ghana and the Ivory Coast, Kenya and Tanzania, Senegal and Gambia, and Zambia and Zimbabwe. Hybrid approaches, which include climate without overemphasizing it, seem appropriate.

In any case, economic theories and those policies suggested by the developed world did little to help the tropics. "The protest movement of the newly independent elite and the sympathetic or diplomatic responses to this protest of Western intellectuals, politicians, and officials called for the ready transferability of knowledge and skills from advanced to 'underdeveloped' (no longer 'backward') or, later, 'developing' countries. The neglect of the role of climate fitted well into the new optimism. It is part of the stages-of-growth mythology that all countries tread inexorably the same path to eventual 'take-off' and self-sustained economic growth. . . ." (Streeten 1976: xi) This may result in part from the ethnocentric views of some American and European scholars, but it also seems to have been welcomed by many Africans. Reality has been disappointing. Some have suggested that dependency and exploitation explain the problems of underdevelopment, but this neglects the successes of the newly industrialized countries (NICs). The NICs are largely temperate zone countries, but differ widely in economic and political structure, suggesting that climate may play an important role in their success. These failings in traditional approaches bring Andrew Kamarck, of the World Bank, to stress climate and its effects on plant and animal life in the tropics. He does not argue for a monocausal explanation, but conditions his discussion on questions of nutrition, health, education, and social organization. (cf. Kamarck 1967) Kamarck's argument is straightforward:

Compared to the Temperate Zones, there are certain effects of the tropical climate that, up to the present, hinder agriculture, handicap mineral exploration, and make the population less vigorous through disease and, possibly, through the direct physiological impact of temperature and humidity. The effects of tropical climate are not an absolute obstacle to economic development, but they do make many of the problems of economic development in the Tropics sufficiently different from those in the Temperate Zone countries so that an additional hurdle has to be overcome and, consequently, all other relevant factors being equal, the pace of development in tropical countries tends to be slower. (Kamarck 1976: 3–4)

The climate affects the distribution of weeds and parasites, wide variations in rainfall, the quality of the soils, and the impact of trypanosomiasis (sleeping sickness). On the other hand, the tropical climate may be turned to advantage, since sunlight energy is sixty to ninety percent higher there, and rain forests can produce three to five times as much organic material each year. If the difficulties can be overcome through research into the particular problems of the tropics, there is room for some optimism.

The climate also has human consequences, especially as it affects public health. "Lack of good health affects a person's attitude toward work, initiative, creativity, learning ability, energy, and capacity for heavy or sustained work or thought." (Kamarck 1976: 57) Of course, climate is not the sole or even primary cause of poor health, except perhaps for river sickness, but it does exacerbate some diseases and parasital infestations. For instance, cold winters in the temperate zones kill many disease-carrying vectors. In addition, while improvements in public health are possible, we must keep in mind the fact that many existing social structures have mechanisms to cope with poor health; better public health will affect the basis of these social structures. Better public health also means a lower mortality rate which, with constant fertility rates, will further exacerbate the population explosion in Africa.

In an earlier work, Kamarck discussed additional related factors. He begins with obstacles of geography, noting that most African rivers have waterfalls relatively near the coast, making them relatively useless for navigation; African navigation also suffers from the shortest coastline relative to area of any continent. Isolation by land has also impeded African development over history, with the Sahara a major obstacle.

The tropical climate is a difficult one. Nine million of the 11.7 million square miles in Africa are in the tropics. Tropical soils are poor and easily depleted, and to make matters worse the rainfall is erratic over much of the continent. The climate also means that tropical diseases are endemic. One especially damaging such disease is trypanosomiasis, which prevented the use of animal transport inland, making it necessary to use inefficient human porters. Not all of these are still problems today, but they have contributed to Africa's problems in the past.

Man has a reciprocal effect on the climate. One issue raised by the reciprocal interaction of man and climate is desertification, especially in the Sahel. This is in part a result of long-term climactic changes beyond man's control, but it also results from cultivation practices,

JUNCTIONS BETWEEN SOCIAL AND LIFE SCIENCES

patterns of rangeland use, the use of wood for fuel, and some uses of inappropriate technologies. For instance, "Crops such as cotton, groundnuts and tobacco have proven to be especially harmful for they have required that vast amounts of land be cleared of its original cover, thereby interrupting the natural cycle of organic replentishment. Once such annual crops have been harvested, moreover, the earth is laid bare and is therefore exposed to the baking action of the sun." (Lofchie 1989: 13) One hybrid study of the problem is *Seeds of Famine* (1980), written by the anthropologist Richard W. Franke and the sociologist Barbara H. Chasin. They argue both that the immediate cause of African famine is the environmental deterioration of the Sahel, and that this degradation is in turn the result of West Africa's colonial legacy, especially the agricultural policies pursued by colonial administrators in order to develop a large-scale export agriculture sector.

For over four decades, climate had been expelled from theories of development. The geographers have remained particularly silent. Beginning in the late 1970s and early 1980s, social scientists, as well as botanists, zoologists, parasitologists, geologists, and other representatives of the natural sciences, began work to resucitate the moribund theories of development spoiled by ethnocentric economists, sociologists, and political scientists. Here, too, interaction of the life sciences and the social sciences has provem to be fruitful.

23

INTERNATIONAL POLITICAL ECONOMY: A FUSION OF SEVERAL SUBFIELDS

Political economy has a venerable tradition, going back to the classical economists. "Indeed, until a century ago, virtually all thinkers concerned with understanding human society wrote about political economy." (Frieden and Lake 1987: 3) The Marxian school of political economy has a continuous and voluminous tradition, while the classical tradition had largely died out after the 1930s. Despite the existence of such a tradition, international political economy is not a cyclical fad, but an upward spiral; as the examples below will show, the concerns of political economy are usually quite different than those of the classics.

Fragmentation and a steady narrowing of focus began to break down the coherence of the field about the turn of the century: "professional studies of economics and politics became more and more divorced from one another. Economic investigation began to focus on understanding more fully the operation of specific markets and their interaction. . . . At the same time, other scholars were looking increasingly at the political realm in isolation from the economy." (Frieden and Lake 1987: 3) Each area of specialization naturally progressed by excluding factors. At the same time, this fragmentation left a series of gaps between various specialties. These gaps eventually proved untenable.

Consider the case of international trade theory. Scholars focused on the redistributive and social welfare effects of trade and tariffs, while neglecting the political decisionmaking which lay behind the choice between protection and liberal trade policies. Economic historians, too, tended to take politics for granted when exploring their economic effects of policies, preferring to concentrate on economic changes such as technology or the increasing scale of markets.

Traditional international trade economics begins with the contention that mutual benefit arises from the pursuit of comparative advantage through free trade, and then examines conditions under which departures from such trade might be justifiable, such as the use of monopsony power, the protection of infant industries, or an attempt to provide social insurance. Whether or not the theory is normatively defensible, it was clearly of little explanatory power in a world in which virtually every country had some tariff on just about everything. It also ignored the use of military coercion to open trade (a neglect going back at least to Ricardo's discussion of Anglo-Portuguese trade), the coercive use of trade explored by Albert O. Hirschman, or the unequal distribution of benefits. These gaps also left room for hybridization.

Both disciplines also fragmented internally. Throughout economics we see a division between theorists and empiricists. Each generally learned little from the other, as historical and contemporary data seemed to have few theoretical implications, and the increasing complexity, and abstraction, of formal theory meant that it was of decreasing utility for economic historians. Barry Eichengreen has discussed the problem in one sub-subfield, the study of the gold standard, as follows:

> Most of the elements needed to paint a complete picture are readily at hand. Completing the picture only requires that we blend the contributions of economic theorists and economic historians. Like the blind man with the elephant, students of the gold standard have derived their views from an awareness confined to individual parts of the beast. . . . Interaction between these two sets of scholars and integration of these two literatures are precisely what is needed to generate fresh insights into how the gold standard worked. (Eichengreen 1985: 3)

Political science has been fragmented along its own lines, which has also hindered research into important topics in what is now international political economy. Before World War II, political science had had a tradition which could have filled the resulting gaps. Perhaps the most important work in the last years of the "old" political economy was E. E. Schattschneider's *Politics, Pressures and the Tariff* (1935). By examining the political behavior of economic actors on a question of economic policy, Schattschneider was able to pinpoint a number of economic features of political interest groups which help determine their relative effectiveness. However, the double perspective of this work was lost, and it became instead a part of subsequent work on interest groups—for instance, the dominance of producer groups over consumer groups, identified by Schattschneider, is an important feature in Theodore Lowi's *The End of Liberalism.*

INTERNATIONAL POLITICAL ECONOMY

Study of the domestic forces behind foreign policy was largely dropped by the field of international relations as it explored the internal logic of a system of anarchic states. The dominance of certain approaches in postwar investigations of international relations meant that the field studied diplomacy and diplomats, largely only with relation to questions of security, military strategies, alliances, and other forms of so-called "high politics." Economic policy was dismissed as "low politics," and was considered about as interesting as visa application processes in consulates. Embassies, not consulates, and political officers, not economic liaisons, were the focus.

This was sometimes astounding in the voids it left. For instance, as recently as the early 1970s, Richard N. Cooper believed it necessary to persuade the readers of *Foreign Policy* that "Trade Policy *is* Foreign Policy" (1972–73). Other divisions also weakened scholarship as research progressed, most notably the separation of comparative politics from international relations. Comparative politics generally ignored foreign policy as something which belonged to the field of international relations, even when the policy was the result of domestic demands. Students of international relations ignored the domestic determinants of foreign policy in turn. This can lead to perverse results. One of us has witnessed a discussion in which participants denied that military organization, doctrine, and policy was a part of either foreign policy or domestic policy—thereby denying its study a home in political science at all. While security studies has not suffered from such views, foreign economic policy did suffer from falling into the cracks, at least until the 1970s.

As a substantive field, international political economy bridges the gap left between these manifold traditions in both economics and political science. The literature on endogenous tariff theory, for instance, is largely the product of economists with links to comparative politics. It seeks to explain tariffs, and foreign economic policy more generally, as the result of competition among economic interest groups. It has rediscovered the Schattschneider tradition, and much improved and expanded it.

Elsewhere in the field, those political economists with their roots in international relations began their work by documenting interdependence, to persuade the postwar generation of specialists in international relations that power-seekers were constrained by the web of economic relationships in the international system. Furthermore, the school argued, states were not the only, and perhaps not even the most important, actors in the international system, but were joined by multinational corporations, transnational actors such as the Catholic Church, and international organizations, among others. This "interdependence" school is best exemplified by Robert O. Keohane and Joseph S. Nye, Jr., in the co-edited volume *Transnational Relations and World Politics* (1970), and the co-authored book *Power and Interdependence* (1977). By looking at both political and economic actors in the attempt to explain both political and economic behavior, this work highlights many important features of the international system which had been neglected.

While not a general theory, interdependence has been both important and useful as a conceptual framework and as a research agenda. It has helped stimulate hybrid research, such as the theories of "regimes" developed by the various authors in *International Regimes* (1983), edited by Stephen D. Krasner. These authors sought to understand regularized cooperation among interdependent state and non-state actors from various perspectives. A parallel body of theory has sought to explain both the preconditions for interdependence and the development of regimes by examining hegemonic leadership of the international economy, in work by Charles Kindleberger, Robert Gilpin, Stephen Krasner, Robert Keohane, and others. These works draw not only from traditional theories about state behavior, but from Olson's "privileged group" model of collective goods, as well as from work in economic history relating to the gold standard.

The field has moved from being self-consciously hybrid to asserting its character in its own right. In the words of Martin Staniland, "It asserts that politics and economics overlap and influence each other and that theoretical analysis should not just take account of this relationship but should be founded on it, should take it as an assumption, and should use concepts that illuminate the relationship." (Staniland 1985: 3) This field is now recognized as a separate specialty within political science, on a formal par with both comparative politics and international relations although it still has far fewer members than either of these older specialties. As it develops as a distinct field, it too will face the problems of density and diminishing marginal productivity. In fact, areas of the new field already show some signs of stagnation. For one thing, security problems relationships—which are of obvious importance for the European "Economic" Community—are largely ignored. There is room for the recombination of international political economy with the field of security studies. The contributors to *Cooperation Under Anarchy* (1986), edited by Kenneth A. Oye, suggest a way of unifying a number of approaches to the study of both economic policy and security policy. The development of such a common language may help make possible an exploration of the interplay between these two kinds of issues.

Others have sought to extend the field more towards comparative politics. This is the impulse behind the current literature on the inter-

INTERNATIONAL POLITICAL ECONOMY

national determinants of domestic policy. An important example is Peter J. Katzenstein's *Small States in World Markets* (1985), which explains corporatism and the rise of the welfare state in small European countries as the result of the instability of the international market. Peter Gourevitch, another scholar working in this area, explains changes in domestic political coalitions largely as the result of international economic crises in his *Politics in Hard Times* (1986), although he includes some domestic-system variables in the analysis as well.

Such work shows the usefulness of combining international relations, comparative politics, and domestic political economy. Work in this latter area exists, and is being integrated into the field of international political economy. It begins with the juxtapositon of the political world of the state and the economic world of the market. As Robert Gilpin has pointed out,

> The parallel existence and mutual interaction of 'state' and 'market' in the modern world create 'political economy'. . . . In the absence of the state, the price mechanism and market forces would determine the outcome of economic activities; this would be the pure world of the economist. In the absence of the market, the state or its equivalent would allocate economic resources; this would be the pure world of the political scientist. (Gilpin 1987: 8)

Early works approached precisely this interaction. Andrew Shonfield's *Modern Capitalism* (1965), for instance, is subtitled "The Changing Balance of Public and Private Power." Shonfield weaves together economic, social, and political causes of the tendency towards pervasive—and successful—government management of the economy. At the same time, he examines the effects of these policies both on the economy and on the institution of parliamentary government. In so doing, Shonfield led in the formation of a research agenda in political economy, beginning with precisely these kinds of substantive issues. New questions have led to innovative research.

One work ultimately stemming from this research agenda is Robert H. Bates' *Market and State in Tropical Africa* (1981), which discusses how state agricultural policies have had damaging effects on individual incentives. Going beyond such an economic critique, he also examines the political reasons behind these policies, especially the need for African leaders to keep their urban bases of support. The result is a work which has been important not just for scholars, but also for policy makers in the American foreign policy community and at the World Bank or International Monetary Fund. Edward R. Tufte's *Political Control of the Economy* (1978), from a different tack, has also sought to explain the choice of economically irrational policies, taking advanced democracies as his cases. He finds, for instance, an electoral cycle of government intervention: American presidents have manipulated the development of disposable income in order to garner votes. Both Bates and Tufte, by exploring the political logic behind economic policies—and some of the effects of these policies on economic actors, and therefore subsequent politics—have woven together innovative explanations of important features of modern politics.

Much of international political economy, like economics, relies upon the methodological assumption of rational choice. Several books have been innovative by applying the methodology of rational choice to huge topics, such as Mancur Olson's *The Rise and Decline of Nations* (1982), and Douglass C. North and Robert Paul Thomas's *The Rise of the Western World* (1981). What distinguishes them from "interdisciplinary" work is that they do not tackle these gigantic topics by throwing every causal factor they can think of into the heap, but rather that they carefully select concepts, methods, and theories from interconnected subfields which they weave into innovative arguments. Olson applies his theory of collective action to predict patterns in political systems over time, in an effort to understand which systems will achieve high rates of economic growth and which will stress instead policies of economic redistribution. North and Thomas apply theories of economic scarcity and factor prices to social orders such as feudalism, in an effort to understand how Western Europe developed modern economic institutions.

The assumption of rational choice, like any other, ultimately has limits. Some we discuss in Chapter 24, with reference to psychology. In addition, the assumption that individuals rationally choose those actions which will best achieve their goals has a serious problem in the realm of preference formation—"there's no accounting for taste." As Robert Keohane has pointed out, "the assumption that individuals are self-interested and rational . . . is ambiguous, since 'self-interest' is defined culturally rather than as an objective given." (Keohane 1983a: 559) Of course, within a relatively stable culture this is not a problem, but with changing conditions even some of the most well-known political economists have fallen into this trap. Samuel Popkin, for instance, in his discussion of the "rational" peasant's decision to revolt, suggests that "So long as the Communists argued only in terms of material incentives and neglected to add an ethnic, Vietnamese content to their discussions of the future, they were unable to present a credible vision of the future to the peasants. . . . The religious movements, on the other hand, brought visions of the future consonant with peasant beliefs. . . ." (Popkin 1979: 54) While the argument is persuasive, it is surprising

INTERNATIONAL POLITICAL ECONOMY

that it comes from a self-proclaimed political economist using strictly "rational choice" reasoning. Hybridization in the direction of political socialization or social psychology would probably prove fruitful.

Furthermore, much current work in the field of political economy, by focusing on individual utility maximization and, at least implicitly, on mutually beneficial exchange theories, excludes power and domination. There is a tendency among some political economists to become too narrowly economic, neglecting politics. Richard Sklar argues that

> economic theories disregard the question of domination, which is left for political scientists to explore with the use of concepts and methods that are distinctive to their own discipline. Proponents of the "new" political economy abjure this traditional division of labor. They are interdisciplinary zealots, who presume to investigate political realities with tools from the laboratory of purely economic science. The concept of power is hardly relevant to their approach, which is predicated upon the voluntaristic presuppositions of classical economic thought. (Sklar 1983: 198)

Not all of this problem is insoluble, however, since there exist economic theories of oligopoly which do include the concept of power. Power is also a notoriously problematic concept and may not present an attractive alternative. Even so, the inclusion of authority systems or ideological hegemony may be warranted.

The field might also benefit from modelling the political economy of conflict. Jack Hirshleifer argues that there is currently a gap between political science and economics in precisely this area. "Political scientists, while they have of course produced an enormous literature on conflict, have only recently been developing a tradition of formal theorizing. And the economists, whose selection and training prepare them for such analysis, have suffered from a 'harmonistic bias' that puts the study of conflict outside their explanatory jurisdiction." (Hirshleifer 1988: 225) Such gaps are, as always, potentially fruitful for innovators.

24

THE HESITANT EXCHANGE BETWEEN ECONOMICS AND PSYCHOLOGY

One way to see how valuable cross-fertilization can be is to examine areas of knowledge that have recognized the need for greater exchange between them but have been unable to achieve it. Analyzing the limits of each field and the obstacles to bringing them together highlights the potential for innovation if they are ultimately brought together. Psychology and economics—or, more accurately, experimental cognitive psychology and formal microeconomic theory—provide an excellent example.

The discipline of economics is the proud owner of the most powerful, and the most widely shared, paradigm in the social sciences. The paradigm assumes rational utility maximization and can be stated with mathematical precision. Like all Kuhnian paradigms, it has accomplished much but has also run up against a number of anomalies which subject it to challenge. As one economist has confessed, "When it comes to rationality, economics as an imperialist discipline finds itself in an unwontedly defensive position. Damaging attacks upon rational man have come from the direction of psychology." (Hirshleifer 1985: 59)

It is obviously true that not all human behavior is rational, and experimental psychologists have successfully demonstrated this in great detail. One famous example with importance for economic theory is that choices involving gains are usually risk-averse, while those involving loss are usually risk-seeking. There is no rational reason for this phenomenon, but it seems to be grounded in psychological concerns. It is also sufficiently robust to warrant inclusion into the economic theory of the firm.

Herein lies both the need for synthesis between experimental psychology and economic theory. At the same time, there are many difficulties in combining the two. As Hogarth and Reder point out, "Whereas psychologists delight in finding anomalous behavior that contradicts received wisdom, economists revel in showing how apparently anomalous behavior is in fact consistent with the maintained hypothesis." (Hogarth and Reder 1986: 5–6) There is a need to modify the economists' assumptions, in light of psychological evidence, in such a way that the power of their paradigm is not lost.

Milton Friedman, in a famous article, argues that it does not matter whether people are "really" rational—what matters is not whether or not the assumptions are correct, but whether they lead to good predictions. The Friedman approach will have succeeded in its own terms when it is the object of the kind of critique the astronomer Bludeville levelled at Copernicus' assumption that the earth moved: "by help of which false supposition he hath made truer demonstrations of the celestial spheres, than ever were made before." (cited in Kuhn 1957: 186)

The argument is not without its force. After all, Newtonian physics assumed that all bodies had their masses concentrated in a single infinitely small point, yet its predictions were excellent. For that matter, until recently most maritime navigation relied on the assumptions of the Ptolemaic astromonical system, knowing full well that these assumptions were false—but useful. At the same time, the assumptions of classical economics have been found to be plausible for a wide variety of circumstances; even chronic psychotics, who one would expect to be "irrational," obey the law of demand, buying less when prices are raised. (Battalio *et al.* 1973) Yet the fact remains that economic assumptions are inconsistent with much of modern psychology. This does not mean that psychology's findings are being exploited by economics: most economists are very fond of Friedman's argument that assumptions do not matter if the predictions are good, while most psychologists dismiss Friedman out of hand.

Part of the reason for the conflict is the distinction between process and outcome. Economists want to explore system-wide outcomes, such as market equilibria. Psychologists want to study the cognitive processes by which individuals make decisions. If cognitive processes do not change the market equilibrium, most economists are not interested in them. If "evolutionary" arguments about economic behavior are correct, that only those firms who behave rationally survive, then the economists' neglect of the failures may be justifiable.

However, the Friedman argument would be more convincing if the assumption of rational utility maximization always lead to a determi-

EXCHANGE BETWEEN ECONOMICS AND PSYCHOLOGY

nate prediction. Unfortunately, it does not—especially when we consider interaction between two or more individuals. Game theory is full of indeterminate games, such as iterated prisoner's dilemma. Arrow's theorem, too, makes prediction impossible. As Jon Elster has pointed out, "games without solution constitute a deep anomaly in the theory of rational behavior . . . (which) has implications for philosophy, psychology and the social sciences in general." (Elster 1979: 123) Although no "rational" solution exists to such games, real-world individuals in such situations do arrive at decisions. Psychological evidence suggest that they use various rules of thumb, heuristics, and biases. The psychologists Daniel Kahnemann and Amos Tversky are major figures in the new area of cross-fertilizing such findings from experimental psychology with the assumptions of formal economic theory. Yet their work is as yet poorly integrated into economic theory even though economists cite it with approval.

The psychological finding that "framing" affects decisions also has profound implications for economics. People will make different medical choices depending on whether risks are presented in terms of mortality or in terms of survival; a 90 percent survival rate is much more acceptable than a 10 percent mortality rate even though they are exactly the same. Most economists need to exploit such observations, although some already have. In an interesting book at the boundaries of economic theory, public policy, and psychology, *Disaster Insurance Protection: Public Policy Lessons,* Howard Kunreuther *et al.* exploit the notion of framing and the empirical finding that people do not buy flood insurance when or where it is rational to do so; instead, people buy flood insurance *after* a flood. This psychological variable is therefore responsible for an important case of market failure in insurance markets, and needs to be incorporated into economic analysis. An analysis of other failures in economic policy led Amitai Etzioni to focus on the importance of psychological variables, suggesting the development of a field he calls "socioeconomics." (Etzioni 1983)

It may be that neither the psychologists nor economists will succeed in forming the hybrid, while others will. The political scientist Herbert Simon won a Nobel prize in economics for work at the intersection of economic theory, public organizations, and psychology. In his book *Administrative Rationality,* which draws from psychology as well as from organization theory, he developed the twin ideas of "bounded rationality" and "satisficing" when individuals are faced with increasingly complex tasks. These concepts have much enriched many subfields of political science as well as the economic theory of the firm but have so far made little dent on formal economic theory more generally— although most recognize the need.

Others outside both economics and psychology are also working in this gap. Snyder and Diesing's *Conflict Among Nations* (1977), written by a political scientist and a philospher, moves from classical realism to game theory and then to information processing and theories of decisionmaking. Other political scientists are also exploring the interaction of rational choice and cognitive psychology.

While we have focused on those psychological findings which undermine the economic assumption of rational utility maximization, the strength of the economic paradigm is no less threatening for the field of experimental psychology. If we can understand outcomes by assuming that people behave "as if" they were rational, then it really doesn't matter much how the cognitive processes they used to arrive at that result. It is certainly interesting, as John Kagel *et al.* have demonstrated, that animals are "rational utility maximizers." This undercuts psychology's traditional focus on the relevance of cognition for behavior.

Psychology, by attacking the foundations of the rationality paradigm, is a dangerous partner for economics. Economics, by arguing that outcomes can be understood without reference to cognitive process, is no less dangerous for psychology. Although everyone knows that intercourse is essential, no one really knows how to go about it without getting hurt. As David Riesman wrote, in a different context, "In intellectual as in other activites, it is worthwhile occasionally attempting to bridge impossible barriers among the disciplines and beyond them, because in the process, though it be by its nature unending and often self-defeating, our understanding grows." (Riesman 1956: 339) As we have seen, the two bodies of theory come from completely different perspectives even though there is considerable overlap of the phenomena they analyze. If each has some truth to it, then both are limited in their explanatory power. If both are partially correct, then both are untenable as they stand. Without hybridization, scientific progress is blocked.

FINAL REMARKS: THE NEW KALEIDOSCOPE OF SOCIAL SCIENCES

It is obvious that the social sciences today are very different than what they were at the beginning—or even the middle—of the century.

Growth has implied fragmentation, specialization, and—of most interest to us—hybridization. The details change continually, as if one was slowly turning a kaleidoscope.

The social sciences have greatly expanded in the last half century. Each domain of knowledge has reached a point at which it became unknowable by generalists and required specialization to master it. As this happened, distinct disciplines, each with their own accumulation of findings, were created. Out of these disciplines, then, new fields grew and split off. Yet the process did not stop with the creation of these fields, for each has itself expanded, and each has fragmented into specialized subfields and sub-subfields.

We may take the example of France, where a centralized administration of scientific research enables us to see the overall picture more clearly. At the Centre National de la Recherche Scientifique in France, there were in 1989 about 45 formal disciplines, each divided into many fields. Depending on the definition, there were between 400 and 500 fields overseeing a total of about 2,500 research units and about 12,000 scholars. These include the natural sciences and humanities as well as the social sciences, which represent about 20 percent of the total number of researchers. In 1950, many social sciences were not even recognized as independent disciplines. A similar process could be observed in less centralized countries as well.

While specialization is essential for the in-depth study of any topic, this process of fragmentation leaves gaps. Many of the most innovative

230 FINAL REMARKS

scholars build on these bodies of knowledge, or patrimonies, by extending them across these voids in the direction of related specialties in neighboring disciplines. If a group of scholars works in a given intersection of subfields, a hybrid subfield is born.

We have shown these processes at work, discussing how scientific advance brings about the fragmentation of a discipline into subfields; how scientific advance may lead to intellectual sterility in core areas through the "paradox of density"; how the search for innovation leads specialists across disciplinary boundaries into the subfields of other disciplines; and how this transfer serves as the basis for innovative exchanges of methods, concepts, and theories.

Notwithstanding the common patterns, there is a great deal of diversity in the paths taken towards hybridization. Some disciplines, such as economics, are methodological imperialists, while anthropology's impact on other social sciences has been more important in its discoveries and in some of its theories designed to explain these discoveries. There is also much diversity in the current state of the disciplines. Economics and linguistics are comparatively unified, while the others are federations of nearly sovereign subfields.

Social sciences do not expand at the same speed and consequently do not interpenetrate each other to the same degree. Like the peripheries of several giant cities in a given region, which by their expansion tend to build a continuous urban area—a polynuclear megalopolis—so too do the walls of the formal social sciences become remnants of outdated divisions. These walls need to be demolished in order to encourage better circulation among the various districts.

Administrative reorganization is not necessarily required. There is little real meaning to any effort to change the existing boundaries between the various social sciences. They are moving anyway. A formal discipline is not like an empire preoccupied with defending its frontiers. No Great Wall is possible, and no such wall could keep the "barbarians" out: scholars move from one territory to the other without passports.

We make no recommendations. Our approach has not been normative, but empirical. It has also not been philosophical. Of course, while looking at the question of innovative hybrids sociologically, we also had occasion to refer to the philosophy of science. We looked at what innovative scientists have actually done, and we trust that this history has its lessons.

If everyone were to cross the official boundaries of their discipline, there would be more scientific innovation. This is the natural conclusion of our analysis. There is nevertheless a danger of creating serious problems in communication, an "Interdisciplinary Tower of Babel." (Riggs 1988) Scientists in one specialty might not know of the existence

FINAL REMARKS

of another, potentially relevant specialty. How many researchers studying comparative political parties know of the literature on endogenous tariff theory? Fortunately, the computer has greatly expanded the memory capacity of science.

Part of the problem is that there are very few individuals in each specialized subfield on any one campus. As Jencks and Riesman note, "the real unit of intellectual work is the subdiscipline, which usually has only one or two representatives on a small campus and seldom more than half a dozen even on a big one." (Jencks and Riesman 1969: 526) These specialized scholars must communicate not only across the boundaries of disciplines but across campuses; this may make it still more difficult for them to know of one another's existence unless a specialized journal can tie them together.

It would be valuable to know more about the shape of research communities. The communication network of an individual scholar could consist of departmental colleagues, scholars from other disciplines at the same university, scholars from the same discipline at other universities, and scholars from other disciplines at other universities. Scholars communicate remarkably little within their department. This is not an impression, but the result of an ongoing informal poll of scholars we meet. Almost all agree that there is very little scholarly interaction within their department, and this is true of all social science departments. If the disciplines are meaningful divisions today, why is there so little communication? Supposedly all political scientists study the same thing, politics; all economists, the economy; all psychologists, the mind; all linguists, language, and so on.

What keeps them apart? Ideologies are one reason, particularly in many European universities. Methodology is another dividing line; some modellers don't take verbal reasoners seriously, and vice versa. The same is true of scholars addicted to statistics and those allergic to them. Subject is a third cleavage; the inability of area specialists to communicate with specialists of other areas is one indication of this cleavage, as are most divisions in history and geography. Theories and paradigms can also keep scholars apart, even in the same subfield. In the study of international relations, scholars often do not communicate across levels of analysis: systems theorists often do not interact with those who find the causes of foreign policy in domestic politics; in many social sciences, functionalists and class analysts do not communicate. Last but not least, there are always personality problems—we cannot give any examples here, but the reader will find many in his or her department without difficulty.

Departments are not crossroads, only empty corridors. Despite the lack of communication in any department, each department has a large mailbox and a large telephone bill. Obviously there is communication with scholars outside the department. Some of this communication is with other specialists, scholars studying the same topic or using related theories. No university can have more than one German philologist, if any, so their communication network is obviously inter-university by necessity. But this is not hybridization.

Many scholars go further, and regularly communicate with scholars from other disciplines, whether at the same university or not. The University of Chicago has a reputation for stimulating such interaction on campus; for scholars elsewhere, inter-university cross-disciplinary communication may be more common. This may be the beginning of a process of hybridization. The extent of this communication varies enormously. The density of some networks of scholarly communication across disciplinary frontiers cannot help but improve the work of all who participate in it.

Many scholars in political theory write books on the great political theorists of the past. However, such books are not read by political scientists outside the subfield of theory. The typical comparativist or Americanist or student of international relations or public administration has little use for information about Aristotle, Locke, Rousseau, Montesquieu, Heidegger, or even Marx. Philosophers, historians, and classicists read such books, but the authors' colleagues in political science do not. This, too, testifies to the internal diversity of each discipline and the manner in which they necessarily form contacts with the outside.

There are dangers to this fragmentation. The growth of specialties may so distort the meaning of borrowed concepts that scholars will have great difficulty communicating with one another across disciplines even if they know of one another's existence. As concepts are imported and exported from one specialty to another, they change their meanings and this is not always beneficial: "failure of communication may well result not only from the use of one word to mean different things, but also from the use of different words to mean the same thing." (Riggs 1988: 1) For example, one of us recently witnessed criticism of a theory by three listeners, each from a different perspective, and each of which referred to the same problem. For one, the speaker's theory suffered from "circular reasoning," the second accused him of treating as "exogenous" a variable which was in fact "endogenous," and the third believed that the combination of variables "exhibited multicollinearity." As the subfield in question is increasingly torn apart by divisions among verbal reasoners, mathematical modellers, and statistical analysts, such superfluity in terminology will grow worse, and communication will not be the better for it. In archaeology, "Efforts to unify

FINAL REMARKS

nomenclature and work out new typologies and new taxonomic methods of classification are haphazard and unco-ordinated, and in some cases lead to worse confusion than before, or even real strife betwen different schools of thought. Different people use the same terms with very different meanings, and those on different sides of discussions seem at times to be talking different languages. . . ." (de Laet 1978: 189) The conceptual usage of some scholars seems to be following the example of the Queen of Hearts, when she insisted to Alice that when she used a word it meant exactly what she intended it to mean, no more and no less, regardless of what the listener thought. The same thing happens in economic anthropology, which "is full of terms which have indeed been throroughly misunderstood. . . ." (Belshaw 1989: 18)

To cope with this problem, some are trying to compile a conceptual dictionary which can serve as a basis for cross-disciplinary communication. The project is designed to break down precisely those communication barriers which block successful cooperation between scholars in different disciplines and countries. (Riggs 1987: 117) Such a project is as important as it is difficult. As an example of the many difficulties involved, we may examine the work of the contributors to *Social Science Concepts: A Systematic Analysis* (Giovanni Sartori, ed.). In this volume, a series of scholars expend much effort in the attempt to clarify important cross-disciplinary concepts such as "consensus," "development," "ethnicity," "integration," "political culture," "power," and "revolution." To do this for all social science concepts would be a daunting task. As Sartori rightly points out in his introduction, "the major reason for the neglect of (conceptual clarification) . . . is, quite simply, its very difficulty." (Sartori 1984: 10)

A further complicating factor is the existence of several major languages of scholarship, to say nothing of minor ones. When a conceptual dictionary must be multilingual, the problems are multiplied. Fortunately, some terms are simple borrowings (*laissez faire, Zeitgeist*) or only slightly modified ones (dependency/*dependencia,* charisma, economy/*economie*). Others have slightly different meanings but the differences are easily mastered (*politique/Politik* versus policy/politics, economy versus *Wirtschaft*). Some others are untranslatable, perhaps blissfully so; what, for instance, shall we do with Martin Heidegger's *Seinvergessenheit* ("oblivion of being")? In such cases the scholarly Tower of Babel feeds on the Babel of the human race more generally, and is much the worse for it.

The problem is so general that even those "two countries separated by a common language" (G. B. Shaw), Britain and the United States, can use concepts differently. Economists must deal with the different meanings of "billion" on either side of the Atlantic, as political scientists face the very different meanings of "social security" in the United States and Europe. The simple reason is that "as soon as those institutions, beliefs, and customs which play a profounder part in the peculiar life of a society make their appearance, the translation into another language, made after the likeness of a different society, becomes an enterprise fraught with dangers. For to choose an equivalent is to postulate a resemblance." (Bloch 1954: 162) For this reason, all scholars in the world will increasingly communicate in written English across distances and in broken English when they meet at conferences. Broken English, as a lingua franca, will facilitate communication across frontiers.

The proliferation of possible meanings for the same term, even within the same language, makes it easier to misuse borrowed concepts. This is a real danger for hybrids. What Margaret Mead said about her fellow anthropologists might in the end be applied equally well to all social scientists: "we fail to use the instruments that are appropriate for our own problems and misuse half-understood instruments from a half-understood field." (Mead 1961: 480) Stanislav Andreski is harsher still, taking aim at all the social sciences: "contacts between subjects often amount to inter-disciplinary cross-sterilization through symposia by mutually uncomprehending specialists. . . ." (Andreski 1972: 113) Borrowing cannot be indiscriminate; some care is necessary, and being a good hybrid is more difficult than being a good unidisciplinary specialist.

Some exploit conceptual complexities to bedazzle the innocent. Stanislav Andreski provides an amusing example:

> During his stay at the court of Catherine II of Russia, the great Swiss mathematician Euler got into an argument about the existence of God. To defeat the voltairians in the battle of wits, the great mathematician asked for a blackboard, on which he wrote:
>
> "$(x + y)^2 = x^2 + 2xy + y^2$ therefore God exists."
>
> Unable to dispute the relevance of the formula which they did not understand, and unwilling to confess their ignorance, the literati accepted his argument. (Andreski 1972: 127)

Euler, of course, knew better. Not all those who misuse the concepts and methods of another discipline are aware of their errors.

Some scholars manage to fool both themselves and others. We all know of scholars who have succeeded in restating or renaming what is already known. We know of a mathematically inclined scholar who truly believes that his models are innovative although his conclusions

FINAL REMARKS

differ in no way from the conclusions of the "classic" author in his subfield, whom he cites repeatedly. Yet this scholar is successful, having published articles in important journals and holding a position at an ivy-league university. The mathematics is good, and his work is doubtless reviewed by other mathematically inclined social scientists unfamiliar with the classic in question. Clearly communication among these different scholars has been hindered by the mathematical jargon. Obviously any specialized language facilitates communication among specialists but not with neighboring subfields. This is another aspect of the Babel problem.

As this example suggests, fragmentation can cause problems by making it more difficult to obtain access to earlier research on a given topic done by scholars from different disciplines. The problem was apparent already in the many collections of the British Museum in the 1840s, when a Royal Commission investigated practices there. As the report noted, "so much of the value to the public of these collections depends upon a good system of indication, calculated to convey to the inquiring mind as much useful information as the limited area of the labels will permit." (British Museum Report 1850: 43–44) The magnitude of the problem today is surely staggering. Computers help immensely, but generally require a common nomenclature: someone researching American tariff policy will have to search under "trade policy," "foreign economic policy," "customs," "duties," and "protection," as well as under "tariff."

Specialization of journals, like fragmentation of fields, can also hinder communication. A given scholar can only follow a few journals, and perhaps with the help of colleagues he or she may be kept abreast of developments in a few more. Most will remain *terra incognita*. This requires skilled librarians and information specialists, to act as interpreters and managers for the rest of us. Let us hope that library science will not itself fragment.

Fragmentation can also lead to intolerance. New perspectives often make scientists dismiss other perspectives as obsolete even if they are still able to produce innovative work. As we all know, Marxists are often very intolerant of non-Marxists, and the feeling is mutual. Mathematically oriented social scientists are often condescending towards the work of colleagues who will not use these methods. Social historians, in reaction against the earlier dominance of narrative history, often deny its relevance; yet there is obviously room for both. In geography, as in other social sciences, model-builders and more traditional inductivists distort one another's positions in their polemics; as Mikesell points out, "the model builder becomes a 'mechanic' and the champion of regional synthesis is exposed as a 'mystic.'" (Mikesell 1969: 241)

Disciplinary sensitivities are also sometimes affected. Classicists are not known for their respect for political theorists who study Aristotle or Plato, simply because they ask different kinds of questions. Many economists hold other social scientists in contempt because of their rudimentary use of mathematics and statistics. Of course, these intolerences are to be deplored, and we agree with David Riesman that "it makes sense to try to reduce the fanaticism, the deadly seriousness of the proponents and opponents of each scheme, including one's own. It also makes sense to train ourselves and our students in the art of translation, so that we can shift easily from one set of metaphors to another, one set of models to another." (Riesman 1956: 338)

Intolerence bred of fragmentation and hybridization presents scholars with a dilemma. Paul Diesing has pointed out that "Increased cohesiveness of a field cuts one off from colleagues in other fields using the same method and thus reduces the wide collaboration that is important for scientific advance. Conversely, wide-ranging collaboration reinforces methodological differences within a field and leads to increased strife and polemics within departments and at field conventions." (Diesing 1971: 22) We can advocate only tolerance, mutual exchange of ideas, and greater clarity in the use of concepts, in this inevitable process of innovation, specialization, fragmentation, and hybridization. As this essay has shown, the interaction of specialties brings many benefits, well worth the price of slightly more difficult communication.

BIBLIOGRAPHY

Note: This Bibliography contains only those works actually quoted, not all those works referred to.

Alker, Hayward R., Jr. 1969. "Statistics and Politics: The Need for Causal Data Analysis." Lipset, ed. 1969: 244–313.

Allison, Paul D. and John A. Stewart. 1974. "Productivity Differences Among Scientists: Evidence for Accumulative Advantage." *American Sociological Review* 39(4): 596–606 (August).

Almond, Gabriel A. 1966. "Political Theory and Political Science." *American Political Science Review* 60(4): 869–879 (December).

American Library Association. 1986. *Titles Classified by the Library of Congress Classification. National Shelflist Count: 1985.* Chicago: American Library Association, Resources and Technical Services Division.

Andreski, Stanislav. 1972. *The Social Sciences as Sorcery.* London: Andre Deutsch.

Annales. 1988. "Histoire et sciences sociales. Un tournant critique?" Annales ESC 43(2): 291–293 (mars-avril).

Apostel, Leo, Guy Berger, Asa Briggs and Guy Michaud, eds. 1972. *Interdisciplinarity: Problems of Teaching and Research in Universities.* Report of the Centre for Educational Research and Innovation (CERI). Paris: Organization for Economic Cooperation and Development.

Aron, Raymond. 1958. "Evidence and Inference in History." *Evidence and Inference,* ed. Daniel Lerner. Glencoe, IL: The Free Press. pp. 19–47.

Aronson, Sidney H. 1969. "Obstacles to a Rapprochement Between History and Sociology: A Sociologist's View." Sherif and Sherif, eds., 1969: 292–304.

Bachrach, Peter. 1968. "Charles H. McIlwain." *Encyclopedia* 9: 511–513.

Baker, Alan R. H. 1973. "Cliometric Note on the Citation Structure of Historical Geography." *The Professional Geographer* 25(4): 347–349 (November).

Baltimore, David. 1978. "Limiting Science: A Biologist's Perspective." *Daedelus* (Spring).

Barnes, Harry Elmer. 1968. "Charles A. Ellwood." *Encyclopedia* 9: 31–33.

Barraclough, Geoffrey. 1978. "History." UNESCO 1978: 277–488.

Barry, Brian. 1978. *Sociologists, Economists and Democracy.* Chicago: University of Chicago Press.

238   BIBLIOGRAPHY

Battalio, R. C., *et al.* 1973. "Experimental Investigation of Consumer Behavior in a Controlled Environment," *Journal of Consumer Research* 1(2): 52–60.

Baum, Lawrence. 1983. "Judicial Politics: Still a Distinctive Field." Finifter, ed. 1983: 189–215.

Beardsley, Philip L. 1974. "Political Science: The Case of the Missing Paradigm." *Political Theory* 2(1): 46–61 (February).

Beck, Jacob. 1968. "Hermann von Helmholtz." *Encyclopedia* 6: 345–350.

Belshaw, Cyril. 1988. "Challenges for the Future of Social and Cultural Anthropology." *International Social Science Journal* 116: 193–202 (May).

———. 1989. "Anthropology in the Spectrum of Knowledge." Unpublished manuscript, International Social Science Council.

Ben-David, Joseph. 1973. "How to Organize Research in the Social Sciences." *Daedalus* 102(2): 39–51 (Spring).

Berelson, Bernard. 1956. "The Study of Public Opinion." White, ed. 1956: 299–318.

Berger, Guy. 1972. "Opinions and Facts." Apostel *et al.*, eds. 1972: 23–76.

Bernard, Jean. 1986. *Le sang et l'histoire.* Paris: Brichet-Chastel.

Besnard, Philippe. 1986. "L'imperialisme sociologique face a l'histoire." *Historiens et sociologues aujourd'hui.* Paris: Editions du CNRS. pp. 27–35.

de Bie, Pierre. 1970. "Problem-focused Research." UNESCO 1970: 578–645.

Bloch, Marc. 1954. *The Historian's Craft.* Manchester: Manchester University Press. Original title *Apologie pour l'histoire ou metier d'historien*, 1949, translated by Peter Putnam.

Boisot, Marcel. 1972. "Discipline and Interdisciplinarity." Apostel *et al.*, eds. 1972: 89–97.

Bottomore, Tom and Patrick Goode, eds. 1978. *Austro-Marxism.* Oxford: Clarendon Press.

Boudon, Raymond. 1970. "Mathematical Models and Methods." UNESCO 1970: 529–577.

———. 1979. "Sociologie et histoire: l'analyse sociologique du singulier." *La logique du social.* Paris: Hachette.

———. 1988. "Will Sociology ever be a *normal science?*" *Theory and Society* 17: 747–771.

——— and François Bourricaud. 1982. *Dictionnaire critique de la sociologie.* Paris: P.U.F.

Boulding, Kenneth E. 1977. "Peace Research." *International Social Science Journal* 29(4): 601–614.

Boxer, Marilyn J. 1982. "For and About Women: The Theory and Practice of Women Studies in the United States." *Signs* 7(3).

Braudel, Fernand. 1962. "Histoire et sociologie." *Traité de sociologie*, ed. G. Gurvitch. Paris: P.U.F. Vol. I, pp. 83–98.

———. 1979. *Civilization and Capitalism, 15th–18th Century. Volume II: The Wheels of Commerce.* (Sian Reynolds, trans., 1982) New York: Harper and Row, Publishers.

Briggs, Asa and Guy Michaud. 1972. "Problems and Solutions." Apostel *et al.*, eds. 1972: 181–277.

BIBLIOGRAPHY

British Museum. 1850. Report of the Commissioners Appointed to Inquire into the Constitution and Government of the British Museum. London: Pares and Sons.

Broadus, Robert N. 1971. "The Literature of the Social Sciences: A Survey of Citation Studies." *International Social Science Journal* 23(2): 236–243.

Brunet, Roger. 1982. "La Geographie." *Les sciences de l'homme et de la societé en France*, ed. M. Godelier. Paris: La Documentation Française, pp. 381–420.

Burke, Peter. 1980. *Sociology and History*. London: George Allen and Unwin.

Burnham, Walter Dean. 1978. "The Politics of Crisis." *Journal of Interdisciplinary History* 8(4): 747–763 (Spring).

Cahnman, Werner J. and Alvin Boskoff, eds. 1964. *Sociology and History: Theory and Research*. New York: The Free Press of Glencoe.

———. 1964. "Sociology and History: Reunion and Rapprochement." Cahnman and Boskoff, eds. 1964: 1–18.

Cairns, Robert B. and Jaan Valsiner. 1984. "Child Psychology." *Annual Review of Psychology* 35: 553–577.

Campbell, Donald T. 1969. "Ethnocentrism of Disciplines and the Fish-Scale Model of Omniscience." in Sherif and Sherif, eds. 1969: 328–348.

de Certaines. J. D. 1976. "La Biophysique en France: Critique de la Notion de Discipline Scientifique." in Lemaine *et al.* 1976: 99–122.

Chang, K. C. 1967. "Major Aspects of the Interrelationships of Archaeology and Ethnology." *Current Anthropology.* 8(3): 227 (June).

Chubin, Daryl. 1973. "On the Use of the *Science Citation Index* in Sociology." *The American Sociologist* 8(4): 187–191 (November).

Clark, Burton R., ed. 1987. *The Academic Profession: National, Disciplinary, and Institutional Settings*. Berkeley and Los Angeles: University of California Press.

———. 1987. *The Academic Life: Small Worlds, Different Worlds*. Princeton: The Carnegie Foundation for the Advancement of Teaching.

Claval, Paul. 1988. "Geography, a Crossroads Science." International Social Science Council, unpublished.

Cloud, Preston. 1983. "Early Biogeologic History: The Emergence of a Paradigm." *Earth's Earliest Biosphere: Its Origin and Evolution*, ed. J. William Schopf, Princeton: Princeton University Press. pp. 14–31.

Cole, Jonathan R. and Stephen. 1972. "The Ortega Hypothesis: Citation Analysis Suggests that Only a Few Scientists Contribute to Scientific Progress." *Science* 178(4059): 368–375 (October 27).

Collins, H. 1983. "The Sociology of Scientific Knowledge: Studies of Contemporary Science." *Annual Review of Sociology* 1983: 265–285.

Crawford, Elisabeth T. and Albert D. Biderman, eds. 1969. *Social Scientists and International Affairs: A Case for a Sociology of Social Science*. New York: John Wiley and Sons, Inc.

Cronin, Blaise. 1981. "The Need for a Theory of Citing." *Journal of Documentation* 37(1): 16–24.

Crosby, Alfred W. 1986. *Ecological Imperialism: The Biological Expansion of Europe, 900–1900*. Cambridge: Cambridge University Press.

240 BIBLIOGRAPHY

Datan, Nancy, Dean Rodeheaver and Fergus Hughes. 1987. "Adult Development and Aging." *Annual Review of Psychology* 38: 153-180.

Davies, James Chowning. 1983. "The Proper Biological Study of Politics." *Political Psychology* 4(4): 731-743 (December).

Davis, Murray S. 1986. "'That's Classic!' The Phenomenology and Rhetoric of Successful Social Theories." *Philosophy of the Social Sciences* 16: 285-301.

Deutsch, Karl W., Andrei S. Markovits and John Platt. 1986. *Advances in the Social Sciences, 1900-1980. What, Who, Where, How?* Cambridge: University Press of America.

Deutsch, Morton. 1983. "What is Political Psychology?" *International Social Science Journal* 96: 221-236.

Diesing, Paul. 1971. *Patterns of Discovery in the Social Sciences.* Chicago: Aldine, Atherton, Inc.

Dingwall, William Orr, ed. 1978. *A Survey of Linguistic Science.* Stamford, CT: Greylock Publishers.

_____ and Harry A. Whittaker. 1978. "Neurolinguistics." Dingwall, ed. 1978: 207-246.

Dogan, Mattei. 1988. "Giant Cities as Maritime Gateways." *A World of Giant Cities*, ed. Mattei Dogan and John Kasarda. Beverly Hills: Sage Publications. pp. 30-55.

_____ and Daniel Derivry. 1988. "France in Ten Slices: An Analysis of Aggregate Data." *Electoral Studies* 7(3): 251-267.

_____ and Dominique Pelassy. 1984. *How to Compare Nations.* Chatham: Chatham House.

_____ and Stein Rokkan, eds. 1969. *Quantitative Ecological Analysis in the Social Sciences.* Cambridge: M.I.T. Press.

Downing, Paul B. and Elizabeth Ann Stafford. 1981. "Citations as an Indicator of Classic Works and Major Contributions in Social Choice." *Public Choice* 37(2): 219-230 (1981).

Easton, David. 1953 (1971). *The Political System: An Inquiry into the State of Political Science.* New York: Alfred A. Knopf.

_____. 1959. "Political Anthropology." *Biennial Review of Anthropology*, ed. Bernard J. Siegal. Stanford: Stanford University Press. pp. 210-267.

_____. 1965. *A Framework for Political Analysis.* Englewood Cliffs, NJ: Prentice-Hall, Inc.

Eckstein, Harry. 1975. "A Critique of Area Studies from a West European Perspective." Pye, ed. 1975: 199-217.

Eichengreen, Barry. 1985. "Editor's Introduction." *The Gold Standard in Theory and History*, ed. Barry Eichengreen. New York: Methuen. pp. 1-35.

Elster, Jon. 1979 (rev. ed. 1984). *Ulysses and the Sirens. Studies in Rationality and Irrationality.* Cambridge: Cambridge University Press.

_____. 1985. *Making Sense of Marx.* Cambridge: Cambridge University Press.

Emmerich, Herbert. 1956. "New Bridges between Theory and Practice." White, ed. 1956: 384-392.

Encyclopedia (International) of the Social Sciences, ed. David L. Sills. 1968. New York: The Macmillan Company and The Free Press. 16 vols.

BIBLIOGRAPHY

Etzioni, Amitai. 1983. "Toward a Political Psychology of Economics." *Political Psychology* 4(1): 77–86 (March).

Farley, Joseph and Daniel L. Alkon. 1985. "Cellular Mechanisms of Learning, Memory, and Information Storage." *Annual Review of Psychology* 36: 419–494.

Fetter, Frank W. 1968. "T. E. Cliffe Leslie." *Encyclopedia* 9: 260–261.

Finifter, Ada W., ed. 1983. *Political Science: The State of the Discipline.* Washington: American Political Science Association.

Firth, Raymond, ed. 1967. *Themes in Economic Anthropology.* London: Tavistock Publications.

———. 1967. "Themes in Economic Anthropology: A General Comment." Firth, ed. 1967: 1–28.

Flenley, R. 1953. "History and Its Neighbours Today." *Canadian Historical Review* 34(4): 324–338 (December).

Fohlen, Claude. 1968. "Émile Levasseur." *Encyclopedia* 9: 261–263.

Freedman, Maurice. 1978. "Social and Cultural Anthropology." UNESCO 1978: 3–176.

Frieden, Jeffry A. and David A. Lake. 1987. "Introduction." *International Political Economy: Perspectives on Global Power and Wealth,* eds. Jeffry A. Frieden and David A. Lake. New York: St. Martin's Press. pp. 1–15.

Gans, Carl. 1987. "Punctuated Equilibria and Political Science: A Neontological View." *Politics and the Life Sciences* 5(2): 220–227 (February).

Garson, G. David. 1974. "On the Origins of Interest-Group Theory: A Critique of a Process." *American Political Science Review* 68(4): 1505–1519 (December).

Gass, J. R. 1972. "Preface." Apostel, *et al.*, eds. 1972: 9–10.

Ghiselin, Michael T. 1987. "Principles and Prospects for General Economy." *Economic Imperialism: The Economic Method Applied Outside the Field of Economics,* ed. Gerard Radnitzky and Peter Bernholz. New York: Paragon House. pp. 21–31.

Gilbert, Edmund W. 1968. "Halford Mackinder." *Encyclopedia* 9: 515–517.

Giles, Micheal W., Francie Mizell and David Patterson. 1989. "Political Scientists' Journal Evaluations Revisited." *PS* 22(3): 613–617 (September).

Gilfillan, S. C. 1935/1963. *The Sociology of Invention.* Cambridge: MIT Press.

———. 1965. "Roman Culture and Dyxgenic Lead Poisoning." *Mankind Quarterly* 5(3): 3–20 (January-March).

Gilpin, Robert. 1987. *The Political Economy of International Relations.* Princeton: Princeton University Press.

Godelier, Maurice. 1974. "Anthropology and Biology: Towards a New Form of Co-operation." *International Social Science Journal* 26(4): 611–635.

Gottschalk, Louis. 1956. "The Historian's Use of Generalization." White, ed. 1956: 436–450.

Greenberg, Joseph H. 1968. "Anthropology: The Field." *Encyclopedia* 1: 304–313.

Greenstein, Fred I. 1969. "Personality and Politics: Problems of Evidence, Inference, and Conceptualization." Lipset, ed. 1969: 163–206.

242   BIBLIOGRAPHY

Greer, Scott. 1969. "Sociology and Political Science." Lipset, ed. 1970: 49–64.

Gunnell, John G. 1983. "Political Theory: The Evolution of a Sub-Field." Finifter, ed. 1983: 3–45.

Hadamard, Jacques. 1945. *The Psychology of Invention in the Mathematical Field*. New York: Dover.

Haefele, J. W. 1962. *Creativity and Innovation*. New York: Rheingold.

Hall, W. G. and R. W. Oppenheim. 1987. "Developmental Psychobiology: Prenatal, Perinatal, and Early Postnatal Aspects of Behavioral Development." *Annual Review of Psychology* 38: 91–128.

Hare, F. Kenneth. 1988. "Canada: The Land." *Daedalus* 117(4): 31–50 (Fall).

Hauser, Philip M. 1956. "Ecological Aspects of Urban Research." in White, ed., 1956: 229–254.

Hayek, F. A. 1956. "The Dilemma of Specialization." White, ed. 1956: 462–473.

Heckhausen, Heinz. 1972. "Discipline and Interdisciplinarity." in Apostel *et al.*, eds. 1972: 83–89.

Hippel, Eric von. 1988. *The Sources of Innovation*. Oxford: Oxford University Press.

Hirshleifer, Jack. 1985. "The Expanding Domain of Economics." *American Economic Review* 72(6): 53–68 (December).

_____. 1988. "The Analytics of Continuing Conflict." *Synthese* 76: 201–233.

Hofstadter, Richard. 1968. "History and Sociology in the United States." Lipset and Hofstadter, eds. 1968: 3–19.

Hogarth, Robin M. and Melvin W. Reder. 1986. "Introduction: Perspectives from Economics and Psychology." *Rational Choice: The Contrast between Economics and Psychology*, eds. Robin M. Hogarth and Melvin W. Reder. Chicago: University of Chicago Press. pp. 1–23.

Inkeles, Alex. 1986. "Advances in Sociology—A Critique." Deutsch, Markovits, and Platt, eds. 1986: 13–31.

Intriligator, Michael. 1985. "Interdependence among the Behavioral Sciences." Paper Presented at the World Congress of Political Science, Paris.

Izard, Michel. 1988. "Presentation." *Revue française de science politique* 38(5), special issue on "L'Anthropologie politique aujourd'hui," octobre.

Janik, Allan and Stephen Toulmin. 1973. *Wittgenstein's Vienna*. New York: Simon and Schuster.

Janis, Irving L. 1968. "Carl I. Hovland." *Encyclopedia* 6: 526–531.

Jencks, Christopher and David Riesman. 1969. *The Academic Revolution*. Garden City, NY: Doubleday-Anchor.

Jensen, Richard. 1969. "History and the Political Scientist." Lipset, ed., 1969: 1–28.

Johnson, Chalmers. 1975. "Political Science and East Asia Area Studies." Pye, ed. 1975: 78–97.

Johnston, William M. 1972. *The Austrian Mind: An Intellectual and Social History*. Berkeley: University of California Press.

Jones, Emrys. 1979. "New Perspectives on an Old Science." Rokkan, ed. 1979.

Kamarck, Andrew M. 1967 (rev. ed. 1971). *The Economics of African Development*. New York: Praeger Publishers.

BIBLIOGRAPHY

———. 1976. *The Tropics and Economic Development.* Baltimore and London: The Johns Hopkins University Press, for the World Bank.

Katicic, Radoslav. 1988. "Some Fundamental Issues in Linguistics." *International Social Science Journal* 116: 231–238 (May).

Kennedy, Paul. 1980. *The Rise of the Anglo-German Antagonism, 1860–1914.* London: George Allen and Unwin.

Keohane, Robert O. 1983a. Review of Olson's *Rise and Decline of Nations. Journal of Economic Literature* 21: 558–560.

———. 1983b. "Theory of World Politics: Structural Realism and Beyond." Finifter, ed. 1983: 503–540.

Khoshkish, A. 1979. *The Socio-political Complex: An Interdisciplinary Approach to Political Life.* Oxford: Pergamon Press.

Kim, Chin-Wu. 1978. "Experimental Phonetics." Dingwall, ed. 1978: 159–205.

Kimpton, Lawrence A. 1956. "The Social Sciences Today." White, ed. 1956: 348–352.

Knapp, Peter. 1984. "Can Social Theory Escape from History? View of History in Social Science." *History and Theory* 23(1): 34-52.

Kuhn, Thomas S. 1957. *The Copernicus Revolution: Planetary Astronomy in the Development of Western Thought.* Cambridge: Harvard University Press.

———. 1962 (rev. ed. 1969). *The Structure of Scientific Revolutions.* Chicago: University of Chicago Press.

———. 1969. "Postscript." Kuhn 1962 (rev. ed.): 194–210.

———. 1970. "Reflection on My Critics." Lakatos and Musgrave, eds. 1970: 231–278.

de Laet, Sigfried J. 1978. "Archaeology and Prehistory." UNESCO 1978: 177–226.

Lakatos, Imre. 1970. "Falsification and the Methodology of Scientific Research Programmes." Lakatos and Musgrave, eds. 1970: 91–196.

——— and Alan Musgrave, eds. 1970. *Criticism and the Growth of Knowledge.* Cambridge: Cambridge University Press.

Laponce, J. A. 1980. "Political Science: An Import-Export Analysis of Journals and Footnotes." *Political Studies*: 401–419.

———. 1983. "Political Science and Political Geography: Neglected Areas, Areas for Development." *International Social Science Journal* 35(3): 549–558.

Lasswell, Harold D. 1956. "Impact of Psychoanalytic Thinking on the Social Sciences." White, ed. 1956: 84–115.

Lazarsfeld, P. F. 1970. "Sociology." UNESCO 1970: 61–165.

Lemaine, G., R. Macleod, M. Mulkay, P. Weigast, eds. 1976. *Perspectives on the Emergence of Scientific Disciplines.* The Hague: Mouton.

Leontief, Wassily. 1948. "Note on the Pluralistic Interpretation of History and the Problem of Interdisciplinary Cooperation." *Journal of Philosophy* 45(23): 617–624 (November).

Lichnerowicz, Andre. 1972. "Mathematic [sic] and Transdisciplinarity." Apostel *et al.*, eds. 1972: 121–127.

Lijphart, Arend. 1974. "The Structure of the Theoretical Revolution in International Relations." *International Studies Quarterly* 18(1):41–74 (March).

244 BIBLIOGRAPHY

Lippett, Ronald. 1968. "Kurt Lewin." *Encyclopedia* 9: 266–271.

Lipset, Seymour Martin. 1968. "History and Sociology: Some Methodological Considerations." Lipset and Hofstadter, eds. 1968: 20–58.

———, ed. 1969. *Politics and the Social Sciences.* New York: Oxford University Press.

——— and Richard Hofstadter, eds. 1968. *Sociology and History: Methods.* New York: Basic Books, Inc.

Lofchie, Michael. 1988. *The Policy Factor: Agricultural Performance in Kenya and Tanzania.* Boulder, CO: Lynne Rienner.

Lorwin, Val R. 1968. "Historians and Other Social Scientists: The Comparative Analysis of Nation-building in Western Societies." *Comparative Research Across Cultures and Nations,* ed. Stein Rokkan. Paris: Mouton. pp. 102–117.

Losco, Joseph and Donna Day Baird. 1982. "The Impact of Sociobiology on Political Science." *American Behavioral Scientist* 25(3): 335–360 (January–February).

Mackenzie, W. J. M. 1970. "Political Science." UNESCO 1970: 166–224.

Marvick, Elizabeth Wirth, ed. 1977. *Psychopolitical Analysis. Selected Writings of Nathan Leites.* Beverly Hills: Sage.

Matos Mar, Jose. 1988. "Anthropology in the Twenty-first Century." *International Social Science Journal* 116: 203–210 (May).

McCormick, Richard L. 1986. *The Party Period and Public Policy: American Politics from the Age of Jackson to the Progressive Era.* New York and Oxford: Oxford University Press.

McHenry, Dean E., Jr. 1988. "Summary and Analysis of a Survey of Graduate Core Courses in Comparative Politics." *The Political Science Teacher* 1(2): 5–6 (Spring).

McKennan, Robert A. 1968. "Roland B. Dixon." *Encyclopedia* 4: 243–245.

Mead, Margaret. 1961. "Anthropology Among the Sciences." *American Anthropologist* 63(3): 475–482 (June).

Merkl, Peter. 1984. "Interdisciplinary Approaches and the Fall of the Weimar Republic." Unpublished manuscript.

Merton, Robert K. 1973. *Sociology of Science: Theoretical and Empirical Investigations.* Chicago: University of Chicago Press.

Meyer, Alfred G. 1975. "Comparative Politics and Its Discontent: The Study of the U.S.S.R. and Eastern Europe." Pye, ed. 1975: 98–130.

Michaud, Guy. 1972. "General Conclusions." Apostel *et al.,* eds. 1972: 279–288.

Mikes, M. 1967. "Acquisition des categoires grammaticales dans le langage de l'enfant." *Enfance* 20: 289–298.

Mikesell, Marvin W. 1969. "The Borderlands of Geography as a Social Science." Sherif and Sherif, eds., 1969: 227–248.

Mitchell, William C. 1969. "The Shape of Political Theory to Come: From Political Sociology to Political Economy." Lipset, ed. 1969: 101–136.

Moore, Barrington. 1966. *Social Origins of Dictatorship and Democracy: Lord and Peasant in the Making of the Modern World.* Boston: Beacon Press.

BIBLIOGRAPHY

Moravcsik, Michael J. and Poovanalingam Murugesan. 1975. "Some Results on the Function and Quality of Citations." *Social Studies of Science* 5: 86–92.

Muensterberger, Warner and Bill Domhoff. 1968. "Géza Róheim." *Encyclopedia* 13: 543–545.

Oden, Gregg C. 1987. "Concept, Knowledge, and Thought." *Annual Review of Psychology* 38: 203–227.

Olson, Mancur, Jr. 1969. "The Relationship Between Economics and the Other Social Sciences: The Province of a 'Social Report.'" in Lipset, ed. 1969: 137–162.

Ordeshook, Peter C. 1986. *Game Theory and Political Theory: An Introduction.* Cambridge: Cambridge University Press.

Oromaner, Mark. 1977. "The Career of Sociological Literature: A Diachronous Study." *Social Studies of Science* 7: 126–132.

Parker, Harold T. 1957. "A Tentative Reflection on the Interdisciplinary Approach and the Historian." *South Atlantic Quarterly* 56(1): 105–111 (January).

Parsons, Talcott. 1965. "Unity and Diversity in the Modern Intellectual Disciplines: The Role of the Social Sciences." *Daedalus* 94(1): 39–65 (Winter).

Patinkin, Don. 1983. "Multiple Discoveries and the Central Message." *American Journal of Sociology* 89(2): 306–323.

Piaget, Jean. 1970a. "The Place of the Sciences of Man in the System of Sciences." UNESCO 1970: 1–57.

———. 1970b. "Psychology." UNESCO 1970: 225–282.

———. 1972. "The Epistemology of Interdisciplinary Relationships." Apostel *et al.*, eds. 1972: 127–139.

Plakans, Andrej. 1986. "History and Anthropology: Trends in Interaction." *Historical Methods* 19(3): 126–128.

Popkin, Samuel L. 1979. *The Rational Peasant: The Political Economy of Rural Society in Vietnam.* Berkeley: University of California Press.

Popper, Sir Karl. 1970. "Normal Science and Its Dangers." Lakatos and Musgrave, eds., 1970: 51–58.

Pye, Lucian W., ed. 1975. *Political Sciences and Area Studies: Rivals and Partners?* Bloomington: Indiana University Press.

———. 1975. "The Confrontation between Discipline and Area Studies." Pye, ed. 1975: 3–22.

Radnitzky, Gerard and Peter Bernholz. 1987. "Preface." *Economic Imperialism: The Economic Approach Applied Outside the Field of Economics,* ed. Radnitzky and Bernholz. New York: Paragon House Publishers.

Rasmussen, Eric. 1989. *Games and Information. An Introduction to Game Theory.* Oxford: Basil Blackwell.

Revel, Jacques. 1986. "L'histoire sociale dans les *Annales*: une définition empirique." *Historiens et sociologues aujourd'hui.* Paris: Editions du CNRS. pp. 169–178.

Riesman, David. 1956. "Some Observations on the 'Older' and the 'Newer' Social Sciences." White, ed. 1956: 319–339.

Riggs, Fred W. 1987. "A Conceptual Encyclopedia for the Social Sciences." *International Social Science Journal* 39(1): 109–125 (February).

——. 1988. "The Interdisciplinary Tower of Babel." Paper at the World Congress of Political Science, Washington, 1988.

Riker, William H. 1962. *The Theory of Political Coalitions.* New Haven: Yale University Press.

Rokkan, Stein, ed. 1979. *A Quarter Century of Social Science.* New Delhi: Concept.

Roose, Kenneth D. 1969. "Observations on Interdisciplinary Work in the Social Sciences." Sherif and Sherif, eds. 1969: 323–327.

Roth, Günther. 1979. "Charisma and Counterculture." *Max Weber's Vision of History: Ethics and Methods.* Günther Roth and Wolfgang Schluchter. Berkeley and Los Angeles: University of California Press. pp. 119–143.

Rukang, Wu. 1988. "Paleontologie et neoanthropologie." *Revue internationale des sciences sociales* 116, May.

Rutman, Darrett B. 1986. "History and Anthropology: Clio's Dalliances." *Historical Methods* 19(3): 120–123 (Summer).

Sartori, Giovanni. 1969. "From the Sociology of Politics to Political Sociology." Lipset, ed. 1969: 65–100.

——, ed. 1984. *Social Science Concepts: A Systematic Analysis.* Beverly Hills: Sage Publications.

Schneider, Benjamin. 1985. "Organizational Behavior." *Annual Review of Psychology* 36: 573–611.

Schorske, Carl E. 1961. *Fin-de-Siecle Vienna: Politics and Culture.* New York: Vintage Books.

Sears, David O. 1987. "Political Psychology." *Annual Review of Psychology* 38: 229–255.

Seignobos, Charles. 1901. *La methode historique appliquee aux sciences sociales.* Paris: Ancienne Librairie Germer Bailliere.

Seyfarth, Constans and Gert Schmidt. 1977. *Max Weber Bibliographie: Eine Dokumentation der sekundär Literatur.* Stuttgart: Enke.

Shapiro, R. J. 1968. *Creative Research Scientists.* Washington: National Institute for Personnel Research.

Sherif, Muzafer and Carolyn W. 1969. "Interdisciplinary Coordination as a Validity Check: Retrospect and Prospects." Sherif and Sherif, eds., 1969: 3–20.

——, eds. 1969. *Interdisciplinary Relationships in the Social Sciences.* Chicago: Aldine.

Shubik, Martin. 1982. *Game Theory in the Social Sciences: Concepts and Solutions.* Cambridge MA: MIT Press.

Simiand, François. 1903. "Methode historique et science sociale." *Revue de synthese historique.* pp. 1–22.

Simmons, Ozzie G. and James A. Davis. 1957. "Interdisciplinary Collaboration in Mental Illness Research." *American Journal of Sociology* 63(3): 297–303.

Sklar, Richard L. 1983. "On the Concept of Power in Political Economy." *Toward a Humanistic Science of Politics. Essays in Honor of Francis Durham Wormuth*, ed. Dalmas H. Nelson and Richard L. Sklar. Lanham: University Press of America. pp. 179–206.

BIBLIOGRAPHY

Smelser, Neil, ed. 1988. *Handbook of Sociology.* Beverly Hills: Sage Publications.

Social Science Research Council. 1954. *The Social Sciences in Historical Study. A Report of the Committee on Historiography.* New York: SSRC, Bulletin 64.

de Solla Price, Derek. 1975. *Science Since Babylon* (enlarged edition). New Haven: Yale University Press.

Somit, Albert, Steven A. Peterson and Denise Peer. 1987. "1986: Boom Year of Biopolitics." *Politics and Life Science* 6(1): 58–63 (August).

Staniland, Martin. 1985. *What is Political Economy? A Study of Social Theory and Underdevelopment.* New Haven: Yale University Press.

Stillings, Neil A., *et al.* 1987. *Cognitive Science: An Introduction.* Cambridge, MA: MIT Press.

Stokes, Donald E. 1983. "Basic Inquiry and Applied Use in the Social Sciences." Finifter, ed. 1983: 581–591.

Streeten, Paul. 1976. "Foreword." Kamarck 1976: ix–xii.

Temin, P. 1981. "Notes on the Causes of the Great Depression." *The Great Depression Revisited,* ed. K. Brunner. The Hague: Martinus Nijhoff.

Thrupp, Sylvia. 1957. "History and Sociology: New Opportunities for Co-operation." *American Journal of Sociology* 63(1): 11–16 (July).

Tilly, Charles. 1981. *As Sociology Meets History.* New York: Academic Press.

Truman, David B. 1965. "Disillusion and Regeneration: The Quest for a Discipline." *American Political Science Review* 59(4): 865–873 (December).

Turner, Henry Ashby, Jr. 1985. *German Big Business and the Rise of Hitler.* New York: Oxford University Press.

Turner, Ralph. 1988. "American Sociology in Search of Identity." Paper presented to the Chinese Academy of Social Sciences.

UNESCO. 1970. *Main Trends of Research in the Social and Human Sciences. Part One: Social Sciences.* Paris/The Hague: Mouton/UNESCO.

———. 1978. *Main Trends of Research in the Social and Human Sciences. Part Two, Volume One. Anthropological and Historical Sciences. Aesthetics and the Sciences of Art. Part Two, Volume Two. Legal Science and Philosophy.* (general ed. Jacques Havet) Hague/Paris/New York: Mouton Publishers/ UNESCO.

Vernant, Jean-Pierre. 1985. Interview in Le Currier du CNRS. Janvier-Mars.

Veyne, Paul. 1971. *Comment on écrit l'histoire.* Paris: Le Seuil.

Ward, Robert E. 1975. "Culture and the Comparative Study of Politics." Pye, ed. 1975: 23–47.

Wasby, Stephen L. 1970. *Political Science: The Discipline and Its Dimensions.* New York: Charles Scribner.

Weingrod, Alex. 1967. "Political Sociology, Social Anthropology and the Study of New Nations." *British Journal of Sociology* 18(2): 121–134 (June).

White, Leonard D., ed. 1956. *The State of the Social Sciences.* Chicago: University of Chicago Press.

Wiegele, Thomas C. 1979. *Biopolitics: Search for a More Human Political Science.* Boulder, CO: Westview Press.

Wilcox, Stephen and Stuart Katz. 1984. "Can Indirect Realism be Demonstrated in the Psychological Laboratory?" *Philosophy of the Social Sciences* 14: 149–157.

Wilkinson, David. 1980. *Deadly Quarrels. Lewis F. Richardson and the Statistical Study of War.* Berkeley and Los Angeles: University of California Press.

Wirth, Louis, ed. 1940. *Eleven Twenty-Six: A Decade of Social Science Research.* New York: Arno Press (Reprinted 1974).

Zoppo, Ciro. 1988. "From Specialization to Interdisciplinarity: Security Studies in International Relations." Unpublished manuscript.

Zuckerman, Harriet. 1977. *Scientific Elite. Nobel Laureates in the United States.* New York: The Free Press.

Zuckerman, Harriet. 1988. "The Sociology of Science." Smelser, ed. 1988.

AUTHOR INDEX

Abraham, David 71
Ader, Robert 101
Adorno, Theodore 71, 74
Akamatsu, Kaname 48
Akerlof, George 26
Alexander, Franz 160
Alexander, Jeffrey 108
Allardt, Erik 179
Allen, R.G.D. 48
Allison, Paul 237
Allport, Floyd H. 69
Almond, Gabriel A. 35, 40, 42, 90–91,
  127–128, 154
Althusser, Louis 103
Anderson, Perry 64
Andreski, Stanislav 21, 32, 118, 138, 234
Angell, J. R. 69
Apostel, Leo 131
Apter, David 13, 35, 77, 80, 144
Arendt, Hannah 35
Aristotle 33, 37, 40, 126, 169, 232, 236
Aron, Raymond 26, 44, 179, 188, 192
Aronson, Sidney 188, 197, 200
Arrow, Kenneth 26, 182, 227
Asbjørnson, Peter Christen 144
Ashley, William James 180
Aubertin, Ernest 24
Axelrod, Robert 208

Babbage, Charles 178
Bachofen, Johann Jakob 68
Bachrach, Peter 67
Bailey, Samuel 86
Baird, Donna Day 203
Baker, Alan R. H. 21
Baltimore, David 69
de Balzac, Honore 88

Banks, Arthur 117
Barnes, Harry Elmer 69
Barraclough, Geoffrey 89, 189, 195
Barry, Brian 136, 158–159
Bastiat, Claude Frédéric 127
Bates, Robert H. 212, 221–222
Bateson, Gregory 92
Battalio, R. C. 226
Baum, Lawrence 75–76, 103
Baur, Ferdinand 73
Bayes, Thomas 26, 99, 182
Beach, F. 99
Beard, Charles 61, 155, 179
Beardsley, Phillip 154
Beck, Jacob 133
Becker, Gary 111
Bellah, Robert 187
Belshaw, Cyril 32, 64, 89, 117, 133, 156,
  167, 233
Ben-David, Joseph 74, 84, 156–157
Bendix, Reinhard 79, 88, 180, 189
Bentham, Jeremy 86
Bentley, Arthur 48, 61, 133
Berelson, Bernard 26, 28, 104
Berger, Guy 238
Berger, Suzanne 13
van den Bergh, George 25
Berliner, Joseph S. 43
Bernard, Claude 144
Bernard, Jean 131, 207
Bernholz, Peter 136
Bernoulii, Johann 26
Besnard, Phillipe 4, 194
von Beyme, Klaus 182
Biderman, Albert D. 3
de Bie, Pierre 84, 117
Bigelow, Julian 127

AUTHOR INDEX

Blanc, Louis 127
Bloch, Marc 46, 58, 66, 94, 116, 188, 192–195, 234
Bloomfield, Leonard 109
Blumberg, Abraham S. 103
Bobbio, Norberto 182
Boff, Leonardo 153
Boisot, Marcel 238
Booth, Charles 189
Bopp, Francis 108
von Bortkiewicz, Ladislaus 134
Boskoff, Alvin 4, 195
Bottomore, Tom 73
Boudon, Raymond 108, 136, 188, 190
Boulding, Kenneth E. 156
Bourricaud, François 108
Bowman, Isaiah 94
Boxer, Marilyn 238
Brahe, Tycho 10
Braudel, Fernand 4, 64, 94, 116, 126–127, 188, 190
Briggs, Asa 84
Broadus, Robert N. 39, 41
Broca, Paul 24, 156
Brock, William 111–112
Brown, Ralph H. 70
van der Brück, Moller 26
Brunet, Roger 97
Bryce, Lord 47
Buchanan, James 183
Bueno de Mesquita, Bruce 136, 180
Bull, Edvard 11
Burdeau, George 182
Burgess, Ernest W. 95
Burke, Peter 4, 190, 198
Burnham, Walter Dean 26
Burnouf, Eugene 108
Butler, David 25, 182

Cahnman, Werner J. 4, 195
Cairns, Robert B. 27
Campbell, Angus 42
Campbell, Donald T. 4, 59–60, 84, 128, 144
Canard, Jean 135
Caplan, G. 101
Carlson, A. J. 156
Carmichael, L. 99
Casesse, Sabino 182
Cassel, J. 101
Cassing, James 149

Castells, Manuel 180
Cavalli, Luciano 180
Chambers, William Nisbet 191
Chandrasekhar, Subrahmanyan 47
Chang, K. C. 93
Chasin, Barbara H. 215
Chaucer, Geoffrey 10
Child, C. M. 151
Chomsky, Noam 39–40, 69, 109–110, 117, 149, 158, 183
Chorley, Richard J. 95
Chubin, Daryl 9, 117
Clark, Burton R. 9, 60
von Clausewitz, Karl 175–176
Claval, Paul 93–94, 167
Cloud, Preston 20
Cobb, S. 101
Coghill, George 99
Cohen, Benjamin 209
Cohen, G. A. 74
Cohen, Nicholas 101
Cole, Jonathan R. 38
Cole, Stephen 38
Coleman, James 80
Colliard, Jean Claude 182
Collins, H. 3
Comte, Auguste 56, 86, 105, 107, 189
de Condorcet, Marquis 21, 135
Conrad, Alfred 191
Converse, Phillip 179–180
Cooley, Charles Horton 48, 176
Cooper, Richard N. 219
Copernicus 10, 19, 22, 57, 126, 155, 157, 226
Coser, Lewis 108, 180
Cournot, Antoine Augustin 48, 135, 177
Crane, Robert 128
Crawford, Elisabeth T. 3
Crosby, Alfred W. 209–211
Crozier, Michel 180
Cunningham, William 69
Curtiss, Susan 205
Cutright, Phillips 48
Cuzzort, Raymond 95

Dahl, Robert 40, 117, 151
Dahrendorf, Ralf 26, 108, 179
Dalton, Melville 46
Daniels, Robert V. 43
Darwin, Charles 14, 24, 40, 69, 90, 98, 125, 150, 152, 204, 206

AUTHOR INDEX

Darwin, Erasmus 125, 206
Datan, Nancy 99, 145
Davies, James Chowning 204
Davis, James A. 132
Davis, Murray S. 47
Debreu, G. 26
de Laet, Sigfried J. 92, 233
Delbruck, Johann 172
Derivry, Daniel 96
Descartes, Rene 101, 132, 171
Deutsch, Karl W. 4, 15–17, 21, 40, 42,
79, 96, 104–105, 158, 180
Deutsch, Morton 101
Dewey, John 69
Diamant, Alfred 71, 180
Diebold, A. R. 109
Diesing, Paul 133, 228, 236
Dingwall, William Orr 205–206
Dixon, Roland B. 182
Djilas, Milovan 26
Doellinger, Johann Josef Ignatz 73
Dogan, Mattei 46, 48, 96, 132, 179–180
Domhoff, G. William 26, 149
Downing, Paul B. 138
Downs, Anthony 25, 42, 95, 135, 159,
178
Dreze, Jacques 26
Duncan, O. D. 95
Dupuit, Jules 178–179
Durkheim, Emile 15, 22, 40, 47, 105,
107, 127
Duverger, Maurice 25

Easton, David 4, 40, 56–57, 75, 91, 104,
125, 128, 144
Eckstein, Harry 80, 159
Eco, Umberto 88
Ehrlich, Eugen 69
Eichengreen, Barry 218
Einstein, Albert 11, 47, 181
Eisenstadt, S. N. 70, 179
Elias, Taslim Olawale 91
Ellul, Jacques 26
Ellwood, Charles A. 69
Elster, Jon 74, 227
Emmerich, Herbert 102
Engels, Friedrich 26, 117, 127, 169
Engerman, Stanley 190
Ervin, S. M. 205
Etzioni, Amitai 227
Eulau, Heinz 26, 180

Euler, Heinz 234
Evans-Pritchard, E. E. 40, 143–144, 151

Faure, Edgar 113
Febvre, Lucien 94
Fechner, Gustav Theodor 134
Fenno, Richard P., Jr. 134
Fermi, Enrico 172
Ferrier, M. 22
Fetter, Frank W. 67
Feuerbach, Ludwig 22
Finberg, H.P.R. 194
Finer, Samuel 182
Finifter, Ada W. 41
Firey, W. 95
Firth, Raymond 4, 70
Fischer, Franz 48
Fiske, Donald W. 128
Flenley, R. 241
Flora, Peter 180
Fogel, Robert 190
Fohlen, Claude 69
de Forbonnais, François Véron 126
Fortes, M. 143–144
Franke, Richard W. 215
Foucault, Michel 103
Fourastie, Jean 26
Fourier, Charles 48
Freedman, Maurice 30, 72, 75, 90, 137,
142, 159
Freeman, Derek 204
Freud, Sigmund 21, 47, 107, 126, 149–
151, 156, 172, 177
Frieden, Jeffry A. 75, 217
Friedman, Milton 39–40, 117, 182, 226
Friedrich, Carl 35, 179
Fromkin, Victoria 205
Fromm, Erich 74

Gadamer, H. G. 103
Galbraith, John Kenneth 26
Galenson, Walter 11
Galilei, Galileo 142, 155
Galtung, Johan 209
Gans, Carl 208
Garson, G. David 155
Geertz, Clifford 91
George, Alexander 11
George, Juliette 150
Gerard, Ralph W. 128
Germani, Gino 179

AUTHOR INDEX

Gerschenkron, Alexander 48, 150, 192–193
Gesell, A. 99
Ghiselin, Michael T. 208, 212
Gibbon, Edward 172
Gilbert, Edmund W. 68
Giles, Micheal W. 163
Gilfillan, S. C. 20, 158
Gilpin, Robert 220–221
Gini, Corrado 124
Girschick, Meyer A. 182
Gödel, Kurt 87
Godelier, Maurice 82
Goguel, François 96
Goldenweiser, Alexander A. 179
Goldthorpe, J. H. 108
Goode, Patrick 73
Goodenough, Ward 110
Gottschalk, Louis 189–190
Gourevitch, Peter 221
Gramsci, Antonio 103
Greenberg, Joseph H. 10, 90, 109
Greenstein, Fred I. 105
Greer, Scott 116
Grimm, Jacob 108, 110, 144
Grofman, Bernard 25
Guillaume, Alfred 153
Gunnell, John G. 61, 64, 73, 103
Gurland, Arkadij 74

Haas, Ernst 96
Habermas, Jürgen 42, 74, 103
Hagerstrand, Torsten 142
Haggett, Peter 95
Hall, W. G. 63, 99
Halle, M. 110, 117
Hamilton, William 208
Hare, F. Kenneth 97
Hare, Thomas 25
Hauser, Philip M. 129
Hawley, A. H. 95
Hayek, F. A. 86, 112, 181
Heberle, Rudolf 180
Heckhausen, Heinz 104, 131
Heckscher, Eli F. 199
Heidegger, Martin 233
Heidegger, Robert 103, 232
Heisenberg, Werner 87
von Helmholz, Hermann 133
Herbolsheimer, Henrietta 128
Hermens, Ferdinand 25

Herrick, C. J. 99
Herrick, C. L. 99
Herskovitz, M. J. 144
Hexter, J. H. 190
Hicks, J. R. 48
Hilferding, Rudolf 179
Hillman, Arye L. 149
Hintze, Otto 187
von Hippel, Eric 20, 155
Hirshleifer, Jack 4, 26, 111, 119, 135–136, 208, 223, 225
Hirshman, Albert O. 124, 178, 218
Hobbes, Thomas 42
Hobhouse, L. T. 98
Hobsbawm, Erik 198
Hobson, J. A. 209
Hockett, C. F. 109
von Hofmannsthal, Hugo 181
Hofstadter, Richard 4, 30, 188
Hogarth, Robin M. 4, 145, 226
von Holst, E. 99
Horkheimer, Max 74
Hotelling, Harold 95
Hough, Jerry F. 43
Hovland, Carl I. 150
Hudson, Michael 11, 80
Hughes, Fergus 99, 145
Huizinga, Johan 176–177
Humboldt, William 108
Hume, David 86
Hung-hsiang, Chou 92
Hunter, Floyd 26, 151
Huntington, Ellsworth 212
Huntington, Samuel 126

Ike, Nobutaka 79
Inglehart, Ronald 42
Inkeles, Alex 15
Intriligator, Michael 126
Izard, Michel 92

Jacobs, Norman 195
Jacobs, Phillip 118
James, William 69
Janik, Allan 181
Janis, Irving L. 150
Janowitz, Morris 179
Jefferson, Mark 12
Jencks, Christopher 84, 231
Jennings, H. S. 151
Jensen, Richard 103

AUTHOR INDEX

Jervis, Robert 150
Jespersen, Jens Otto 72
Jevons, W. S. 86
Jewitt, Kenneth 43
Jodice, David 12
Johnson, Chalmers 79
Johnston, William M. 181
Jones, Emrys 242
Jones, William 108
Joravsky, David 43

Kagel, John 228
Kahnemann, Daniel 227
Kalecki, Michael 25
Kamarck, Andrew M. 209, 213–215
Kant, Immanuel 73
Kaplan, Morton 128, 158, 181–182
Katicic, Radoslav 33
Katz, Stuart 3
Katzenstein, Peter J. 221
Kehr, Eckart 187
Keller, Susanne 26
Kelsen, Hans 151, 181
Kennedy, Paul 73, 197–198
Keohane, Robert O. 154, 220, 222
Kernberg, O. F. 40
Key, V. O. 40–42
Keynes, John Maynard 25, 40, 86, 112, 156, 182
Kim, Chin-Wu 75
Kimpton, Lawrence A. 84, 98
Kinder, Donald 147
Kindleberger, Charles P. 193, 220
King, Anthony 182
Kirchheimer, Otto 74, 180
Kleinman, Arthur 92
Kluckhohn, Clyde 92
Kluckhohn, Florence 92
Knapp, Peter 4, 188, 191–193
Knight, Frank 26
Knorr-Cetina, Karin 3
Kondratieff, NoDo 48
Krasher, Stephen 205
Krasner, Stephen D. 220
Krauss, Karl
Kroeber, Alfred 12, 149
Kuhn, Thomas S. 11, 19, 40, 57–58, 64, 103, 154, 157–158, 176, 225–226
Kunreuther, Howard 227
Kuo, Z. Y. 99

Lakatos, Imre 157–158

Lake, David A. 75, 217
Lakeman, Enid 25
de Lamarck, Jean Baptiste 206
Lambert, James 25
di Lampedusa, Giuseppe 88
Lancelot, Alain 96
Landau, Lev Davidovich 47
de Laplace, Marquis 47, 134
Laponce, Jean A. 41, 96, 165, 180
Larson, Deborah Welch 150
Lashley, K. 99
Laski, Harold 155
Lasswell, Harold D. 26, 41, 149–150, 179
Latour, Bruno 3
Launhardt, Wilhelm 178
Lavoisier, Antoine Laucet 46
Lazarsfeld, Paul F. 21, 34, 104, 107, 131, 181
Le Bon, Gustave 24, 176
Lehmbruch, Gerhard 13
Leibnitz, Gottfried 24
Leites, Nathan 11, 156
Lemaine, G. 29, 68
Lemarchand, Rene 180
Lenin, Vladimir Ilyich 15, 40, 209
Lenneberg, E. H. 205
Leontief, Wassily 40, 148, 182
Lerner, Daniel 12
Leslie, T.E. Cliffe 67
Levasseur, Émile 69
Lévi-Strauss, Claude 30, 35, 127, 134
Lewin, Kurt 67
Lewin, M. 43
Lexis, Wilhelm 134
Lichnerowicz, Andre 112
Lifton, Robert 79
Lijphart, Arend 13, 25, 158, 180
Lindahl, Erik 24–25
Lindblom, Charles 117, 179
Linz, Juan 179–180
Lippett, Ronald 67
Lipset, Seymour Martin 4, 11, 39–40, 42, 118, 179–180, 187–188, 195, 197
Locke, John 37, 86, 171, 232
Loeb, Jacques 69, 150
Lofchie, Michael 215
Lombroso, Cesare 177
Lorenz, Konrad 98, 206
Loria, Achille 151
Lorwin, Val R. 13, 81, 194
Losco, Joseph 203

AUTHOR INDEX

Lounsbury, Floyd 109–110
Lovelock, James 208–209
Lowi, Theodore 218
Lubbock, John 150
Lukács, György 103
Lynch, Michael 3

Mabillon, Jean 89, 132
McClelland, David 79
McCormick, Richard L. 191
McGraw, M. 99
Mach, Ernst 73, 180
McHenry, Dean E., Jr. 66
Machiavelli, Niccolo 126
McIlwain, Charles H. 67
MacIver, Robert 179
McKennan, Robert A. 182
Mackenzie, W.J.M. 78
Mackinder, Halford 68, 96
McLennan, John Ferguson 68
McNeill, William 211
McPhee, W. N. 104
McRae, Kenneth 13
Madsen, Douglas 207
Magee, Stephen 111–112
Mahan, Alfred Thayer 178
Maier, Charles 187
Maine, Sir Henry Sumner 67, 127
Malinowski, Bronislaw 1, 40, 90, 126,
    128, 143–144, 149
Malthus, Thomas 24–25, 56, 206
Marble, D. F. 95
Marcuse, Herbert 177
Markovits, Andrei S. 4, 15, 105
Marschak, Jacob 128
Marshall, Alfred 135, 179
Marvick, Dwaine 26
Marvick, Elizabeth Wirth 196
Marx, Karl 15, 22, 39–40, 42, 73–74, 79,
    90, 107–108, 117, 126–128, 148, 153,
    157, 169, 187, 217, 232, 235
Masters, Roger D. 207
Matos Mar, Jose 31
Matthews, Donald 26
Mauss, Marcel 143, 177
Mayhew, David 136
Mayntz, Renate 182
Mead, Margaret 4, 10, 126, 204, 234
Meadows, Donella 26
Meisel, James 26
Mendel, Gregor 48

Merkl, Peter 70, 180
Merriam, Charles 126, 149
Merritt, Richard 55
Merton, Robert K. 2–3, 15, 24, 40, 43,
    47, 172
Meyer, Adolf 151
Meyer, Alfred G. 42–43
Meyer, John 191
Michaud, Guy 84
Michels, Robert 26, 175, 179
Mikes, M. 204
Mikesell, Marvin W. 94, 96, 159, 235
Mill, James 86
Mill, John Stuart 22, 25, 86, 169
Miller, George 109, 149
Miller, James G. 105, 128
Miller, W. R. 205
Mills, C. Wright 26, 108
Misselden, Edward 22
Mitchell, John 47
Mitchell, William 244
Mizell, Francie 163
Moe, Jörgen Ingebretsen 144
Montaigne, Michel Eyquem 171
Montesquieu, Charles 22, 86, 232
Moore, Barrington 79, 135, 187–188
Moravcsik, Michael J. 38
Morellet, André 126
Morgan, C. Lloyd 69, 96
Morgenstern, Oskar 21, 26, 117
Mosca, Gaetano 175
Muensterberger, Warner 149
Muir, Sir William 153
Müller, Johannes 10
Mumford, Lewis 26
Mun, Thomas 22
Murdock, G. P. 127
Murugesan, Poovanalingam 38
Musil, Robert 181
Myrdal, Gunnar 25, 42, 156

Neumann, Franz 74
von Neumann, John 21, 26, 117
Neustadt, Richard 182
Neville, John 86
Newcomb, Simon 135
Newell, A. 99
Newton, Sir Isaac 11, 19, 22, 24, 64, 143,
    226
Niebuhr, Barthold Georg 73, 89
North, Douglass C. 222

AUTHOR INDEX

Nozick, Robert 103
Nye, Joseph S., Jr. 220

Offe, Claus 74
Ogburn, William F. 149
Ohlin, Bertil 24, 199
Olson, Mancur, Jr. 40, 42, 148, 153, 178, 222
Oppenheim, R. W. 63–64, 99
Ordeshook, Peter C. 31
Oromaner, Mark 14, 23
Ortega y Gasset, José 26
Ostrogorski, Moisei 21, 26
Oye, Kenneth A. 220

Paige, Glenn 150
Palmer, Harold 72
Pang, Kevin D. 92
Pareto, Vilfredo 26, 40, 135
Park, Robert E. 95
Parker, Harold T. 190
Parsons, Talcott 15, 22, 30, 35, 39, 58–59, 90, 97, 105, 107, 109, 127–128, 131
Passy, Paul Éduouard 72
Patinkin, Don 245
Patterson, David 163
Pauli, Wolfgang 87
Paulsen, Friedrich 69
Pavlov, Ivan 96, 101, 126, 151
Peer, Denise 207
Pelassy, Dominique 132
Peltzman, Sam 111
Peterson, Steven A. 207
Peuerbach, Georg 10
Piaget, Jean 3, 63, 66, 68, 69, 86, 99, 129, 145, 177, 206
Pike, Kenneth 109
Pirenne, Henri 48
Plakans, Andrej 4
Plato 33, 40, 134, 236
Platt, John 4, 15–17, 105
Platt, John R. 128
Poincare, Jules Henri 131
Poisson, Siméon Denis 134, 177
Polanyi, Karl 181
Polsby, Nelson 151, 182
Polybius 94
Popkin, Samuel L. 136, 222
Popper, Sir Karl 103, 159, 181
Posner, Richard 91

Postal, P. 110
Powell, G. Bingham 13
Pratt, John 26
Proudhon, Pierre Joseph 127
Przeworski, Adam 74
Putnam, Robert 26
Pye, Lucian W. 77, 79, 81, 180

Quesnay, François 126
Quételet, Lambert Adolphe 134
Quillian, Ross 100

Radcliffe-Brown, A. R. 10, 40, 90, 93, 127–128
Radnitzky, Gerard 136
Rae, Douglas W. 25
Raiffa, Howard 26
Ramsey, Frank 48
von Ranke, Leopold 12, 89, 195
Rapoport, Anatol 128
Rapoport, David 153
Rasmussen, Eric 137–138
Ratzel, Friedrich 178
Rawls, John 42, 74, 103
Reder, Melvin W. 145, 226
Reich, Wilhelm 177
Revel, Jacques 87,
Ricardo, David 22, 24–25, 56, 124, 148, 172, 218
Richardson, Lewis F. 133, 135
Riesman, David 84, 228, 231, 236
Riggs, Fred W. 180, 230–232
Rigler, David and Marilyn 205
Riker, William H. 103–104, 136
Robinson, W. S. 12, 46
Rodeheaver, Dean 99, 145
Rodinson, Maxim 153
Roemer, John 74
Rogers, Thorold 180
Roheim, Geza 149
Rokkan, Stein 11, 41, 46, 96–97, 118, 179–180
Romanes, G. J. 98
Roose, Kenneth 246
Rosberg, Carl 80
Rose, Richard 182
Rosecrance, Richard 128
Rostow, W. W. 212
Roth, Günther 107, 180, 194
Rothschild, Michael 26
Rousseau, Jean Jacques 37, 232

Rukang, Wu 93
Russett, Bruce 12, 96, 158
Rustow, Dankwart 180
Rutman, Darrett B. 88–89

von St. Paul, U. 99
Samaran, Charles 194
Samuelson, Paul D. 12, 40, 48, 182
Sapir, Edward 149
Sarton, George 70
Sartori, Giovanni 116, 135, 179–180, 233
de Saussure, Ferdinand 127
Sauvy, Alfred 125
Say, Jean-Baptiste 22
Scharnhorst, Gerhard von 175
Schattschneider, E. E. 42, 218–219
Schelling, Thomas 178
Scheuch, Edwin 47
Schlegl, Frederick 108
Schleiermacher, Friedrich 73
Schmidt, Gert 119
Schmitter, Phillippe 13
Schmoller, Gustav 69, 180
Schneider, Benjamin 101–102
Schneirle, T. C. 99
Schnore, L. F. 95
Schönberg, Arnold 181
Schorske, Carl E. 181
Schultz, Henry 46
Schumpeter, Joseph 26, 40, 209
Schwartz, Anna 59, 117
Sears, David O. 101
Sechenov, Ivan 96
Sedgwick, Henry 86
Segall, N. H. 144
Seligman, E.R.A. 92
Senghaas, Dieter 15–17
Seyfarth, Constans 119
Shapiro, R. J. 35
Shaw, J. 99
Sherif, Muzafer 144, 180
Sherif, Carolyn W. 144
Shonfield, Andrew 221
Shubik, Martin 136–137
Siegfried, André 47, 96, 179
Sills, David L. 171
Simiand, François 246
Simmons, Ozzie G. 132
Simon, Herbert 99–100, 112, 138, 178, 227
Simon, Richard 132

Singer, J. David 136, 158
Skinner, B. F. 40
Sklar, Richard L. 80, 223
Skocpol, Theda 180
Slutsky, Eugen 48
Small, Albion 69
Small, Melvin 136
Smelser, Neil 13, 15, 59, 105–106, 108
Smith, Adam 22, 56, 86, 172
Snyder, Glenn H. 228
de Solla Price, Derek 11, 22, 33, 43, 46, 65
Sombart, Werner 47, 127, 187
Somit, Albert 207
Spearman, Charles 134
Spencer, Herbert 127, 189–190
Sperry, Roger 128
Spinoza, Baruch (Benedict) 132
Ssu-ma Ch'ien (Sima Qian) 20
Stafford, Elizabeth Ann 43, 138
Staniland, Martin 220
Staub, Hugo 150
Steinbruner, John 137
Steiner, Jürg 13
Stewart, John A. 237
Stigler, George, Jr. 111, 182
Stiglitz, Joseph 26
Stillings, Neil A. 100
Stokes, Donald E. 42
Stouffer, Samuel 118
Streeten, Paul 213
Sullivan, Harry Stack 151
Sutch, Richard 190
Sutherland, Edwin H. 46
Sweet, Henry 72

Tarde, Gabriel 24
Taylor, Charles 12, 32
Temin, P. 59
Textor, Robert 117
Thomas, Robert Paul 222
Thomas, W. I. 69, 151, 196
Thorndike, Edward L. 69, 150
Thrupp, Sylvia 4
Thucydides 20, 209
Thurstone, L. L. 134
Tilly, Charles 4, 88, 132, 187–188, 190–191, 194, 197
Tinbergen, Jan 98
de Tocqueville, Alexis de 37, 47
Toulmin, Stephen 181

AUTHOR INDEX

Toynbee, Arnold 126, 180
Toynbee, Arnold J. 64, 126, 148, 177
Troeltsch, Ernst 177
Tufte, Edward R. 221–222
Tullock, Gordon 40
Truman, David B. 48, 104, 154
Turner, Frederick Jackson 12, 151, 187, 195
Turner, Henry Ashby, Jr. 200–201
Turner, Ralph 32, 53, 67, 107
Tversky, Amos 227

Ullman, Edward 95–96

Valsiner, Jaan 27
Veblen, Thorstein 26, 175
Verba, Sidney 35, 40, 42
Verhulst, Adriaan 134
Vernant, Jean-Pierre 93
Vernon, Raymond 48
Veyne, Paul 107
Vico, Giambattista 171
Vidal de la Blache, Paul 10, 40
Voltaire, François Marie 65

Wallace, Alfred Russell 24
Wallerstein, Immanuel 128, 177
Wallerstein, Michael 74
Walras, Léon 135
Waltz, Kenneth J. 40, 128, 182
Ward, Robert E. 81
Wasby, Stephen L. 147
Washburn, Sherwood 128

Waterton, Charles 48
Watson, J. B. 99, 151
Weber, Eugen 88
Weber, Max 15, 21–22, 26, 39, 42, 47–48, 79, 90, 105, 107–108, 119, 125–126, 129, 169, 172, 174, 177, 183, 191, 193
Weil, André 134
Weingrod, Alex 151
West, Edward 24–25
White, Leonard D. 4
Whitaker, Harry A. 206
Wiatr, Jerzy 179
Wiegele, Thomas C. 70, 203
Wiener, Norbert 127
Wigforss, Ernst 156
Wilcox, Stephen 3,
Wildavsky, Aaron 153
Wilkinson, David 133
Windle, W. 99
Wirth, Louis 95
Wittfogel, Karl 64, 70
Wittgenstein, Ludwig 87, 181
Woolgar, Steve 3
Wright, Gavin 191
Wright, Quincy 46, 118, 134–135

Yamey, B. S. 70
Young, Crowford 80
Young, Leslie 111–112

Znaniecki, Florian 151, 196
Zoppo, Ciro 66
Zuckerman, Harriet 24–25, 56

SUBJECT INDEX

abstraction 198–199
Académie Française 48
acoustics 133. *See also* linguistics,
 acoustic
adat 156. *See also* Indonesia; law
administration (university) 84–85, 106,
 113, 186, 230. *See also* business;
 universities
adulthood 99, 196. *See also* aging
Africa 34, 55, 77, 80, 91, 115, 144, 194,
 212–214, 221
 East 210
 South 79, 210, 213
 West 79, 215
 see also area studies; development,
  economic; *individual countries*;
  "Third World"
aging 100, 107. *See also* adulthood
agriculture 215
 and archaeology 93
 and political economy 151
 sociology of 106
 U.S. Department of 212
 see also peasants
AIDS (Acquired Immuno-Deficiency
 Syndrome) 24
alcoholism 34, 207
anarchy 151, 219–220. *See also*
 international relations; sociology of
 world conflict
animacy 10. *See also* linguistics
animals
 behavior of 148
 domestic 211
 ecology of 129
 language of 205

rationality of 228. *See also* game
 theory, and biology; rational choice
 see also biology; ethology; primatology;
 psychology, comparative
Les Annales 87–88, 94–95, 194–195
anomalies 157, 189
 in economics 225
 in game theory 227
 and innovation 157–158
 sources of 158
 and theories 158
 see also paradigms
anthropology 4–5, 17, 27, 33, 35, 38, 54–
 55, 58, 61, 63–64, 68–70, 75, 77, 89–
 93, 129, 166–167, 176, 179
anthropogeography 27. *See also*
 geography, cultural
anthropometrics 182. *See also*
 quantification
antiquarianism 89, 92. *See also*
 archaeology
 and art 90
 biological 72, 92
 and biology 84, 89–92, 150, 178, 207
 and chemistry 92–93
 citation in 39–40
 cognitive 90
 comparative 90
 concepts in 42, 126–129, 233
 criminal 55, 177
 cultural 35, 58, 60, 67–68, 84, 90–92,
  107, 151, 173, 182
 of development 90
 discoveries in 144, 167, 230
 and ecology 91
 economic 70, 90–91, 95, 134, 143, 174
 and egyptology 89

SUBJECT INDEX

and epigraphy 93
ethnomusicocology 75, 142. *See also* anthropology, and music; music
and ethology 207
and evolution 68, 90
field observation in 22, 90. *See also* anthropology, methods of; observation
fragmentation of 55, 89
functionalism in 16, 165
and game theory 72–73
and geography 89, 91–92, 96, 178
and geology 89
historical 73, 92
and history 88–90, 176
hybridization in 89–93
and innovation 16, 38
and law 89, 90–91, 129, 151, 156, 159
and linguistics 90, 92, 109, 165
and mathematics 134, 137
and medicine 89, 92, 207
methods of 55, 84, 92, 133–134
and migration 91
and music 89
and papyrology 93
and peasants 91
and perception 92, 144
and pharmacology 207
and philology 93
and philosophy 89, 92
physical 55, 58, 60, 90, 182. *See also* archaeology; physiology
political 72, 90–92, 102, 143–144, 166, 174
and political science 42, 90–92, 103–104, 133, 151, 165
and psychiatry 92
and psychoanalysis 92
psychological 173
and psychology 89–92, 144, 149
and sociology 89–92, 105–107, 133, 151, 165
structuralism in 35
structual-functionalism in 90–91
theories of 92, 230
urban 91
see also archaeology; culture
archaeology, 5, 54, 66, 89–90, 92, 141, 176, 233
and agriculture 93
and geology 92–93

hybridization in 89–90
and mathematics 178
and medicine 93
and natural sciences 93
and paleography 93
and paleontology 90, 92–93
and palynology 93
and technology 141
and theology 132
and zoology 93
architecture 95. *See also* art; cities; urban studies
area studies 27, 77–82, 92, 102
and fragmentation 77–82, 231
and geography 27
and hybridization 77, 81
institutionalization of 78
limitations of 78
and political science 27
theories in 79, 81
see also individual continents and regions
art 5, 90, 106, 176. *See also* humanities; literature
artificial intelligence 66, 100
and linguistics 109
see also cognition; computers; cybernetics; information; psychology, cognitive
Asia 55, 115, 194
Central 68
East 79, 195
South 78–79
Southeast 34, 80, 136, 141
see also area studies; *individual countries*
astrology 56, 155
astronomy 21, 57–58, 92–93, 135, 177, 226. *See also* NASA; physics
astrophysics 64
Athens 34, 180, 209. *See also* Greece
Australia 10, 79–80, 195, 210–211. *See also* aborigenes; area studies
Austria 71
and Austro-Marxism 73, 181
see also Europe
authoritarian personality 70–71, 79. *See also* bureaucracy; rational-legal authority; totalitarianism

Babel, Tower of 118, 230–231, 233, 234

260 SUBJECT INDEX

balance of power 35, 165. *See also*
  anarchy; international relations
behavior
  animal 148
  economic 226
  electoral 179, 199
  organizational 101–102, 227
  purposive 99. *See also* game theory;
    public choice; rational choice
Bible 20, 132, 153
  criticism of 73
  see also religion; theology, *various*
    religions
biofeedback 101
biology 17, 69, 129, 166, 181, 186
  and anthropology 84, 89–92, 150, 178,
    207
  biochemistry 19, 64, 68
  biogeography 94
  biogeology 19
  biophysics 68
  biopolitics 70, 166, 207
  concepts in 127–129
  and criminology 177
  and demography 206
  developmental 63, 99
  and economics 111–112, 206, 208
  and ethology 206
  evolutionary 90, 152, 204, 206
  and game theory 208
  genetic 72. *See also* DNA
  and geology 73
  and history 207
  and imperialism 209–212
  and linguistics 204–206
  and mathematics 178
  molecular 56, 63, 68–69. *See also*
    chemistry; physics
  and natural sciences 208–209
  neurobiology 63. *See also* nervous
    systems; neurology
  paleobiology 19
  and political economy 208
  and political science 207
  and power 207
  and psychology 84, 97, 100, 150, 203,
    206
  reductionism in 204–205
  social 111. *See also* Social Darwinism;
    sociobiology
  and social psychology 101

and social sciences 203–211
and sociology 106, 207
and theology 73
bipolarity 198. *See also* balance of power;
  international relations; systems,
  international
botany 66. *See also* biology; ecology
boundaries, disciplinary 2, 60–61, 67, 83,
  148, 174, 230, 236
  artificiality of 113
  and fragmentation 59–61
  of history 88
  and hybridization 85
  and innovation 59–60
  institutionalization of 59–60
  links across 84–85, 172–173. *See also*
    communication; hybridization
  see also frontiers; gaps; hybridization;
    marginality
brains 24, 100, 127, 156, 204. *See also*
  biology; nervous systems
Brazil 80, 95, 195, 210, 212–213
  see also Latin America; Newly
    Industrial Countries
Britain, Great 9, 34, 47, 55, 80–81, 92,
  115, 192, 198, 210, 233
  geography in 94
  naturalists in 98
  sociology in 34
  see also England; Royal Society
bureaucracy 165
  bureaucratic-authoritarianism 123. *See*
    also authoritarianism; systems,
    political
  see also administration (university);
    organizations
business 33
  administration 107
  schools of 102. *See also* universities
  see also economics, industrial
    organization; organizations

calculus 24, 135, 138–139. *See also*
  mathematics; statistics
capitalism 81–82, 95, 126–127, 135, 151,
  195, 221. *See also* class, working;
  economics; political economy
cardiology 149. *See also* medicine
cataloguing. *See* classification; library
  science
Catholics 71, 219. *See also* religion

SUBJECT INDEX

causation
in history 89, 192, 195
in sociology 191, 193, 195, 198
Celtic languages 110
center-periphery relations 97
ceteris paribus 192. *See also* theory
charisma 125, 172, 191, 233. *See also*
authoritarianism, rational-legal
authority; leadership
chemistry 20, 56, 58, 133
and anthropology 92–93
bio- 19, 64, 68
China 79, 87, 92, 180, 195
Great Wall of 230
see also area studies; Asia
citation 9, 14–15
and age of research 45–46
analysis of 37–43. *See also* sociology of
science
in anthropology 39–40
of "classics" 23, 37, 43
in economics 39–41
in geography 40
and hybridization 41, 43
of multiple-authored works 117. *See
also* research, team
in natural science 37–38, 43
norms of 38
and obsolescence 23, 45–46
and paradigms 37–38
and paradox of density 38
and patrimonies 37–38
perfunctory 37–38, 43
in political science 39–40
in psychology 40
qualitative studies of 43
quantification of 38–41
in sociology 39–41
see also halo effect
cities 48, 65, 95, 97, 141, 211, 230. *See
also* urban studies
class 61, 74
relationships among 128
ruling 34. *See also* elites
working 74. *See also* capitalism; trade
unions
"classics" 53
citation of 23, 37, 43
and patrimonies 22, 33. *See also*
paradigms
Roman and Greek 68, 92, 153, 232

classification 57, 97, 102, 108, 111, 134,
190, 191, 194, 198
in libraries 27, 71–72, 235. *See also*
library science
of objects 123, 125. *See also* concepts
of scholars 27, 171
cleavages
ideological 107
social 104, 189
in sociology 107
clientelism 35, 81, 91, 166
climate
and development 212–215
and geography 94
and imperialism 210
and mathematical models 212
climatology 94–95
cognition 97, 99–101
and international relations 150
and language 109
and political science 104, 228
processes of 226, 228
see also artificial intelligence
cognitive dissonance 165
Cold War 150, 155. *See also* international
relations
collective action 22, 24, 104, 136, 154,
193, 222. *See also* public choice;
public goods
collective goods. *See* public goods
communication 96, 104, 141
between scholarly communities 31, 77,
164, 181, 231–232. *See also*
hybridization; "invisible college";
journals
and concepts 127–128, 232
difficulties of 159, 230–232. *See also*
jargon; obfuscation
and fragmentation 232
and political science 104, 128
and psychology 150
sociology of 106
within scholarly communities 31, 104,
110–111, 231–232
see also Babel, Tower of; language;
linguistics
Communism 71, 79–80, 222
communities, scholarly 31–32, 85, 121
isolation of 31. *See also* fragmentation
see also conferences, academic; density;
"invisible college"; research, team;
scholars

262 SUBJECT INDEX

comparative advantage, law of 218. *See also* trade, international

comparative politics. *See under* political science

comparative primatology. *See* primatology, comparative

computers 142, 149, 164, 235

computer science 66, 86, 99–100. *See also* artificial intelligence; technology

computer simulation 99–100, 208
and innovation 16

concepts 30, 98, 121, 123, 134–135
borrowing of 124–125, 152
changing meanings of 124, 128, 232, 234
and communication 127–128, 232
conceptual dictionaries 233. *See also* libraries, library science
conceptual frameworks 35, 58, 220. *See also* paradigms
and discoveries 123
and hybridization 123–130
and innovation 16, 41–42, 124–125
see also analogies; jargon; *under individual disciplines*

conferences, academic 58

conflict 22, 223
and economics 136, 208
sociology of 108, 137

consciousness 21

consensus 22
and sterility 152

conservatism 96

constitutions 126, 136. *See also* systems, political

constructivism 3

consumer's surplus 123, 179. *See also* economics

contagion, mental 24

content analysis 196. *See also* methodologies

controversy and innovation 152. *See also* consensus; paradigms

cores 7, 23, 32, 75, 173
of economics 23, 110–111, 119, 166
of geography 94, 97
of history 88–89
of linguistics 23, 109–110, 183
of psychoanalysis 149
of psychology 99
of social-cultural anthropology 22–23

of social sciences 85, 119
of sociology 22, 53, 61, 105, 107–108
see also density; margins; paradigms

corporations 85. *See also* business; capitalism; organizations

corporatism 226
neo- 13

cost-benefit analysis 179

creativity 7, 35, 48–49. *See also* innovation

criminology 66
and biology 177
criminal anthropology 55, 177
and economics 106, 111
and psychoanalysis 150
and sociology 106
see also law; psychology; social psychology

crisis 62
political 96
see also cycles, economic

critical methods 73, 132. *See also* history, methods of

critical theory 74

criticism, cultural 74

crystallography 69

culture 23, 79–80, 90, 144, 179, 182
change of 96
cultural ecology 91, 96
cultural history 87
cultural imperialism 209
and environment 182
evolution of 68, 150, 208
political 35, 166
regional 92. *See also* geography, cultural
see also anthropology, cultural

cumulative advance. *See* innovation, incremental nature of; patrimonies

cybernetics 127, 137
and geography 96
and political science 42
and psychology 99
sociocybernetics 106
see also artificial intelligence; information

cycles, economic 48, 54, 221–222. *See also* crisis

Darwinism. *See* Social Darwinism

data 111, 128, 132, 135

SUBJECT INDEX

aggregate 46, 96, 132
citation 38–41
collection of 10, 81, 118, 134, 196
survey 132, 197
see also ecological analysis; statistics
dating methods 92. *See also* archaeology;
technology
Dead Sea scrolls 33, 57
decision-making 62, 100–101, 165, 182
Bayesian 99, 182. *See also* economics;
formal models; psychology
see also rational choice
deduction 67, 95, 159, 180, 199. *See also*
induction
demand 57, 110, 112, 148, 179, 226. *See
also* economics; price; supply
democracy 112, 135–136, 154, 187–189,
221–222
capitalist 74, 166
consociational 13
and economics 136, 158–159
and sociology 158–159
see also political science
demography 5, 132, 134
and biology 206
and economics 206
historical 152, 174
and mathematics 137
and political economy 151
and sociology 61, 107
and statistics in 21, 134
density 4, 30, 31, 32, 33–34, 35, 67, 75
and citation 38
in the core 32
and graduate training 33
in history 34
and hybridization 35–36
and innovation 38, 59–60
in international political economy 22
and jargon 31
and margins 36. *See also* boundaries;
gaps; margins
paradox of 1, 29–36, 37, 173, 230
departments, in universities 65, 83–84,
231–232
dependence 34, 80, 124, 166, 192–193,
213, 233
inter- 219–220
deterrence, nuclear 137, 156. *See also*
Cold War; war
development 48, 80

adult 99, 196
anthropology of 90
biological 63
child 145, 205
and climate 212–215
developmental biology 99
economic 16–17, 48, 63, 78–79, 111,
156, 166, 192–193, 209, 212–215
and geography 214–215
linguistic 205
physiological 66
political 17, 48, 166, 212
psychological 27, 42, 63, 97, 99–100,
206
theories of 79, 212–213
see also modernization
dialects 109. *See also* language; linguistics
diminishing returns, law of 24–25
in research 29, 67, 152, 220. *See also*
density; research
and theories 151
diplomacy 219. *See also* history,
diplomatic
disciplines 38, 58–59, 230, 232
and administration 84–85
boundaries of 60–61, 148
cores of 7, 173
disciplinary associations 60
differences among 153
history of 54–56, 229
imperialism of 83
and intolerance 236
norms of 23
perspectives of 153, 200. *See also*
paradigms
and promotion 85
reviews of 83–114. *See also individual
disciplines*
and teaching 85
disease 211, 214. *See also* health;
immunology
dispute resolution 103
division of labor 78
divorce 101, 137
DNA 72, 123, 129. *See also* genetics

ecological analysis 12, 46, 96
and innovation 41
see also data, aggregate; survey research
ecology 129
and anthropology 91

cultural 91, 96. *See also* anthropology, cultural; culture; geography, cultural
human 27, 129, 141
and imperialism 209–212
social 91, 106
economics 4–5, 17, 27, 33, 43, 54, 56, 61, 63, 66–67, 69–75, 81–82, 101, 110–113, 169, 174, 177, 181, 182–183
anomalies in 225
and anthropology 90–91
applied 55
and biology 111–112, 206, 208
citations in 39–41
concepts in 112, 126–128, 233
and conflict 136, 208
core of 23, 110–111, 119, 166
and crime 106, 111
and democracy 136, 158–159
and demography 206
econometrics 16, 32, 74, 182. *See also* data; statistics
and development 16–17, 48, 63, 78–79, 111, 156, 166, 192–193, 209, 212–215
and engineering 178–179
and evolution 226
and formal models 101, 218, 227. *See also* game theory
fragmentation of 217
and game theory 136, 165, 227
and gaps in 112, 217
and history 111, 136
hybridization of 110–113, 119, 218, 220, 228
imperialism of 111–112, 119, 136, 166, 225, 230
and innovation 16
and international relations 181–182
journals in 41, 161–162
and law 111, 136
macro- 110, 182
marginal analysis 73, 131, 135
and mathematics 21, 48, 111, 132, 178, 225
methodology of 67, 111–112, 131, 133–134, 136, 166
micro- 110, 225
and noncapitalist societies 81–82, 91
See also anthropology, economic; capitalism
obsolescence in 45
paradigm of 154, 225–226, 228

and philosophy 86
and political science 42, 61, 104, 111–112, 138, 147, 165–166, 186, 217–219. *See also* political economy
and psychology 100–101, 138, 165–166, 225–228
publication in 27, 39
quantification in 32
revivals in 48
and sociobiology 208
socio- 227
and sociology 105–106, 111, 138, 165, 227
specialization in 57
statistics in 55, 111, 134
subfields in 54–55
theory of 54–55, 84, 110–111, 199, 225–227
and urban studies 95
welfare 136, 178
economy, as concept 233
education 5
sociology of 106–108
egyptology 89
elections 10, 34–35, 136. *See also* political science
electoral geography 96
elites, study of 15–17, 26, 166, 179
empirical analysis 53–54
endocrinology 72
endogamy 68
engineering 95, 166
and economics 178–179
and psychology 125
and urban studies 95
see also technology
England 54, 69, 124, 135, 200. *See also* Britain, Great
English language 54, 79, 110, 117, 233–234
environment 98, 203–204
and culture 182. *See also* anthropology; ecology, social
and geography 94
and scarcity 208
epistemology 3, 61, 103, 86
and fragmentation 53, 61–62
genetic 72
and history 89
and political theory 103
see also philosophy

SUBJECT INDEX

equilibrium 35, 136, 177, 226
  punctuated 208. *See also* biology;
  evolution
erklären 190
ethics 86–87, 206
ethnocentrism, in history 34
ethnography 10, 90, 137. *See also*
  anthropology; ethnology
ethnology 54–55, 60, 89. *See also*
  anthropology; ethnography
ethnomusicology 75, 142. *See also*
  anthropology, and music
ethology
  and biology 206
  and geography 97
  and political science 207
  and psychology 98–99, 206
Europe 55, 60, 96, 115, 124, 151, 174–
  175, 179, 187, 194–196, 211, 213, 231
  Eastern 34, 43, 79–80
  Western 42, 80–81, 222
  see also area studies; *individual
  countries*
evolution 20, 125, 208
  and anthropology 68, 90
  biological 90, 152, 204, 206
  cultural 68, 150, 208
  in economics 226
  intellectual 176
  and political science 207
  and psychology 98
experiments 100, 133, 206
  and innovation 14

factor analysis 134, 165. *See also* statistics
fads 33, 74–75, 187
  and patrimonies 75
  in political economy 217
family 91
  sociology of 61, 66, 106, 198
feudalism 135, 151, 195, 222. *See also*
  capitalism; history, medieval
field observation 133–134
  in anthropology 22, 90
  in linguistics 10, 57
  in political science 134
folklore studies 27, 67, 144. *See also*
  anthropology; linguistics; literature
foreign policy 62, 78
  and public choice 62
  see also international relations; political
  economy, international

formal models 62, 95, 133–135, 137, 138,
  163
  and economics 101, 218, 227
  and geography 235
  and international relations 62, 137
  and Marxism 74
  and organizational behavior 26
  and psychology 26
  and social psychology 101
  see also game theory; mathematics;
  rational choice
fragmentation 1–2, 4–5, 28, 35, 51, 53,
  54–56, 83, 229–230
  and administrative needs 84
  analytical 77–82
  of anthropology 55, 89
  and disciplinary boundaries 59–61,
  229–230
  of economics 217
  and epistemology 53, 61–62
  by geographical area 77–82, 231. *See
  also* area studies
  of geography 93–94
  of history 87, 89, 187–188
  and hybridization 66
  and ideology 53, 59, 107, 231
  and innovation 59
  and intolerance 31, 137–138, 235–236
  and methodologies 53, 132, 231
  of natural sciences 72
  and paradigms 231
  and patrimonies 53, 56, 59–60, 65
  of political science 61–62, 102, 217, 232
  of psychology 98–99
  of sociology 58–59, 105, 107, 187–188
  and specialization 58
  and statistics 231
  see also specialization
France 24–25, 69, 81, 192
  language 54, 79
  geography 93–94, 96
  politics 54
  sociology in 113
frontiers 195
  American 151, 187, 195
  intellectual 2, 68, 74. *See also*
  boundaries; gaps
functionalism 127, 166
  in anthropology 16, 165
  and innovation 16
  in linguistics 157

266 SUBJECT INDEX

see also structuralism; structural-
functionalism

Gaia hypothesis 208–209
Galapagos Islands 24, 90
game theory 54, 117, 136, 182, 189, 227–
228
anomalies in 227
in anthropology 72–73
and biology 208
and economics 136, 165, 227
and history 190
and international relations 151
and political science 104, 137, 165
and public choice 136–137, 165
and social psychology 137
and sociology 137, 165
see also formal models; mathematics
gaps, intellectual 65, 67–68, 149, 203
and economics 112, 227
and formal models 138
and fragmentation 229–230
and international relations 219
and linguistics 110
and political science 217, 219
see also boundaries; margins
generalists 59, 133, 166, 169, 182, 189–
191. *See also* theories, grand
genetics 19, 72
and psychology 33, 150
and transformational-generative
grammar 33
see also biology; DNA
geochemistry 20
geography 5, 27, 40, 64–65, 93–97, 129,
166–167, 214
anthropo- 27
and anthropology 89, 91–92, 96, 178
area studies in 27
bio- 94
citation in 40
classification in 97
and climatology 94
concepts in 42, 129
cultural 94–96, 159. *See also*
anthropology, cultural; ecology
and cybernetics 96
economic 94–95, 173
electoral 96. *See also* geography,
political; political science
and ethology 97

and formal models 235
fragmentation of 93–94
and geology 97
historical 21, 70
and history 88, 94–95
hybridization of 93–97
and induction 235
innovation in 21
and international relations 96. *See also*
geopolitics
journals in 162
and natural sciences 84, 94, 97
obsolescence in 45
and political science 96–97. *See also*
geopolitics
and psychology 96
social 106. *See also* anthropology;
ecology
and sociology 94–95, 97, 159. *See also*
urban studies
urban 94, 97
geology 19, 23
and archaeology 92–93
bio- 19
and biology 73
and geography 97
innovation in 23
and theology 73, 132
see also geochemistry; plate tectonics
geopolitics 96. *See also* geography;
international relations
Germany 9, 60, 70–71, 73, 81, 97, 125,
178, 187, 190, 192
geography in 93–94, 96
language 54, 108, 154
Social Democratic Party of 71, 119,
175, 194
see also Europe
graduate training 22, 49, 59, 77, 119, 131,
166, 197, 200
and paradox of density 33
recovery from 32
see also teaching
grammar 10, 57, 108, 109
comparative 154
as field 56, 66
generative. *See* transformational-
generative grammar
transformational. *See* transformational-
generative grammar
gravity 148, 155, 193. *See also* physics

SUBJECT INDEX

267

Greece, language in 54, 57, 108, 205

hair-splitting, theoretical 29–30. *See also* obfuscation
halo effect 38. *See also* citation; "star system"
health 101, 214. *See also* disease; immunology
heartland theory 68, 96. *See also* geography; geopolitics; international relations
hegemony 198, 220, 223. *See also* Marxism; Realism; systems, international
heuristics 99–100, 227. *See also* cognitive science; psychology
historical sociology 73, 87–88, 188–199
historicism 190. *See also* positivism
history 5, 20, 27, 43, 46, 54, 63–64, 66, 67, 69–71, 79, 87–89, 132, 174, 190
  ancient 20, 207
  and anthropology 88–90, 176
  and biology 207
  boundaries of 88
  causation in 89, 192, 195. *See also* epistemology; philosophy; science, philosophy of
  classification in 190, 198
  comparative 194–195
  concepts in 42, 128–129, 197
  core of 88–89
  critical methods in 73, 132
  cultural 87. *See also* historical sociology; history, social
  demographic 174
  economic 54–55, 59, 87, 95, 173–174, 180, 188, 199, 217
  and economics 111, 136
  and epistemology 89
  fads in 187
  fragmentation of 87, 89, 187–188
  and game theory 190
  and geography 88, 94–95
  and humanities 84, 88
  hybridization of 87–89, 115–116, 169, 188. *See also* historical sociology
  and innovation 21
  intellectual 54, 71, 87, 176
  and intolerance 235
  narrative 88–89, 195, 200, 235
  patrimony of 20, 187

  and philology 89, 176–177
  and philosophy 86
  political 87, 178, 195, 197, 199
  and political science 41–42, 54–55, 61, 64, 103, 147, 153, 166, 177, 179, 188, 197–198
  and psychology 150
  and quantification 197
  schools of 30, 89, 180
  social 27, 54, 67, 87–88, 95, 176, 194–196, 235. *See also* historical sociology
  and sociology 4, 56, 61, 88, 105, 107, 176–177, 186–201. *See also* historical sociology
  specialization in 187, 189
  and theology 88–89, 132. *See also* theology
  theory of 15, 74, 89
  tunnel vision in 190
humanities 5, 33, 84
  and geography 94
  and history 84, 88
  and linguistics 109
  and social science 181
  and urban studies 95
  see also art; literature; music
hybridization 2, 4–5, 51, 62, 63–76, 85, 229
  of archaeology 89–90
  and area studies 77, 81
  and concepts 68, 123–130, 152
  and density 35–36
  and discoveries 143–145
  of economics 110–113, 119, 218, 220, 228
  and fragmentation 66
  of geography 93–97
  of history 87–89, 115–116, 169, 188
  and innovation 16–17, 39
  institutionalized forms of 51, 63. *See also* administration; institutionalization
  and journals 161–164
  of linguistics 108–110
  and methodologies 16, 73, 79, 131–139
  of natural sciences 72
  of philosophy 86–87
  of political science 102–104, 218, 220
  and problem-solving 156–157
  of psychology 97–102, 228
  quantification of 41, 72

and research foundations 35
in sociology 105–108, 188
and team research 117
theoretical 16, 147–152

ideologies 71, 223
and fragmentation 53, 59, 107, 231
and intolerance 235
in sociology 59, 107, 113
idiography 189
see also description; generalization;
nomothesm
immunology 210–211
psychoneuro- 101
see also disease; health
imperialism 133, 166, 167, 209–212
and biology 209–212
and climate 210
disciplinary 83. See also hybridization
and hybridization 83
in sociology 113, 209
sociology of 106
India 79, 210
languages of 109
see also Indo-European peoples,
languages of
individualistic fallacy. See under fallacies
Indo-European peoples 66
languages of 110
induction 95, 180, 199, 235. See also
deduction
industrial relations. See under economics
industrial revolution. See revolution,
industrial
inequality 124. See also distribution
information 129
and game theory 228
processing of 100–101, 127, 228. See
also cognitive science
see also artificial intelligence; cognitive
science; computers; cybernetics
innovation 1, 4, 7–17, 23, 38, 152, 208,
230
and anomalies 157–158
and concepts 16, 41–42, 124–125
and density 38, 59–60
difficulty of 34–35
and disciplinary boundaries 59–60
distribution of 7, 142. See also cores;
density; marginality
and fragmentation 59

and hybridization 16–17, 39
incremental nature of 9, 19–20, 28
and interdisciplinary research 26
and margins 32–33. See also
boundaries; gaps; margins
as mass phenomenon 13, 29, 37
and methodologies 21, 57, 100
and obsolescence 46
and paradigms 153, 157
and patrimonies 7, 20–25, 45, 48, 65
process of 58–59
quantification of 37, 40
ranking of 40
simultaneous 24–25
and specialization 1, 57–58, 116
and structuralism 16
see also discoveries; under individual
disciplines
instinct 98, 148, 203. See also nature
interdisciplinary research 1, 4–5, 13, 16,
115–119, 222
and innovation 16
and problem-solving 104
synthesis in 2
weaknesses of 65, 78
see also hybridization;
monodisciplinarity
interest groups 30, 42, 48, 111–112, 124,
128, 137, 154–155, 166, 218–219. See
also parties, political
International Encyclopedia of the Social
Sciences 125, 171, 175–176
international relations 54, 56, 150, 151,
198, 219–220
core of 62
and economics 181–182
and formal models 62, 137
and game theory 151
and geography 96
paradigm of 154, 158
and political science 181–182
and psychology 181–182
and social psychology 181–182
and sociology 107, 181–182
and statistics 134
see also political economy,
international; political science
intersections, of disciplines. See
hybridization
intolerance 24
and fragmentation 235–236

SUBJECT INDEX

and disciplines 235, 236
"invisible college" 65, 70, 181. *See also* communication, scholarly; research, team

jargon 29-31, 136
  in anthropology 30
  in political science 30
  in sociology 30-31
journalism 125-126. *See also* media, mass
journals, academic 45, 65, 70, 72, 121
  in cognitive science 100
  and communication 231, 235
  in economics 41, 161-162
  in geography 162
  and hybridization 161-164
  in law 161-162
  and patrimonies 162
  in political science 41, 162
  in psychology 161-163
  in sociology 41, 162-163
  specialization of 161-163, 235
  see also publication
jurisprudence. *See* law

Keynesianism 112, 156. *See also* economics
kinship 90-91, 110, 197. *See also* anthropology; clientalism; sociology of family
kula 10, 143. *See also* anthropology; economics

language 30, 31, 66, 100-101, 109, 205
  classification of 108
  and cognition 109
  and jargon 30. *See also* jargon
  universals in 10, 109, 157
  see also dialects; linguistics
Latin America 34, 54-55, 79-80, 115
law 54, 58, 60, 66, 68, 74, 76, 91, 129, 174
  and anthropology 89-91, 129, 151, 156, 159
  comparative 156
  concepts in 125-126, 129
  and economics 111, 136
  journals in 161-162
  legal-institutional approach 61, 103
  and mathematics 137
  and medicine 177

and political science 54-55, 60, 76, 102-103, 129, 166, 179
and psychoanalysis 150
and psychology 41
sociology of 69, 106
learning 67, 101, 125. *See also* education; teaching
library science 235
  classification in 27, 71-72, 235
life sciences. *See* biology
linguistics 5, 33, 40, 55, 69, 108-110, 127, 129, 142, 157, 158, 166, 205
  acoustic 75, 109
  and anthropology 90, 92, 109, 165
  and artificial intelligence 109
  behavioral 108
  and biology 204-206
  and cognition 109, 204
  comparative 55
  and computers 100
  core of 23, 109-110, 183
  and discoveries 123, 144
  and folklore studies 144
  gaps in 110. *See also* boundaries; gaps
  historical 55, 60, 66-67, 109-110, 125. *See also* Indo-European peoples, languages of
  and humanities 109
  hybridization of 108-110, 154, 204-206
  and innovation 16
  and mathematics 109
  methods of 110. *See also* methodologies
  and natural sciences 109
  paradigm of 154
  patrimony of 57
  and philosophy 74, 86
  phonology 55, 72, 75, 109-110
  and physiology 72, 75, 204
  and psychology 98-101, 109
  socio- 106-107, 109-110, 137, 173, 198
  and sociology 109
  specialization in 110
  structural 16, 35, 109
  syntax 66, 106, 109-110
  theory of 149
  see also dialects; grammar; transformational-generative grammar; language
literature 70, 179, 181
  comparative 67
  and history 88

and music 181
and philosophy 181
see also art; "classics," Roman and
Greek; humanities
logic 56, 66, 86–87, 109
Lotka-Price law of productivity 14–15,
27. *See also* citation; obsolescence;
productivity; publication

marginality 75
of hybrid scholars 177
and density 36
and innovation 32–33
see also boundaries; cores; creativity;
gaps
marketing research 134
markets 26, 35, 227. *See also* economics
Marxism 73–74, 108, 128, 148–149, 217,
235
and formal models 74
and theology 173
see also capitalism; class, working;
political economy
mathematics 56, 64, 66, 70, 72, 127, 133,
149, 159, 181
and anthropology 55, 84, 92, 133–134,
137
and archaeology 178
and biology 178
and climatology 212
concepts in 125–127
divisive nature of 31, 137–138, 235. *See
also* fragmentation
and economics 21, 48, 111, 132, 178,
225. *See also* economics; formal
models; game theory
and innovation 16, 134
and international trade theory 29–30
and linguistics 109
and natural science 178
and philosophy 86
and political science 39, 166
and psychology 134
maximization 138–139, 223, 225–228. *See
also* mathematics
mechanics 177. *See also* engineering
media, mass 12. *See also* journalism
medicine 69, 94, 104, 106, 133, 166, 227
and anthropology 89, 92, 207
and archaeology 93
and law 177

and problem-solving 104
and psychoanalysis 150
and psychology 97
and sociology 106
see also cardiology; paleopathology
meteorology 133, 149. *See also* climate
methodological individualism 190
methodologies 86–87, 121, 151
application of 131–132
borrowing of 73, 79, 131–139. *See also*
hybridization
comparative 166
and fragmentation 53, 132, 231
and hybridization 16, 131
imperialism of 133, 166
improvements of 11, 46, 132. *See also*
innovation
and innovation 21, 57, 100
and paradigms 157
and patrimonies 21, 28, 131
see also formal models; observation;
under individual disciplines
migration 72, 127, 180
and anthropology 91
of fields 75
Germanic 113
intellectual 175–180
sociology of 106
military 66, 136, 137, 219
history 66
sociology of 106, 166
see also security studies
modernization 78, 126, 156. *See also*
development
molecular biology. *See* biology, molecular
monetarism 59, 117. *See also* economics;
Keynesianism
monodisciplinarity 65, 67, 115
and monocausality 57, 148, 178
scholars of 39–40, 173, 182
see also fragmentation; hybridization;
innovation; interdisciplinarity
music 56, 74–75
and literature 181
and sociology 106

NASA (National Aeronautics and Space
Administration) 92, 209. *See also*
astronomy
nationalism 96, 104
nation building 194

SUBJECT INDEX

natural sciences 5, 19–20, 33, 70, 84, 123, 176–177
 and archaeology 93
 and biology 208–209
 citation in 37–38, 43
 discoveries in 143
 fragmentation of 72
 and geography 84, 94, 97
 hybridization of 72
 innovation in 20, 23
 and linguistics 109
 and mathematics 178
 methodologies of 86–87
 and psychology 97
 publication in 38–39. *See also* journals, academic
 and social sciences 203
 and urban studies 95
 see also individual disciplines
nervous systems 98–99, 177. *See also* biology; neurology
neurology 100
 hybridizations of 68, 72, 97–98, 101, 156, 205–206
 and linguistics 104
Newly Industrialized Countries (NICs) 78, 213
Nobel prize 23–24, 37, 47, 56, 68–69, 100, 112, 138, 227
nomothesm 189. *See also* ideography
norms 2–3, 23, 24, 38
 of citation 38
 and economics 136
 and violence 204
North America 55, 151, 211

obfuscation 29–30. *See also* hair-splitting, theoretical; jargon; quantification
observation. *See* field observation
obsolescence 23, 46–49
 and citations 23, 45–46
 of hybrid fields 73, 76
 and innovation 46
 and patrimonies 46
 see also under individual disciplines
ontogeny 205. *See also* biology
organizations 101–102, 106
 and economics 227
 and formal models 26
 industrial. *See* economics, industrial organization

and psychology 101–102, 227
and social psychology 101
theory of 134, 165
see also public administration

paleobiology. *See under* biology
paleography 93
paleontology 90, 92–93
paleopathology 93. *See also* archaeology; medicine
palynology 93
papyrology 93
paradigms 53, 154, 176
 and citation 37–38
 and concepts 157
 and discoveries 157
 and fragmentation 231
 and innovation 153, 157
 and methodologies 157
 synthesis of 155
 and theories 157
 see also anomalies; cores; patrimonies; science, normal; *under individual disciplines*
parties, political 21, 71, 95–96, 154, 166, 191, 231
 competition among 111, 135, 154
 history of 41–42
 systems of 11, 25, 118
 see also behavior, electoral; democracy; political science; voting
pathology, psycho- 98
patrimonies 7, 19–28, 51, 230
 and citation 37–38
 of "classics" 33
 definition of 19
 and discoveries 143
 and fads 75
 and fragmentation 53, 56, 59–60, 65
 growth of 45, 53, 56–57
 and innovation 7, 20–25, 45, 48, 65
 and journals 162
 and methodologies 21, 28, 131
 and number of scholars. *See* density
 and obsolescence 46
 in public opinion 26–27
 quantification of 26–29
 and specialization 56–57
 and theories 147, 152
 see also under individual disciplines
patron-client relations. *See* clientelism

peace research 156. *See also* international relations

peasants 70, 79, 136, 151, 196, 222
  in anthropology 91
  in sociology 107

perception 67, 99–100
  and anthropology 92, 144
  and geography 96
  and international relations 150
  see also cognition; psychology

personality 71, 97–98, 101, 104
  and anthropology 91
  and political science 147
  see also psychology

pharmacology 97–98, 207

philology 54–55, 60
  and anthropology 93
  comparative 55, 176
  and history 89, 176–177
  and psychology 99
  see also grammar; language; linguistics

philosophy 5, 56, 64, 66, 69, 72–74, 86–87, 132, 169, 179
  and anthropology 89, 92
  and economics 86, 136
  and history 86
  hybridization of 86–87
  and linguistics 74, 86
  and mathematics 86
  patrimony of 86
  and physics 86–87
  political 103, 207, 232
  and political science 42, 65, 165, 179, 232
  and psychology 54–55, 86, 97–98
  and sociology 86
  specialization in 86
  and theology 86
  see also causality; epistemology

photography 141

phylogeny 205. *See also* biology

physical sciences. *See also* natural sciences

physics 58, 64, 69, 129, 133, 149, 181, 226
  bio- 68
  concepts in 129
  nuclear 66
  and philosophy 86–87
  quantum 87
  theoretical 38, 176

see also astronomy; gravity; natural sciences; philosophy, natural

physiology 66, 150
  comparative 205. *See also* animals; biology
  and linguistics 72, 75, 204
  neuro- 68, 72. *See also* neurology
  and psychology 55, 98–99

planning
  economic 81, 111. *See also* capitalism; economics; welfare
  urban 95. *See also* urban studies

plate tectonics 20, 23, 56. *See also* geology

pluralism 154–155

policy 233
  economic 219
  studies 102, 104, 156, 227. *See also* political science

political anthropology 72, 90–92, 102, 143–144, 166, 174

political development 17, 48, 166, 212

political economy 24–25, 56, 64, 75, 102, 127–128, 173, 212
  and agriculture 151
  and biology 208
  and demography 151
  and density 22
  as fad 217
  international 22, 62, 186, 198, 217–223. *See also* international relations
  Marxist 73–74, 217
  see also economics; political science

political geography 94, 173. *See also* geography; geopolitics

political history 87, 178, 195, 197, 199

political philosophy 103, 207. *See also* political science, theory

political psychology 70, 98–102

political science 4–5, 10, 17, 27, 33, 35, 40, 43, 58, 60–64, 67, 69–71, 74–75, 77, 102–104, 129, 169, 174, 176, 191, 232
  and anthropology 42, 90–92, 103–104, 133, 151, 165
  area studies in 27
  behavioral 42, 103–104
  and biology 207
  biopolitics 70, 166, 207
  citation in 39–40
  and classics 153

SUBJECT INDEX

classification in 102
and cognition 104, 228
and communication 104, 128
comparative politics 41–42, 48, 97, 102, 106, 166, 219–220. *See also* area studies; case studies; geography; sociology, comparative
concepts in 125–129, 198
and cybernetics 42
and economics 42, 61, 104, 111–112, 138, 147, 165–166, 186, 217–219
and ethology 207
and evolution 207
field observation in 134
fragmentation of 62, 102, 217
and game theory 104, 137, 165
gaps in 217, 219
and genetics 103
and geography 96–97
and history 41–42, 54–55, 61, 64, 103, 147, 153, 166, 177, 179, 188, 197–198
hybridization of 102–104, 218, 220
innovations in 16, 34
journals in 41, 162
and law 54–55, 60, 76, 102–103, 129, 166, 179
mathematics in 39, 166
methodologies in 102–103, 134
and natural sciences 42
obsolescence in 45
paradigms of 154–155
and philosophy 42, 61, 165, 179
and problem-solving 156
and psychoanalysis 149–150
and psychology 42, 100–101, 104, 132, 147, 166, 179, 228
publication in 27, 39. *See also* journals, academic
and quantification 163
and social psychology 42, 104, 147
and sociobiology 207
and sociology 41–42, 60–61, 103–107, 132, 147, 165–166, 177, 179–180, 194
and statistics 73
structural-functionalism in 16. *See also* functionalism; structures; structuralism
and theology 153
theories in 198
and urban studies 95

see also elections; international relations; public opinion; voting
political socialization 66, 91, 104
and anthropology 91
see also political science, political sociology; socialization; sociology
political sociology 42, 65, 102, 104, 106, 166, 179, 198–199
see also political science, political socialization; sociology
political theory 39, 67, 71, 73, 102–103, 179, 232
politics, as concept 233
praxis 15, 155–157
sociological 106
theological 153
see also policy studies; problem-solving
primary sources 195–196. *See also* history; methodologies
primatology 205–206
comparative 91, 207
see also animals; biology
problem-solving
and fragmentation 157
and hybridization 156–157
and interdisciplinarity 104
see also under individual disciplines
production
factors of 35–36
means of 126–127
modes of 70, 79
psychiatry 58, 97, 177
and anthropology 92
and sociology 107
psychoanalysis 74, 150
and anthropology 92
core of 149
psychological sociology 69. *See also* social psychology
psychology 5, 17, 27, 38, 58, 66–67, 69–70, 74, 79, 97–102, 129, 133, 166, 176–181
abnormal 55, 106. *See also* criminology; sociology of deviance
and anthropology 89–92, 144, 149
behavioral 97, 99, 101
bias 123, 227
and biology 84, 97, 100, 150, 203, 206
citation in 40
clinical 66, 97. *See also* psychiatry; psychoanalysis

274 SUBJECT INDEX

cognitive 67, 97, 99, 101, 104, 225. *See also* artificial intelligence; cognition; cognitive science; computer science; perception
comparative 54–55, 69, 98, 205–206. *See also* behavior, animal; primatology
and computer science 99–100
concepts in 42, 125–127, 129
core of 99
cybernetics 99
developmental 27, 42, 97, 99–100, 206
discoveries in 144
and economics 100–101, 138, 165–166, 225–228
and endocrinology 98
and engineering 125
and ethology 98–99, 206
experimental 5, 54–55, 225–226
and formal models 26
fragmentation of 98–99
and genetics 33, 150
and geography 96
Gestalt 99, 127–128. *See also* structures
and history 150
and hybridization 97–102, 228
industrial 101–102. *See also* economics, industrial organization
and innovation 38, 99–100
and international relations 181–182
journals in 161–163
and linguistics 98–101, 109
and literature 181
and mathematics 134
and medicine 97
methods in 100, 133–134
and natural sciences 97
neuro- 97–98. *See also* nervous systems; neurology
"new psychology" 150
and organizational behavior 101–102, 227
perception 67, 99–100. *See also* cognitive science
and philology 99
and philosophy 54–55, 86, 97–98
physiological 98
and physiology 55, 99
political 70, 98–102
and political science 42, 100–101, 104, 132, 147, 150, 165–166, 179, 228

and problem-solving 99–100
publication in 27, 39. *See also* journals, academic
and quantification 150
and social psychology 174
and sociology 98, 107, 144, 165, 177
specialization in 99
and statistics 134
theory of 149–150
public choice 39, 95, 112, 138, 182–183
citation in 43
and foreign policy 62. *See also* international relations
and game theory 136–137, 165
and political science 104
see also political science; rational choice
public goods 12, 42, 104, 136, 200. *See also* collective action; economics; policy studies; political economy; political science; public choice
public opinion 32, 78
patrimony of 26–27
see also survey research
publication 13–14, 45, 81, 164
in economics 27, 39
in natural sciences 38–39
norms of 38
in political science 27, 39
in psychology 27, 39
see also journals, academic
"publish or perish" 14, 81

quantification 29, 31–32, 197
of citations 38–41
of hybridization 41, 72
and innovation 16, 39–40
and patrimonies 26–29
see also under individual disciplines
quantum mechanics. *See* physics
quotas, import 29–30. *See also* trade, international

rational choice 82, 107, 135–136, 137–138, 147, 189, 203, 221–223, 226–227
and geography 96
rationality 24, 101–112, 205, 226
of animals 228. *See also* behavior, animal; psychology, comparative
bounded 138, 227
of scholars 145

SUBJECT INDEX

see also cognitive science; psychology
rational-legal authority 191. *See also*
   bureaucracy
Realism 154, 228
recombination of disciplines and
   subfields. *See* hybridization
reductionism, biological 204–205
reflex 98–99, 101, 206. *See also* stimulus
reinforcement, negative 31. *See also*
   psychology
religion 78, 80, 87, 222, 234
   anthropology of 90
   and mathematics 137
   sociology of 106, 198
Renaissance 20, 23, 155
research 14, 23, 34, 46
   agendas for 220–221
   centers for 9
   diminishing returns to 29, 67, 152, 220.
      See also density
   foundations for 35
   interdisciplinary. *See* interdisciplinary
      research
   team 117–118
   see also foundations; hybridization;
      innovation; interdisciplinary research;
      specialization; universities
review, peer 13. *See also* publication;
   "publish or perish"
revivals 11, 48, 187
revolution 126, 166, 195
   industrial 115, 126
rhetoric 47, 56
risk 26, 225, 227. *See also* economics;
   insurance; psychology
Royal Society 48, 65. *See also* Britain,
   Great

Sanskrit 57, 108, 176. *See also* Indo-
   European peoples
satisficing. *See* rationality, bounded; *under*
   rational choice
scholars 171–174, 175
   classification of 27, 171
   critical mass of 180–181
   generalists 59, 133, 166, 182, 189
   hybrid 173, 175–177
   ideal types of 171–174
   irrationality of 137–138, 189
   monodisciplinary 39–40, 173, 182
   rationality of 145

schools (intellectual) 154, 172
   Fischer 48
   Frankfurt 74, 101
   of history 30, 89, 180
   ideological 113
   Lausanne 135
   of *Les Annales. See Les Annales*
   Marxist 107. *See also* Marxism
   Weberian 107
   see also graduate training; teaching;
      universities
science
   history of 48, 55–56, 176, 229
   normal 11–12, 20, 154, 158. *See also*
      anomalies; paradigms
   norms of 2–3, 24
   philosophy of 3, 61–62, 70, 74, 103,
      136, 145, 154, 176, 230. *See also*
      epistemology; philosophy
   revolutionary 11–12, 19–20. *See also*
      paradigms
   sociology of 2–3, 37, 65, 106
   see also humanities; innovation; library
      science; natural science; political
      science; social sciences
scissiparity 58. *See also* fragmentation
security studies 62, 66. *See also*
   international relations
slavery 191
social choice. *See* public choice
Social Darwinism 152, 203–204
social history 27, 54, 67, 87–88, 95, 176,
   194–196, 235. *See also* historical
   sociology; sociology
social psychology 5, 54, 56, 58, 64, 66,
   69, 74, 98, 100–101, 106, 173, 176,
   180
   and biology 101
   concepts in 42
   discoveries in 144
   and formal models 101
   and game theory 137
   and group behavior 67, 98, 100, 102,
      142, 147
   and international relations 181–182
   methods of 133
   and political science 42, 104, 147
   and psychology 174
   and sociology 105, 107, 151, 174
social sciences 33, 54–57, 58, 83, 84–85
   and biology 203–211

core of 85, 119
definition of 5
discoveries in 143
and ethics 86–87
"golden age" of 83
and humanities 181
and natural sciences 203
publication in 39. *See also* journals,
    academic
Western nature of 81, 180
see also individual disciplines
Social Sciences Citation Index 14, 37,
    39–40, 161, 163
socialization 16, 22, 71, 91, 100–102, 105,
    123, 126
  political 66, 104
  see also political science; psychology;
    social psychology; sociology
sociobiology 203
  and economics 208
  and political science 207
sociological history. *See* historical
    sociology
sociology 4–5, 17, 27, 35, 43, 54–55, 58–
    59, 61, 63, 66–67, 69–70, 72, 74, 77,
    105–108, 112, 129, 169, 174, 176, 179
  and anthropology 89–92, 105–107, 133,
    151, 165
  behavioral 105–106. *See also* behavior
  and biology 106, 207
  boundaries of 88
  causation in 191, 193, 195, 198
  citation in 39–41
  comparative 106, 189, 194
  concepts in 42, 84, 124–129, 197
  core of 22, 53, 61, 105, 107–108
  and criminology 106
  and demography 61, 107
  of deviance 106, 108. *See also*
    psychology, abnormal; psychology of
    deviance
  discoveries in 144
  and economics 105–106, 111, 138, 165,
    227
  environmental 104. *See also* ecology,
    social
  fads in 187
  of family 61, 66, 106, 198. *See also*
    family; kinship
  fragmentation of 58–59, 105, 107, 187–
    188

and game theory 137, 165
of gender 106, 108, 151
and geography 94–95, 97, 106, 159
historical. *See* historical sociology
and history 4, 56, 61, 88, 105, 107,
    176–177, 186–201. *See also* historical
    sociology; history
hybridization of 105–108, 151, 188, 203
ideologies in 59, 107, 113
imperialism of 105, 113
innovations in 15, 32
and international relations 107, 181–182
jargon in 30–31
journals in 41, 162–163
of law 69, 106
of leisure 106, 198
and linguistics 107, 109–110, 137, 173,
    198
and mathematics 106
of mental health 101, 106
methodology of 41, 105–107, 113, 134,
    197
military 106, 166
obsolescence in 23
of organizations 106
paradigms in 32–33. *See also*
    paradigms; revolutionary science
patrimony of 21, 53, 187
and philosophy 86
political 42, 65, 102, 104, 106, 166,
    179, 198–199
and political science 41–42, 60–61, 103–
    107, 132, 147, 165–166, 177, 179–180,
    194
praxis in 106
and psychiatry 107
and psychology 98, 107, 144, 165, 177.
    See also social psychology
quantification in 32, 197
of religion 106, 198
rural 94, 106–107. *See also* agriculture
of science 2–3, 37, 65, 106
specialization in 187, 189. *See also*
    fragmentation; specialization
and statistics 73, 105. *See also* survey
    research
structural-functionalism in 16, 105. *See
    also* structural-functionalism
theory of 105–106, 108, 191–192, 200–
    201
of violence 166

SUBJECT INDEX

of work 101, 198
of world conflict 107
specialization 1–2, 5, 13, 51, 53–62, 85,
  115–116, 229
  and discoveries 144
  and fads 75
  and fragmentation 58
  and innovation 1, 57–58, 116
  and journals 161–163, 235
  and patrimonies 56–57
  see also under individual disciplines
Staatswissenschaften 60, 174
"star system" 23–25
statistics 32, 54, 69, 74, 134, 182
  concepts in 126, 128
  and demography 21, 134
  and density 31
  and economics 55, 111, 134
  and fragmentation 231
  and innovation 14, 16, 31, 134
  and international relations 134
  and political science 73
  and psychology 134
  and sociology 73, 105
  see also data; factor analysis;
    mathematics; quantification
stimulus 98–99, 101, 144. *See also*
  psychology; reflex
stratification, social 34, 61, 65, 80, 106
structuralism 72, 165
  in anthropology 35
  and economics 80
  and imperialism 209
  and innovation 16
  and international relations 155
  in linguistics 16, 35, 109
  see also structural-functionalism
structural-functionalism
  in anthropology 90–91
  and innovation 16
  and political science 16, 151
  in sociology 16, 105
  see also structuralism
subfields 2, 7, 13
  cores of 7
  in economics 54–55
  hybridization of 2
  institutionalization of 69–70
  see also cores; fragmentation;
    hybridization; specialization;
    individual disciplines and subfields

survey research 12, 34–35, 47, 105, 133–
  134, 165
  and innovation 16, 41, 132
  see also data; ecological analysis;
    market research; mathematics; public
    opinion
symbolism 68, 90
synthesis 2, 58–59, 148
  in geography 93–94
  in history 64
  and hybridization 64
  of paradigms 155
systems 104, 128, 166
  biological 17, 128. *See also* biology
  international 151, 181
  political 11, 25, 80, 118, 126, 144, 222.
    See also political science
  social 16, 101, 165
  world 128, 192–193

tariffs 29–30, 71, 149, 217–218
  endogenous tariff theory 219, 231
  see also foreign policy; political
    economy; trade, international
teaching 33, 85, 106, 113
  and density 34
  and disciplines 85
  and research 34
  see also education; graduate training;
    learning
team research. *See* research, team
technology 20, 25, 96, 133, 141–142
  and archaeology 141
  innovation in 20, 46, 141, 155, 158
  spatial diffusion of 142
  see also computers; natural science;
    science; social science
telephones 133
telescope 141
textbooks 35, 39, 83. *See also* teaching
theology 73, 88–89, 125–126, 132
  and archaeology 132
  and biology 73
  and geology 73, 132
  of liberation 153
  and Marxism 153
  medieval 88
  and philosophy 86
  and political science 153
  and praxis 153
  see also religion

theory 81, 121, 144–145, 148–149
and anomalies 158
and area studies 79, 81
borrowing of 147–152, 209. *See also*
hybridization
diminishing returns to 151
of economics 54–55, 84, 110–111, 199,
225–227
formal. *See* formal models
and fragmentation 53
and gaps 149
grand 47, 58. *See also* synthesis
and hybridization 16, 147–152
and imperialism 167
of international trade 29–30. *See also*
under economics
and paradigms 157
and patrimonies 147, 152
see also hair-splitting, theoretical
hypotheses; synthesis, theoretical;
under individual disciplines
thermodynamics 129. *See also* energy
"Third World" 125, 212
totalitarianism 35, 79. *See also*
authoritarianism; Communism;
fascism
trade
balance of, between disciplines 165–167.
See also hybridization
concentration of 124. *See also*
distribution
international 29–30, 54, 85, 104, 111,
124, 199, 217–218
see also economics; international
relations; political economy,
international; tariffs
trade unions 71, 106
see also capitalism; class, working
transformational-generative grammar 33,
109, 145, 149, 154, 157–158
and genetics 33
see also linguistics
transportation 176, 178
"tunnel vision" 119, 190

uncertainty. *See* risk
uncertainty principle 87
UNESCO (United Nations Economic,
Scientific, and Cultural Organization)
4, 64–65, 90
universities 113, 181, 230
administration of. *See* administration
and communication 231
see also business schools; departments;
disciplines; education; graduate
training; teaching
urban studies 5, 61, 65–66, 91, 95, 97,
106–107. *See also* architecture;
geography, urban
urbanization 12, 80

valence 123. *See also* linguistics
values 100, 104–105, 118, 129, 147, 155,
199
postindustrial 123
verstehen 190, 196. *See also erklären*
violence 166, 204
voluntary export restraints 29–30. *See
also* trade
voting 135–137, 155, 191. *See also*
elections; behavior, electoral; parties,
political; political science; public
opinion

war 46, 133–134, 178. *See also*
international relations
welfare 16
economics 136, 178
state 35, 70, 221
see also democracies, capitalist
women's studies 61, 70
Wirtschaft 233. *See also* economics
working class. *See* class, working; capital;
labor; sociology of work
World Bank 156, 212–213, 221

Zeitgeist 233
zoology, and archaeology 93